# BOGOLAN

# BOGOLAN

## Shaping Culture through Cloth

### IN CONTEMPORARY MALI

VICTORIA L. ROVINE

SMITHSONIAN INSTITUTION PRESS

Washington and London

© 2001 by the Smithsonian Institution
All rights reserved

COPY EDITOR: Robin O. Surratt
PRODUCTION EDITOR: Duke Johns
DESIGNER: Amber Frid-Jimenez

Library of Congress Cataloging-in-Publication Data
Rovine, Victoria.
Bogolan : shaping culture through cloth in
contemporary Mali / Victoria L. Rovine.
p.   cm.
Includes  bibliographical references and index.
ISBN 1-56098-942-4 (alk. paper)
1. Bogolon cloth.   2. Bambara (African people)—
Clothing.   3. Resist-dyed textiles—Mali.
4. West African strip weaving—Mali.   I. Title.
DT551.45.B35 R68 2001
391—dc21                    2001020697
British Library Cataloguing-in-
Publication Data available

Manufactured in the United States of America
08 07 06 05 04 03 02 01   5 4 3 2 1

∞ The paper used in this publication meets the
minimum requirements of the American National
Standard for Information Sciences—Permanence of
Paper for Printed Library Materials
ANSI Z39.48-1984.

For permission to reproduce illustrations appearing
in this book, please correspond directly with
the owners of the works, as listed in the
individual captions. (Uncredited photographs are
by the author.) The Smithsonian Institution Press
does not retain reproduction rights for these
illustrations individually or maintain a file of
addresses for photo sources.

*This book is dedicated to artists long classified as "traditional" in Mali and other parts of the world. I hope that my work will introduce readers to contemporary worlds too rarely associated with non-Western cultures.*

# CONTENTS

# ILLUSTRATIONS

## Maps

## Plates *(following page 36)*

# ACKNOWLEDGMENTS

I have a great many people to thank for their time, assistance, support, and insightful responses to my work. First, my thanks to the many artists, merchants, administrators, and students in Bamako who so generously gave of their time in answering my seemingly endless queries. I have been constantly amazed and gratified by the warmth and insight of the people I encountered over the course of my time in Mali. I hope that this book will provide one form of thanks to them, by making wider audiences aware of the country's vibrant contemporary arts. I am grateful to all of the people who appear in this book, but I would like to single out several for special thanks: Klétigui Dembélé, Lalla Tangara Touré and her family, Kandiora Coulibaly, Brehima Konaté, Rokiatou Sow, Boureima Diakité, Hama Guro, and Sidicki Traoré. I am also grateful to Chris Seydou for sharing his time with me. I very much hope that this work will contribute to his legacy.

As importantly, I am very grateful to the friends and colleagues who made my time in Mali so pleasurable as well as fruitful. First, my thanks to my Malian family, the Sissokos of Medina Coura. Special thanks to Nandi and Assa, to their parents, sisters, and extended family; I am very proud to have a home with them. Many, many thanks to Oumar Konipo of the U.S. embassy. Issa Traoré, Gaoussou Mariko, and their colleagues at the U.S. Information Service provided much assistance and levity. The Musée National du Mali—in particular, its director, Samuel Sidibe—the Institut des Sciences Humaines, and the Institut National des Arts (INA) provided much institutional assistance. Thanks also to Eros Sissoko, who first introduced me to students and teachers at INA, Pauline Duponchel, Thierry Alzieu, and Mansour Ciss. Eric Silla was a wonderful housemate during my time in Bamako. Barbara Durr and R. B. Deal provided morning coffee. Mary Curtain was a great motivator.

In the United States, I thank Patrick McNaughton and Roy Sieber for their many years of good advice. Thanks also to Bill Siegmann and the Department of Africa, Oceania, and the Americas at the Brooklyn Museum, where I located shortly after my return from a year in Bamako. Thanks to each of my colleagues at the University of Iowa Museum of Art (UIMA), all of whom had a hand in facilitating this book and the exhibition that preceded it, *Renewing Tradition: The Revitalization of Bogolan in Mali and Abroad*. Howard Collinson, director of the UIMA, provided precious time as I completed this project. Current and past

Africanists at Iowa, including Chris Roy, Bill Dewey, Al Roberts, and Polly Roberts provided a stimulating atmosphere that helped me shape my ideas.

My travel to Mali was made possible by funding from several sources, including a Fulbright-IIE Pre-Dissertation Research Grant in 1992 and two University of Iowa sources in 1997, the International Travel Fund Program and a Mary Jo Small Staff Development Grant. My travel to Mali in 2000 was made possible by the generosity of a museum donor. Both the Rockefeller Foundation and the National Endowment for the Arts provided funding for *Renewing Tradition,* which shaped my thinking about bogolan and its many incarnations. My thanks also to the Stanley Foundation, which has provided funding for many of my activities and acquisitions at the UIMA. The University of Iowa Office of the Vice President for Research facilitated the completion of this book.

My thanks also to Kathy Rovine, Teri Sowell, Mary Jo Arnoldi, and Emily Vermillion for their support and thoughtful responses to my work. Barbara Frank, Julie McGuire, Irene Lambrou, Melissa Anderson, Liz Brown, and Maggie Maluf kept me well stocked in clippings, catalogues, and other records of mudcloth products. Kim Marra and Meredith Alexander supplied bogolan coffee and a careful reading of early versions of this project. Keith Achepohl inspired me with his work ethic (and with many a fine meal). As I neared completion of this book, Sarah Brett-Smith, Tavy Aherne, and Julianne Freeman responded to urgent requests for information from their work in Mali. Thanks also to Ann Starck, Michael Annus, Karla Dennis, Bill Blair, and others who shared their bogolan paintings and clothing with me. Will Thomson skillfully made the maps of Mali and Bamako. The Smithsonian Institution Press enlisted readers who provided insightful suggestions for which I am grateful. And many, many thanks to Florence Babb, who has carefully read every word I have written and provided support, humor, and affection in countless ways.

I ni ce kosèbè!

# INTRODUCTION

## Bogolan's Biography

Le Chic Bogolan
de Chris Seydou:
Habillez-vous Chris
Seydou, pour être
à l'heure de la
valorisation de nos
tissus traditionnels:
cotonade et bogolan.
(Chris Seydou's Chic
Bogolan: Wear Chris
Seydou to be up-to-
date in the revival
of our traditional
textiles: cottons
and bogolan.)
*Promotional feature,*
*Nyeleni*

In Bamako, the capital of the West African country of Mali, a single textile, identified variously as bogolanfini, bogolan,[1] and mudcloth, has in the past decade been the object of dramatic technical, stylistic, and functional innovations at the hands of Malian artists and art merchants. Like a river overflowing its banks into distant lakes, streams, and oceans, bogolan's distinctive black and white geometric patterns have surged into diverse markets both in Mali and abroad—from village marketplaces to airport souvenir shops, exclusive boutiques, mail-order catalogues, and museums. Although bogolan's distinctive patterns are likely familiar to many North Americans, few are aware of its origins, its rich history, and its important role in the lives of innumerable Malians. The quotations to the right, the first from a popular Malian magazine, the second from an article in an American academic journal, reflect the vast diversity of "personalities" this uniquely Malian textile projects, from a chic fashion accessory to a carefully encoded repository of secret knowledge and power. In its varied guises, bogolan shifts between rural and urban locales, between African and Euro-American artistic styles, between tourist art markets and exclusive art galleries. The cloth's many incarnations in Bamako and abroad encompass every aspect of the global economy, in which African art now circulates. Bogolan is also global in its symbolic reach, its story a dramatization of the changing role of tradition, authenticity, and identity in contemporary urban Africa.

My investigation of bogolan's changing fortunes focuses on the cloth's varied roles and on the associations it carries for the Malians and non-Malians who make and consume it. Their perceptions of the cloth reveal much concerning the cultural engines that have propelled bogolan's late-twentieth-century revival. In the chapters that follow, artists, designers, and entrepreneurs tell the story of the cloth's meanings, its histories, and its prospects for the future. Where these stories diverge, they reveal bogolan's rich potential to contain many meanings simultaneously, absorbing the diverse desires of those who see themselves reflected in its patterns and colors. Bogolan is traditional for some, modern for others; it is deeply religious in some contexts, secular and trendy in others. In sum, the subject at hand is not a unified one. My interest in bogolan's story is in this diversity of interpretations rather than in the telling of a single history.

A brief introduction to bogolan's properties here leads us into the world of contemporary artistic expression in Mali. The word *bogolanfini,* and *bogolan,*

In Bamana society
unintelligibility or
"obscurity" (*dibi*)
is a sought after
achievement. The
purpose of the code,
whether it be the
sign system of a
secret association
or the patterns of
a mud cloth, is to
record knowledge
for the initiated
while simultaneously
blocking the approach
of the uninitiated.
*Sarah Brett-Smith,*
*"Speech Made Visible"*

Map 1. Mali's location in Africa.

indicates the cloth's close association with the Bamana,[2] Mali's most populous ethnic group and the group most closely associated with bogolan production. In Bamanakan, *bogo* means "clay" or "mud," *lan* means "with or by means of," and *fini* or *finin* means "cloth." Throughout this book, I will refer to the cloth being adapted to new markets in the Malian capital of Bamako as *bogolan,* reflecting both the current usage of the term among artists and merchants and distinguishing the urban phenomenon from the rural, "classic," versions of the cloth known as *bogolanfini.* The American adaptations of the cloth, produced in Mali and elsewhere, are here referred to as *mudcloth.*

Because bogolan today is made in myriad styles using a wide range of techniques, a thorough description of its formal attributes here would be impossible. Instead, I begin with an inventory of the characteristics that, almost without exception, can be traced through all of these incarnations. These traits represent only the outlines of a complex and dynamic artistic tradition, yet this inventory will provide a foundation for more comprehensive discussions of bogolan's many manifestations:

> *colors*—earth tones, including blacks, browns, grays, tans, rusty reds, and mustard, as well as the white of the undyed fabric
> *dyes*—a mordant or fixative made from leaves of the *n'gallama* tree; moist earth from the banks of rivers or ponds used as brown or black pigment
> *fabric support*—locally woven cotton strips of four to six inches (ten to fifteen centimeters) wide, sewn into rectangular cloths
> *motifs*—geometric forms, including dots, circles, crosses, triangles, and zigzag lines, with some modern bogolan incorporating representational imagery and using geometric motifs as backgrounds or borders
> *stories*—explanations of bogolan's uniquely Malian origins, its uses in "traditional" contexts, and the significance of its symbols

The artists and entrepreneurs who have adapted new techniques, created new styles, and pursued new markets for bogolan have occasionally omitted one or more of these basic characteristics. If the artists leave behind one too many traits, they risk removing their work from the category of bogolan, leaving behind the many associations that accompany the cloth and that have helped to make it an ubiquitous feature of Bamako's many markets.

In Bamako today, bogolan is the most popular textile in tourist markets and the medium of choice for most of the city's successful visual artists. The cloth is also worn by increasing numbers of young people in the form of hats, vests, dresses, and shirts. It is carried to school by Malian schoolchildren, who have it emblazoned on their notebooks (Figure 1). Yet, not long ago, the future of this art form was in doubt.

An article in 1970, one of the first discussions of bogolan in English, predicted a bleak future for the cloth:

> The failure of younger women to learn the art and the gradually increasing preference of young people for European styles and factory-made cloth creates concern for the survival of this art form beyond the next few generations, unless new interest is generated in it and new demands made for it.[3]

The new interest and new demands that were to develop in the decades that followed this lament have taken bogolan in directions that could scarcely have been imagined thirty years ago. The number of young people currently producing bogolan paintings, clothing, housewares, and other items suggests that the technique will continue to thrive with its present vigor for some time to come.

Any investigation of bogolan's contemporary manifestations must encompass a dizzying variety of styles, technical innovations, and markets, for the cloth today traverses geographical and conceptual boundaries usually held separate in studies of non-Western cultures. The art of urban, contemporary Africa, epitomized by bogolan's dramatic transformations, often blurs conceptual categories long accepted by students of African art. The separation of "tradition" from "modernity," "African" from "Western," and "local" from "international" is complicated by the richly layered cultures of the cosmopolitan setting in which bogolan flourishes today. Woven through this study is an examination of the notion of tradition in contemporary urban Mali. Bamako has a distinct role in the creation and transmission of the country's "traditional" practices.[4] The city's discos, factories, and most recently Internet cafes, all but absent in rural Mali, exemplify its modernization and, in turn, the apparent demise of the country's traditional cultures. Simultaneously, Bamako's museums, cultural centers, and festivals provide access for both visitors and Malians to "traditional" Mali as part of the construction and promotion of a national culture. Bogolan exemplifies the ways in which Bamako's artists and entrepreneurs produce and modify "tradition" to operate effectively in the economic and political climate of a large urban center. For urban Malian audiences and foreign audiences alike, the cloth serves as a tool for the representation of preexisting traditions as well as for the creation of new traditions. By examining the varied markets for bogolan, the artists who create bogolan for these markets, and the varied forms the cloth takes, I seek to look behind categories to find motivations. Henry Drewal advocated such an approach, noting the potential insights that may accompany an examination of these motivations: "If, as I believe, the concepts of reality, deception, and authenticity are continually negotiated, rhetorically constructed categories, then what is most interesting is to explore the reasons behind various constructions in order to understand how and why certain views emerge, hold sway, or decline."[5]

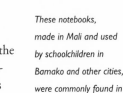

Figure 1. Bogolan-patterned notebooks. Bamako, 1997.

*These notebooks, made in Mali and used by schoolchildren in Bamako and other cities, were commonly found in markets and stationery stores in the late 1990s.*

The revitalization of bogolan is taking place in a number of markets, from tourist art to fine art, all of which are in continual flux; the artists, merchants, and consumers change constantly, as do the styles of the cloth itself. Igor Kopytoff's analysis of commodification provides a useful model for contemporary bogolan's myriad manifestations. He defines a commodity as a "thing that has use value and that can be exchanged in a discreet transaction for a counterpart."[6] All commodities, like the people who exchange them, have multiple histories and shifting identities. Kopytoff advocates an acknowledgment of this complexity by treating objects as "culturally constructed entit[ies], with culturally constructed meanings, and classified and reclassified into culturally constituted categories."[7] He calls this approach—treating the material world as an active, continually shifting subject—cultural biography. This examination of bogolan's cultural biography will elucidate the diverse yet related styles and forms that develop as the cloth travels beyond rural settings, entering national and international marketplaces where it is reconstructed and reclassified to carry new meanings and to suit the needs of new audiences.

Kopytoff's approach to the study of objects also acknowledges the important role of commodification in the construction of objects' biographies, and it recognizes their inherent instability:

> Out of the total range of things available in a society, only some of them are considered appropriate for marking as commodities. Moreover, the same thing may be treated as a commodity at one time and not at another. And finally, the same thing may, at the same time, be seen as a commodity by one person and as something else by another.[8]

This condition is exemplified by bogolan and its recent incarnations: bogolanfini wraps are worn by women and hunters in villages and exhibited in museums abroad; bogolan cloth produced for the tourist trade is sold from hotel gift shops; bogolan paintings are exhibited in art galleries; and bogolan-patterned factory cloth is made into clothing worn by both Malians and non-Malians. Following bogolan's trajectory, this biography also describes the cloth's changing forms and fortunes as it is adapted to North American markets, where the cloth is reclassified, distanced from its distinctly Malian identity to serve as a symbol of broadly ethnic and exotic cultures. In each of these contexts, the cloth's status as a commodity shifts, from the commodification of the tourist art market to the rarified atmosphere of museums and galleries. Patterns of production and consumption differ widely in these varied markets. By viewing these developments as separate elements of a complete biography, I maintain the focus on a single subject while embracing its complexity and its capacity for change.

The story of bogolan's contemporary incarnations has significant implications for the study of African art and, more broadly, for an understanding of the changing roles of tradition and its frequent corollary, authenticity, at the beginning of the twenty-first century. Bogolan's presence in divergent markets offers an exceptional opportunity to follow a single art form through varied negotiations and adaptations of tradition. Remarkably, the cloth's revival has occurred both in concert with and in opposition to consumers' expectations of "authentic, traditional" Malian arts.

All of the artists I worked with in Mali, and most of the people I knew there, were aware of the prevalent Western view of Africa as a continent of traditions, embodied by remote villages in which artists work in the same highly localized "tribal" styles as their ancestors, making statues and masks for ritual use. Visitors to Mali are often enticed with the promise of experiencing "authentic" cultures. One travel agency representative recently exhorted travelers to visit before that authenticity slips away: "[N]ow is the time to go to Mali, while it is still in its authentic state, not ten years from now."[9] Though this prediction of authentic Mali's imminent disappearance was written in 2000, nearly a century ago a similar warning was sounded by anthropologist Franz de Zeltner following a visit to Mali, which was then part of the French colony of Haut-Sénégal-Niger.[10] Thus, as westerners first encountered local practices, they assumed that they were seeing the last gasp of a way of life, observed and recorded just before it slipped away. "Authentic Africa" and its arts retain their value by always remaining, in James Clifford's incisive description, "just prior to the present (but not so distant or eroded as to make collection or salvage impossible)."[11] Contemporary arts, thus, do not gain legitimacy until they fade into the past, where they may acquire new status as traditional.

The "salvage paradigm," to use Clifford's phrase, has been addressed by numerous scholars who critique the sequestering of non-Western cultures into an impossibly static, hermetically sealed world of tradition.[12] The circular logic of authenticity, in which the past is always deemed more authentic than the present and where innovation is viewed as loss, is summarized by John Picton in a special issue of *Third Text:* "It appears that people in Africa can never win, for if they remain attached to the traditions of the past, they are innocent and exotic, and if they move into the present, they are merely foolish."[13] In the same issue, David Koloane's discussion of South African art goes to the deeper implications of such logic:

> This expectation [that one's art reflect one's authentic cultural identity], however, does not appear to apply to white artists as well. The fact that white artists can quote and assimilate wide and varied sources and cultures without feeling any qualms and without fear of being accused of appropriation or misappropriation, or of losing their identities, insinuates that Black artists lack the capacity for creative diversity.[14]

Drawing attention to this inherently contradictory and distinctly discriminatory position is crucial if the art market (and, by extension, the popular media) is ever to fully admit and evaluate the world's artists in an equitable manner. Beyond the importance of recognizing these racialized expectations, our understanding of contemporary artistic production in Africa is enriched by examining how this circumstance has also yielded astoundingly creative adaptations by artists and entrepreneurs in Mali and elsewhere, manipulating the odds stacked against them. At the core of these manipulations is their understanding of the international art market and African art's ostensible place within it as an emblem of steadfast tradition. The present study investigates some of the many strategies by which artists operate successfully within this system, sometimes turning expectations of "traditional" art in on themselves to market wholly new forms that incorporate the stereotypical elements of tradition.

Each of the three major markets in which bogolan's revival is taking place—tourist art, studio art, and fashion—represent distinct responses to the problem of creating and selling art in an environment laden with expectations that one's work be recognizably "traditional," that is, an "authentic" cultural production. The implications of this demand for authenticity have particularly dramatic consequences for artists in the studio art market whose work aims to make a distinctly contemporary statement. Some artists and merchants use references to tradition as a marketing technique, deliberately employing the tropes of tradition—low-technology production, local materials, ritual use, and other elements of the inventory of bogolan's basic traits—in order to meet the demands of their market. Others shun affiliation with the traditional, which they view as an obstacle to their entry into international art markets; the latter artists seek out media and iconography that cannot be directly tied to local practices. Most artists in Bamako today have an ambivalent relationship with "traditional," or "classical," Malian art, exemplified by the carved wooden figures and masks displayed in museums and in the homes of collectors. Many celebrate traditional arts as a part of their heritage, yet for most, traditional art also represents the past, a foundation from which they must move forward as they create art relevant to the concerns of contemporary Mali.

Several distinct conceptions of tradition and authenticity may be at play in a single moment of artistic creation: the artist's own conceptions, those that viewers bring to their encounters with an artist's work, and the artist's interpretation of his or her audience's expectations. These multiple understandings of tradition are at issue, to varied effect, in the major markets for contemporary bogolan. The work of many of the artists and designers participating in bogolan's revival has been shaped by their awareness not only of their audiences' preferences but also of the implications that lie behind those preferences: What does the common preference of non-Malians for "traditional" art imply about that audience's view of the country and its people? The tourist art market, as we shall see, provides a readily apparent illustration of the adaptations artists make to suit the expectations of their intended consumers. In each of bogolan's other markets the same careful evaluation of and adjustment to audience is evident. As Janet Wolff describes in her seminal work, *The Social Production of Art,* no work of art is unshaped by its audience: "The reader, viewer or audience is actively involved in the construction of the work of art, and without the act of reception/consumption, the cultural product is incomplete. This is not to say that consumption is simultaneous with production, but that it complements and completes it."[15]

The balance of power between artist and audience may be played out in the realm of "the traditional." That is, through the lens of artistic production, tradition and authenticity become means of both control and of resistance, as Marvin Cohodas' analysis of the marketing and reception of early twentieth-century Native American basket maker Elizabeth Hickox illustrates. He describes the control wielded by Western audiences: "The constructions of 'authentic tradition' imposed on indigenous peoples of North America were disempowering because they were descriptions of an imaginary past lifestyle that no living Native American could attain."[16] From the other side of this relationship, Cohodas indicates that Elizabeth Hickox and other Native American artists subversively resisted that control:

Native curio producers continuously negotiated the ambiguous and shifting Euro-American boundary between "tradition" and "innovation," adapting creatively to Western tastes and changing definitions of their own "authenticity" while avoiding overt signs of innovation that would jeopardize the value of a curio product as a metonym for the premodern.[17]

Bogolan tells a similar story of accommodation and resistance. The cloth has been successfully adapted to contemporary art markets, employed by both artists for whom tradition serves as a selling point and by those who seek to distance themselves from associations with the past.

Bogolan is profoundly embedded in traditional Malian practices, worn during Bamana women's initiation ceremonies and used by hunters as spiritually charged protective garments. In villages where the cloth is still made for local consumption, bogolan is woven by men and decorated by women using symbolic patterns that refer to Bamana history and mythology. Today in Bamako, bogolan dyes made of carefully prepared mixtures of earth, leaves, and bark are used to paint elaborately detailed landscapes, images from Malian history, and abstractions. The cloth is also fashioned into flowing robes as well as Western-style miniskirts, and quickly produced versions of bogolan are sold by the hundreds in tourist markets in Mali and abroad. In addition, bogolan's adaptations to American markets exemplify its role in the recent American celebration of multiculturalism. In its many incarnations, bogolan provides a fascinating illustration of the role of art in identity politics, its meanings shifting with the same fluidity as its forms.

My efforts to trace the many paths of bogolan's revival are informed by research conducted in Bamako over the course of approximately sixteen months, spanning nine years, from 1991 to 2000. In 1991 I spent the summer in Bamako working at the U.S. embassy as a Department of State intern. I entered the world of bogolan on meeting two art students, participants in the student-led uprising that mere weeks prior to my arrival overthrew the twenty-three-year dictatorial government of Moussa Traoré. The popular uprising, the culmination of years of resistance and violently suppressed opposition politics, cost the lives of more than one hundred students and other protesters in Bamako, some of whom died in the streets, others in detention following their arrests.[18] Their heroism, and that of the other Malians who died during the événements, the Malian term for the coup, is commemorated in several monuments throughout the city. During the months after Traoré's removal from power, the country entered a phase of national reinvention, creating a new system of government, drafting a new constitution, and eventually electing a new president, Alpha Oumar Konaré, in June 1992.[19]

The dramatic nature of Mali's political transformation had ramifications in nearly every aspect of Malian life. The two young men I met in 1991 were resuming classes long suspended by strikes at Mali's only art school, the Institut National des Arts (see Map 3), where bogolan classes were being taught. They eagerly embraced the technique and its characteristic patterns as a reflection of their pride in their Malian identity, which was heightened in the aftermath of the coup d'état. This was my first encounter with bogolan's aesthetic and associative powers.

I returned to Bamako in 1992 on a Fulbright pre-doctoral grant in art history to spend a year studying the training of artists and the marketing of visual art in a contemporary, multiethnic urban center. Bogolan was then, as it is now, a prominent icon in Bamako's visual landscape whose ubiquity soon led me to make it the central subject of my research. Documenting bogolan's biography required a range of approaches to examine the cloth's transformations at the hands of myriad artists, its celebration as an aspect of the newly democratic nation's cultural patrimony, and its growing role abroad as a symbol of the nation. Through observations and interviews conducted in museums, galleries, shops, studios, schools, and cultural events, I found that bogolan's presence (and, in some instances, its absence) provided fodder for spirited discussion; nearly everyone I encountered had opinions about and explanations for bogolan's growing popularity. Records in Mali's Archives Nationales and in libraries and research institutes provided documentation and further elucidation of bogolan's ascent to its current pinnacle of popularity.[20]

Returning to the United States in 1993, I found that I could continue unabated my investigation of bogolan's revival, for the cloth was also becoming an extraordinarily visible icon in U.S. markets as an element of fashion and housewares. Bogolan-patterned sheets, wrapping paper, vests, hats, and countless other items sold in North American shops, boutiques, and catalogues demonstrated the cloth's appeal and its relevance even an ocean away from its place of origin. Bogolan's associations with Malian culture, however, were largely absent, replaced by connections to other concepts and identities, including African American cultural pride for some consumers and a vague association with the "exotic" for others. The strength of bogolan's formal properties—its bold patterns and distinctive colors—enabled it to be altered yet remain undiluted, both stylistically and literally, by the distances it traveled.

On its journey from villages to international fashion, bogolan had to overcome an inauspicious introduction to non-Malian publics in the first few decades of the twentieth century. The earliest description of bogolanfini in a European publication is Franz de Zeltner's 1910 technical overview of the cloth's production,[21] which highlights its unique properties, while, already at this early date, despairing of its apparently inevitable disappearance in the face of Western imports:

> The Bambaras seem to be the only ones who know this decorative technique . . . the Bambara villages of the right bank of the Niger River have dyers who continue to make the cloth. Probably the commerce in European cottons tends to limit the use of indigenous cloth . . . one might imagine that the future of this type of dyeing is limited.[22]

As early as the 1920s, Henri Clouzot published illustrations of bogolanfini cloths from the Trocadéro Museum that had been collected by de Zeltner. Clouzot cites de Zeltner's description of the cloth's production, but Clouzot's lack of enthusiasm for the fabrics likely did little to encourage further research and collection:

Unfortunately, their designs are among the most rudimentary, at least among the pieces assembled by de Zeltner. The regular repetition of motifs, circles, chevrons . . . squares, crosses, zig-zagged and crossed lines, always arranged at right angles, don't do great honor to the inventive spirit of the Bambara.[23]

Other early references to bogolanfini are scarce, yet awareness of the cloth among non-Malians is indicated by records in the Archives Nationales, which contain a wealth of documents concerning French administration of the former colony. Telegrams and letters provide detailed accounts of the collection of artifacts for display in the numerous colonial expositions, the European equivalent to the American World's Fairs of the same period, from the middle of the nineteenth to the early twentieth century. Telegrams from regional governors in Dakar and Paris contain requests for specific items from certain regions. The planners of the Salon de la France d'Outre Mer in 1940 and the Exposition Coloniale Internationale in 1937, both held in Paris, requested *bogharafini*[24] and "*pagnes* [wraps] dyed with mud—black and white designs"[25] from regions that are still today known for bogolanfini production, including San and Kolokani.

Not until the 1970s did sustained interest in bogolan become evident in academic journals and popular publications on African art and fabrics.[26] The revival of bogolan in Mali had to wait, however, until circumstances in Bamako became conducive to new ways of thinking about Malian identity and until new markets for Malian arts gained a foothold in the city. It also had to wait, of course, until talented artists in the city recognized the cloth's potential.

The transformation of bogolanfini arguably could only have occurred in the urban, culturally heterogeneous, internationally oriented environment of Bamako, by far Mali's largest and most diverse community. The city offers a cultural, political, economic, and ethnic environment distinctly different from any other Malian city, town, or village. An introduction to Bamako's population and its other "vital statistics" provides insight into the revitalization of bogolan. Only in Bamako do artists have a range of outlets for their work (though all of the artists I know would agree that far more are still needed). These include hotel boutiques that cater to tourists, textile stalls in the large downtown market that sell the cloth wholesale to retailers and exporters, and a national museum whose rotating exhibition space provides a forum for the display of work by professional artists.

Bamako's large population places the city in a completely different social, political, and economic realm from the rest of the country. Conservative estimates place the population at more than seven hundred thousand inhabitants, though the city's many "unofficial" neighborhoods[27] and its hundreds of transient inhabitants may place the population as high as one million.[28] The concentration of people, industry, and governmental bureaucracy in this sprawling city is particularly dramatic in light of Mali's predominantly rural population. In 1992, the country's population was estimated at 9.82 million, with more than 90 percent of its inhabitants residing in rural areas.[29] These figures describe a nation whose urban population is concentrated in a single city, Bamako, which contains approximately 7 to 10 percent of the country's population.

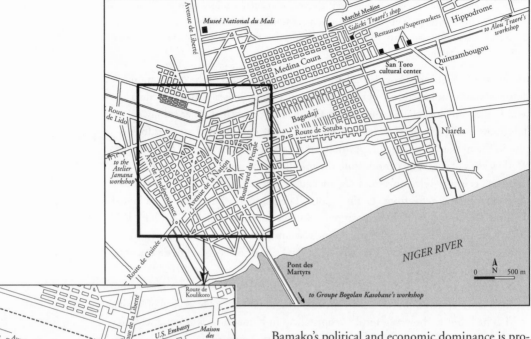

Top: Map 2. Bamako's
central neighborhoods.
Bottom: Map 3. Central
Bamako, detail.

Bamako's political and economic dominance is proportionately even greater than its population. As the country's capital, Bamako is home to all the national ministries, the site of policy development, and the focus of political campaigns as well as most political protests and unrest. Bamako is also the nation's education center, the location of all post-secondary institutions, including, as noted earlier, the Institut National des Arts. A similar dominance is evident in business and financial sectors; all embassies, international aid organizations, and banking institutions are based in the capital. Communications too are concentrated in the urban center; radio, television, and the vast majority of newspapers are based in Bamako, though some have correspondents and bureaus in other urban centers, such as Mopti, Segou, and Sikasso (see Map 1).

The average age of Mali's population is another factor particularly germane to the subject at hand: More than 60 percent of the country's population is under twenty years of age,[30] and a sizeable concentration of youthful Malians lives in Bamako. A large population of students has been drawn to the city's many schools, and large numbers of other young people have left their villages seeking employment in Bamako's factories, markets, restaurants, and other urban businesses. In this milieu, bogolan production has emerged as another source of income for young Malians. Additionally, young people provide a large portion of the market for some forms of bogolan.

Since the early twentieth century, Bamako has also been home and temporary host to numerous foreigners, who have been an important impetus and audience for artistic innovations. In 1908 the French selected Bamako as the capital of their colonies in the French Sudan, moving from the heat and sand of Kayes, northeast of Bamako, to what was then a small town whose location on the Niger River had already made it an entrepôt and a military base.[31] Because Bamako was the administrative capital, French foreign service officers and military personnel, and the tradesmen who provided services for them, moved to Bamako. The European population grew over time; the city today has by far the country's largest population of non-Malians. These non-Malians, from European (primarily French), Asian, North and South American, and African countries, have played an important role in the development of bogolan's current popularity.

Bamako's size, its diverse population, and its extensive connections with non-Malian cultures create both needs and potentialities particular to an urban setting. Of special relevance to the biography of contemporary bogolan is the role of urban centers in the creation of symbols of nationality, which may play important roles in both constructing and reflecting a nation's identity. Recent scholarship in the fields of sociology, history, and cultural studies has examined the complexities of identity construction in the increasingly globalized environment of the late twentieth century.[32] National identities are of necessity based on commonalities more diverse and complex than identities based on familial bonds, language, or ethnicity.[33]

Mali, for example, is a nation whose population comprises diverse ethnic groups, each of which speaks a distinct language, or, as in the case of the Dogon, several distinct linguistic dialects. The country's deserts are populated by nomads, its savannas by farmers, and its riversides and towns by fishermen, traders, and other specialists; each group is ethnically and culturally distinct. Although varied ethnic groups live side by side in towns and villages, trade with each other, and intermarry, many markers of ethnic identity remain distinctive, from languages and clothing styles to family names and occupations.

Forging a national identity of these varied ethnic and regional identities is a particularly crucial process in urban Bamako, the seat of national government, where the external forces of trade, international aid, tourism, and the like complicate the city's ethnic mix. The urban "cauldron" in which Malians and foreigners of varied ethnicities coexist may in fact intensify rather than diminish the distinctions between the local and the foreign. B. Marie Perinbam's thorough and illuminating investigation of Bamako in the nineteenth century reveals that the city has long been a place of identity formation in opposition to exterior forces. In fact, the significance of the ethnic label "Bambara," or "Bamana," was shaped by the interface between the French and local inhabitants of the then-French Sudan.[34] In the face of non-Malian influences, national identity becomes a unifying force. Esther Pasztory describes the emergence of identificatory artistic styles as a means of unifying a group to set themselves apart from external forces: "Ethnic or polity styles emerge primarily as a way of dealing with others, and their purpose is the creation of difference. The socio-political conditions essential for them is the close proximity of other independent groups."[35]

When the peoples with whom one coexists are members of local ethnic groups, national identity becomes less important than the ethnic identity that distinguishes one from one's neighbors. In Bamako, where one's neighbors, coworkers, supervisors, teachers, friends, and public figures may be American, French, Nigerian, or Russian, Malian identity becomes a source of difference. John Tomlinson, among others, has noted the increasing importance of identity construction in the modern world: "The fact that the nation-state is the most significant political-economic unit into which the world is divided means that there is often a good deal of 'cultural construction' involved in the making of national identities."[36] One means by which these national identities are constructed is through the revival and celebration of traditions that can be generalized to provide a common sense of cultural unity. Among the seminal collection of studies on the phenomenon of identity construction in the modern world is Eric Hobsbawn and Terence Ranger's *Invention of Tradition,* which addresses revivals and adaptations of traditional clothing, music, and ritual to suit the needs of modern nation-states.[37] Bogolan provides such a tradition. It has been generalized in Bamako from its specifically Bamana (and, less well known, its Dogon, Minianka, and Senufo) origins to serve as broadly Malian. Nakunte Diarra, a highly regarded bogolanfini artist, produces cloth in a distinctly Bamana context. Yet, as Tavy Aherne notes, Diarra appreciates her cloth's increasing adaptation to the needs of national rather than ethnic identity:

> Nakunte is very aware of the changes occurring in bógólanfini production. In fact, she differentiates between those designs she considers old, "the bógólan of old men," which existed before Mali's 1960 independence, and those which were created after this date. The former she calls "Bamana," the latter "Mali." . . . She also includes in the "Mali" category San cloths [quickly produced bogolan from the city of San that is made for the tourist trade], stenciled examples, and bógólanfini paintings by trained artists.[38]

Clearly, bogolan's biography is a complex assemblage of diverse yet congruent forms. The cloth's many "personae" coexist, appearing in varied markets simultaneously. Quickly produced bogolan aimed at the tourist trade is sold from street stalls not far from the Musée National du Mali (see Map 2), where bogolan from nearby villages is displayed alongside treasured ancient terra-cottas from Djenne,[39] while bogolan clothing is worn in Bamako's nightclubs and bogolan-patterned sheets are sold in Chicago department stores.

In a reflection of its multilayered subject, this book is presented in a series of overlapping chapters. The six chapters at its core are paired sets, each addressing one of the three major incarnations of bogolan's revival in contemporary Malian markets. Each pair opens with a chapter that defines the broad outlines of the subject at hand, laying the theoretical groundwork for discussions of bogolan's adaptations to the worlds of tourist art, studio art, and fashion. Flanking these discussions are chapters that address bogolan's roots and its farthest branches: the "traditional" bogolan of rural villages and the cloth's adaptations to the U.S. market. Each of these chapters addresses one of bogolan's contemporary manifestations, yet each acknowledges the blurred boundaries of its subject. The present chapter has set the stage for bogolan's biography. Here, a crucial character was introduced: Bamako, home to the vast majority of the artists, entrepreneurs, designers, and consumers who animate the cloth's revival. Bogolan made elsewhere in Mali also finds its primary markets in Bamako, where rural origins add to its salability. Like urban centers the world over, Bamako is in the forefront of cultural transformations, an incubator of new styles and a port of entry for non-local influences.

Chapter 2 introduces the "classic" version of the cloth that has inspired the present explosion of bogolan-related arts. An overview of the cloth's forms and the techniques of its production lays the groundwork for the discussions of contemporary bogolan's many urban manifestations, all of which are rooted (to varying degrees) in the techniques and iconography of rural bogolanfini. In villages and small towns throughout the southern third of Mali, women make bogolanfini wraps and tunics for use in specific ritual contexts. Although this cloth's ritual functions and rural origins might lead observers to expect that it is made in a conservative, insular environment, a closer examination of its contexts reveals much innovation, often in response to market demands and to individual artists' inspiration, much like the innovations of Bamako's bogolan revival. The rural production of bogolanfini is more than the passive inspiration for bogolan's recent urban manifestations; many of the women who make bogolanfini are directly linked to the technique's adaptations to painting, haute couture clothing, and tourist art in Bamako. Some of the women who make the cloth for local use also teach the technique to artists and entrepreneurs from Bamako, and others receive commissions from Bamako or farther afield to make cloth for collectors and entrepreneurs. Thus, the "traditional" versions of the cloth have a direct effect on urban, international markets far beyond the villages and small towns where they are created.

Chapters 3 and 4, the first paired set, address the bogolan of Bamako's tourist art market, which abounds wherever foreigners congregate in the city. "Tourist art" has long been maligned by participants in the fine art trade, the term itself often considered to be synonymous with fakery and mass production. With few exceptions, scholars and collectors of African art have turned their attention to tourist art only in order to elucidate the characteristics of "authentic" art objects. The stacks of bogolan in tourist market stalls, not surprisingly, have been virtually ignored by students of Malian visual culture. Yet, any survey of bogolan's contemporary manifestations would be woefully incomplete without an investigation of this deceptively simple adaptation of the cloth. Tourist market bogolan incorporates a variety of technical and conceptual innovations, all aimed at efficiently meeting the desires and expectations of its audiences. My discussion of these adaptations centers on two distinct iconographic strategies by which associations with tradition are signified. I have labeled these strategies mimetic and reproductive adaptations. The cloth made for sale in the tourist market is often sold along with information that ties it to tradition, a layering on of references that supplement the varied styles of bogolan itself. The tourist market offers arguably the most vivid illustration of the negotiation and renegotiation of "tradition" on an international stage.

Another important arena for the shaping of Malian "tradition" is the studio art, or fine art, market, increasingly populated by artists using bogolan materials and iconography. Chapters 5 and 6 center on several of the artists whose work exemplifies the innovative adaptation of bogolan to painting in a wide range of styles. Unlike the producers of bogolan for the tourist art market, these artists have adapted the medium as a means of self-expression, with marketing concerns occupying a secondary level of motivation. Each seeks to express a personal vision and to distinguish his or (more rarely) her work from that of other artists, from the bogolan made for sale to tourists, and from the rural versions of the cloth associated with Malian tradition. Several of these artists also use bogolan to create clothing and housewares, thus blurring the boundaries between fine art and fashion.

Chapters 7 and 8 examine the uses of contemporary bogolan as clothing, harkening back to its original function, yet here appearing in dramatically innovative forms. My discussion of bogolan fashion distinguishes between two strains, each reflecting a distinct relationship to the traditions that bogolan embodies: the "fine art" and "couture" schools. Because garments are highly visible and directly associated with the person who wears them, bogolan clothing offers a particularly vivid opportunity for designers and their patrons to express diverse attitudes toward "traditional" Malian culture. Worn by both Malians and non-Malians, bogolan skirts, vests, hats, and other garments may connote both urban modernity and rural traditionalism. Here too, boundaries between bogolan's varied "personae" are porous: cloth made for sale in the tourist market may be tailored to create fashionable clothing for Malian markets; artists who create elaborately worked paintings for sale in galleries may rely on sales of quickly produced bogolan scarves and hats to support themselves.

Chapter 9 follows bogolan abroad to the United States, where the cloth has in the past decade gained popularity among audiences quite distinct from those who make, wear, and purchase bogolan in Mali. In the United States, bogolan has undergone dramatic formal transformations yet still retains crucial ties to the cloth that is its inspiration. Here, bogolan's abstract designs and its black and white hues are its defining features. Although bogolan-inspired products may not be identified as Malian, they are consistently associated with Africa or, more broadly, with distant, "authentic" cultures. In some contexts, bogolan is marketed as an emblem of African American identity, while in others the cloth is presented as broadly "ethnic." These most distant manifestations demonstrate bogolan's formal strength and the power of its symbolic associations, altered but not lost as the cloth moves across an ocean.

Bogolan is at play in the negotiation of tradition and modernity in contemporary Mali, and it is used as a tool in the formation of numerous identities, from prototypically "authentic" Malian culture to the "global" blending of cultures. Bogolan is extraordinary for its presence in so many distinct markets, for its popularity in its place of origin and abroad, and for its capability to carry diverse yet related meanings wherever it travels. As we shall see in the chapters that follow, bogolan offers invaluable insight into the complexity of contemporary Mali's relationship with its "traditions." Simultaneously, the cloth illustrates the strategic adaptations of those traditions to Western tastes, both in Mali and in the United States.

# 2

# THE RURAL ROOTS
# OF BOGOLAN

Nous assistons à une évolution et à la dilution d'une tradition millénaire, confrontée à une diffusion de masse. Malgré ce phénomène, peu de personnes connaissent l'origine et la technique du bogolan. (We are witness to an evolution and to the dilution of an age-old tradition that is encountering a popular diffusion. In spite of this phenomenon, few people are familiar with bogolan's origins and its technique.)
*Pauline Duponchel,*
*Bogolan Traditionelle*

The bogolan that is today being adapted to a wide range of new markets carries with it powerful associations—images of women gathering leaves and dyeing cloth in village settings, hunters wearing bogolanfini tunics as they stalk dangerous game in the forest, and young girls clad in bogolanfini wraps ritually transformed from childhood to adulthood. These associations and others accompany the cloth into the marketplace, whether it is sold in Bamako or abroad. Kandiora Coulibaly, founder of the atelier Groupe Bogolan Kasobane, eloquently expressed the profound connection between Malians and bogolan when he stated that bogolan is literally made of the earth, forests, rivers, and sun of Mali.[1] Coulibaly's comment is true both literally and figuratively. Bogolan's powerful associations with Malian culture and with the land itself are a crucial aspect of the revival and revitalization of bogolan in Mali today. Thus, one cannot hope to understand the bogolan baseball caps and pillows sold in Bamako and beyond without first exploring the cloth's rural roots.

Bogolan's precise history is not known, though the people who make and use the cloth speak of it as an ancient art form. The oldest examples of bogolanfini in European museums date from the early twentieth century, with the oldest documented cloth, from 1900, in the Musée de l'Homme in Paris.[2] The collection of the Musée Ethnographique du Bâle in Switzerland includes a cloth that dates from 1908,[3] and Sarah Brett-Smith illustrates a cloth in the Museum für Völkerkunde in Munich that was collected in 1915.[4] Renowned German anthropologist Leo Frobenius collected four pieces of bogolanfini in 1910, all adorned with patterns that resemble those still in use today.[5] The similarity this cloth bears to contemporary bogolanfini indicates the continuity of the practice and hints at the long history that lies behind these early examples, part of a complex, already fully developed tradition. Bogolan's adaptations to Bamako's diverse art markets are but the most recent developments in this long history.

Even as bogolanfini has been adapted to new products and new markets, the cloth in its original forms clearly remains relevant in Mali today. Bogolan is a rare example of an artistic tradition that thrives simultaneously in its original form and in modern, global incarnations; the roots from which Bamako's bogolan emerges continue to grow, as do its farthest branches. Rural bogolanfini is not a stage in the evolution of urban bogolan; the diverse aspects of bogolan's biography are at the same time experiencing a revival on the international market.

As noted in Chapter 1, the distinctive manner by which bogolanfini is made is described, in elegant simplicity, by the Bamana word itself, which means "cloth made of earth or mud." My use of the term *bogolanfini* refers here to the cloth's rural, "traditional" incarnations, made of local materials for local use, painstakingly designed and created by women who have learned their skills during long apprenticeships to older female friends and relatives.

The bogolanfini heartland is the Beledougou region north of Bamako, generally considered the cloth's place of origin.[6] The Beledougou region, whose population is primarily Bamana, is renowned for the tenacity of indigenous religions, which are marked by initiatory societies and belief in wilderness spirits. These aspects of Bamana heritage were long ago displaced or modified by Islam, the professed religion of 90 percent of the country's population.[7] Bogolanfini is thoroughly rooted in the societal practices of Bamana animism, so the Beledougou region's reputation for the production of bogolanfini is tied to its population's perpetuation of non-Islamic (or, more precisely, extra-Islamic) practices. In fact, claiming a cloth's origins in the Beledougou has become a selling point for merchants in Bamako.

Bogolan has long been made in other regions as well, by Bamana artists as well as by members of varied ethnic groups, including the Bozo, Dogon, Minianka, and Senufo. Each of these groups is, in theory, distinguished by its own styles, though those distinctions have become much more fluid in recent years. The Bamana are, however, the best-known producers of bogolanfini and, not surprisingly, Bamana versions of the cloth are most often illustrated and displayed in publications, museums, and galleries, coming to serve as the "classic" style of the cloth. Scholarship, too, has overwhelmingly focused on Bamana production. Within the sphere of Bamana bogolanfini, one of several substyles has come to stand for the tradition as a whole, both in Mali and abroad: *kanjida,* or "white bogolanfini." The style's relevance to many innovative artists and entrepreneurs is in its reference to an immediately recognizable prototype through its patterns. The cloth's range of functions in initiations and as hunter's garb, as well as its relative visibility, is equally important, for it predisposes this type of bogolanfini to multiple adaptations.

Brett-Smith divides bogolanfini into three categories—red, black, and white— noting that Bamana color categories do not correspond to Western conceptions. "Red" might describe cloths that range from yellow to dark brown, and "black" might include indigo-dyed blue and green cloths as well as dark-hued bogolanfini. In the realm of bogolanfini, the color classification of cloth can be as much a function of its patterns and its intended uses as a reflection of the cloth's hue. All bogolan in the red category (*basaie,* or *bileman*) serve ritual functions and have protective powers, while white cloths are used in secular contexts. Each color category carries symbolic associations: red with blood and transformation, black with fertility and productivity, and white with both death and purity.[8] The well-known artist Nakunte Diarra divides bogolanfini into four categories: white, black, gray, and red. Kanjida cloth, Diarra explains, is the most common type and may be worn by anyone. Black and its variations, including gray cloth, are not common styles: "Black . . . is worn in similar contexts to white and is chosen over white as a personal preference, while gray may be worn as camouflage by hunters in the bush."[9] Red bogolanfini, dyed in a bath of boiled bark from the *n'beku,* or *m'peku,* tree, is also associated with hunters' shirts.

Because kanjida might acceptably be worn at a wide range of events, and is not as specialized in its functions as other varieties of bogolanfini, it lends itself to the secular markets of contemporary Bamako. This white style is so thoroughly accepted as representative of the bogolanfini tradition that it is rarely identified as part of a subgroup; for all intents and purposes, kanjida is the classic style of bogolan. The contemporary revival of bogolan that is the focus of this study is most frequently modeled on kanjida.

## MAKING BOGOLANFINI: COTTON AND EARTH

Bogolanfini is distinguished by its highly contrasting black, brown, and white hues as well as its geometric patterns (Plate 1). The pigments that give the cloth its distinctive appearance are applied in an extraordinarily labor-intensive manner that, not surprisingly, has been modified to speed production for artists at work in Bamako today. Every aspect of bogolanfini's production involves specialized expertise and great patience; successful bogolanfini artists may spend a lifetime learning all of the subtleties of the cloth's production and its symbolism.

Bogolanfini begins with the cleaning, carding, and spinning of cotton, tasks performed by women. Although all women might be expected to possess the basic skills required for these tasks, spinning requires experience and a sure hand to create thread of consistent strength and thickness. The next step in the process, the weaving, is the exclusive purview of male professionals. Working on horizontal looms, weavers transform the cotton thread into long rolls of fabric strips approximately six to eight inches wide (fifteen to twenty centimeters) (Figure 2).[10] These strips are then sewn into cloth called *tafé* or *taafé* in Bamanakan and *pagnes* in French,[11] usually six or seven, and rarely eight, strips wide. Locally woven cloth, *finimougou,* is readily distinguishable from factory-produced cloth, because the seams between the narrow strips are clearly evident, and the cloth has the natural irregularities of hand-spun and woven cloth.

Although men weave the cloth from which bogolanfini is made, women do the work that transforms it into a distinctly Malian art form, for they gather, process, and apply mineral and vegetal pigments to create its colors and patterns. Rural women learn the technique from older female relatives, observing and later assisting in the creation of the cloth. Because the lives of women are filled with responsibility for children, with tending gardens and fields, and with household chores, bogolanfini is generally produced during the dry season, when farming responsibilities are temporarily suspended. Older women, past their childbearing years and relieved of some responsibilities by their now-grown children or by their increased frailty, may have the time and the talent to devote to bogolanfini production. As Julianne Freeman notes, bogolanfini production offers a rare opportunity for elderly women to continue to contribute to their families' economic well-being, while most "older women are challenged by the loss of the productivity in which they used to engage as younger women."[12] Similarly, women who have never had children may also become bogolanfini artists.[13]

Figure 2. Weaver at
work. Bamako, Mali,
1993.

*On a side street in Ba-
mako's Quinzambougou
neighborhood, a weaver
produces strips of cotton
cloth on a single-heddle
loom. The warp stretches
out in front of the loom,
weighted by a sledge that
moves slowly toward him
as he weaves.*

The complex and labor-intensive nature of bogolanfini has been the object of fascination among students of African textiles. Claire Polakoff, in her survey of African
textiles, singles out bogolanfini's technical complexity, stating,

> Among the most elusive and difficult to classify of all the fabrics in Africa—both in a tech-
> nical as well as a design sense—has been the mud cloth of the Bambara (Bamana) peoples
> of Mali. . . . Mud cloth has confused textile historians because the designs seem to indicate
> procedures used in other fabric design techniques.[14]

Polakoff likely refers to the resemblance of bogolanfini's light patterns on a dark
ground to resist-dyed fabrics such as batiks. Looking closely at the cloth's surface, one
might well imagine that bogolan's patterns were covered with wax or some other im-
permeable material and the entire cloth dyed in a dark pigment; in batik or *adire*[15]
cloth, the resist would then be removed to reveal the still-undyed patterns. In fact, the
technique used to make bogolanfini more closely resembles a reversal of resist techniques, painstakingly applying the background instead of the patterns themselves.

Bogolanfini artist Nakunte Diarra will serve to illustrate the production of bogolanfini. Diarra is from Kolokani, a small town in the heart of the Beledougou region. She epitomizes the success of bogolanfini in the international market: she is
routinely commissioned by European and American visitors to create cloths for museums and private collections; she teaches young men from Bamako and elsewhere in

Mali who seek to earn a living from the production of bogolan in the new, urban markets; and she has allowed numerous researchers to document her techniques and her opinions.[16]

Tavy Aherne, in the 1992 catalogue that accompanied the U.S. exhibition of Diarra's work, describes the many aspects of Diarra's circumstances that would likely lead observers to classify her work as "traditional." Trained by the side of her mother and grandmother, steeped in the lore of Bamana history and culture, Diarra seems to demonstrate the stasis of tradition perpetuated by artists who receive and pass on an unchanging set of beliefs and practices. Yet, as Aherne notes, this apparent conservatism conceals the essence of her success: Diarra has skillfully incorporated new forms and new iconography, fusing them seamlessly with the skills she learned from her mother and grandmother.[17]

Nakunte Diarra's method of working serves as a typical example of bogolanfini production. The dyeing process begins with the mashing and boiling, or soaking, of leaves from the n'gallama (*Anogeissus leiocarpus*) and *n'tjankara* (*Combretum glutinosum*) trees to create a dye bath.[18] After soaking in the bath, the cloth is dried in the sun. The dye causes the cloth to take on a yellowish tint, which is more pronounced on the side of the cloth facing the sun, whose light activates the dye; the yellow of the n'gallama thus becomes more vivid if the sun is particularly intense on the day the cloth is dyed.[19] Though this tint will be barely visible on the finished cloth, the dye bath is a crucial preparatory step in the process that readies the cloth for the application of pigment.

Diarra then carefully considers the distribution of designs, measuring off the sections into which the cloth will be divided. Bogolanfini wrappers are generally divided into five distinct sections, each dominated by a motif, although the same motif may appear in more than one section. Each section has a name:

> left border—*sokono bolo* (the hidden border), the end of the cloth that is tucked under when worn as a wrap and is thus not visible
> right border—*kenema bolo* (the outer border)
> top border—*finitayoro* or *fini siri bolo* (the section that is attached), the portion wrapped around the waist that may be folded down
> bottom border—*senkorola* or *duguma bolo* (the section that is closest to the ground or to the feet)
> central section—*fini ba* (the big cloth or the mother of the cloth) or *ba so*[20]

The motif that adorns the central section is the most important and receives the most weight in evaluating a cloth's quality.

Although not all bogolanfini wraps conform to this system of organization—because individual artists or clients may choose to work with fewer distinct segments—as a general rule the cloth may be "read" as five related sections. In discussing the characteristics of a fine cloth, Diarra notes that she admires "creativity, manifested in the manipulation of known motifs in new and different ways."[21] Combinations of motifs, distributed among the five sections of the cloth, often relate to one another. Patterns that describe bravery, familial harmony, or some other general subject may be used together.

Figure 3. Nakunte Diarra's tools and mud pigment. Kolokani, 1992. Photograph by Tavy D. Aherne.

*Like most bogolanfini artists, Nakunte Diarra uses wooden or iron tools to apply a concoction of fermented mud to her cloth.*

Bogolanfini's patterns are applied using a *binyé,* a pointed iron spatula, or a *kala,* a wooden stick, dipped in a highly concentrated earth or mud concoction (Figure 3). The mud is collected from riverbeds, and individual artists usually favor the particular earth of a particular place. Pascal James Imperato and Marli Shamir describe the gathering of mud:

> The mud used for creating the designs is obtained from the centers of large ponds which have dried up at the height of the dry season in April. Essentially, the mud is collected from that central portion of the pond's bottom which has had water in it for the longest period of time.[22]

The intensity and, correspondingly, the effectiveness of the mud is enhanced by its fermentation in clay jars, often for months, further decomposing the organic materials in the mixture. Some of the artists who have adapted bogolan to new markets in Bamako have personal "recipes" for the preparation of mud.

The mud is carefully applied to the cloth, worked into the surface with the binyé, kala, or occasionally a feather quill, until it covers nearly the entire face. The artist usually works seated on the ground, often beneath a tree for shade. Freeman draws attention to the position in her analysis of older women's work: "Ntifè [Ntifè Tarawèlè, an elderly bogolanfini artist], as other women I have seen, paint while sitting on the ground, legs spread out in front of her. This posture is often associated with greater leisure and older women often have the pleasure of being able to sit in this manner."[23] On her lap, the artist holds an inverted calabash bowl, with the cloth draped over its curved surface. She works on one portion at a time, keeping the entire composition of the cloth in mind though the curved surface on which she works distorts her view of the whole. The straightness of the lines on the finished cloth is all the more impressive when one considers the spherical calabash on which they are painted (Plate 2).

The artist creates bogolanfini's distinctive patterns in negative space, painting the mud around her intended designs. Thus, the motifs in white are created by applying the dark mud to the background from which they emerge. Once applied, the mud is permitted to dry to a gray, crackly consistency. The cloth is then washed in clean water to remove the mud. Wherever it has been applied, the mud darkens the cloth, leaving in its place a brown or gray tone. John Donne's chemical analysis of the cloth elucidates this reaction: "Chemical tests carried out on a recent specimen of bogolanfini confirmed that the technique consists of mordanting the cloth with tannic acid and then painting it with an iron oxide to produce a black or dark brown colour."[24] That is, the yellow-tinted dye bath of n'gallama and n'tjankara leaves produces tannic acid, a basic element in compounds used to tan leather, that serves as a mordant or fixative. The highly concentrated mud that is applied contains iron oxide, which reacts with the tannic acid to permanently darken the cloth. To attain deep, saturated browns and blacks, women may coat the surface with several layers of mud, each applied after the cloth has been washed of the previous layer's dried mud and, importantly, again dyed in the n'gallama or n'tjankara bath. These successive layers compound bogolanfini's labor intensiveness, each applied to cover precisely the same areas, cleanly outlining the motifs.

A variety of other materials may be used to apply color to the cloth—too many to name here. Each region, village, and individual artist may use specific combinations of leaves, roots, bark, or various other ingredients to create distinctive effects. Often, the detailed "trade secrets," as Aherne describes this knowledge, are known only to the artist and, perhaps, to the girls and young women she instructs:

> [D]uring an initial step in the preparation of the mud dye, Nakunte uses a species of leaf different from that commonly used by bógólanfini artists; this leaf helps her achieve the very dark coloration of the mud dye for which her cloth is known. She does not disclose the name of the leaf to other artists.[25]

The final step in bogolanfini production is, somewhat paradoxically, the removal of the color created by the first step. Using a locally produced soap made of millet bran, caustic soda, and ground peanuts, artists retrace the designs to remove the yellow created by the dye bath so that the motifs emerge in white on a brown or black ground.[26] This task is often given to young girls, part of the process by which they learn the technique.[27] Imperato and Shamir describe the elaborate process by which the yellow pigment is removed by some of the artists in the Beledougou region:

> The artist carefully passes over the designs with the tip of a thin stick which is dipped with each stroke into the savon de sodani [locally produced soap] solution. The yellow designs turn brown on contact with the preparation. Once all the designs have been passed over, the cloth is placed out in the sun for a week. Ordinary water is then thrown onto it, and most of the soap is thus washed off. . . . Then water which has been used for washing large millet after the bran is removed is thrown onto the cloth, and then simple water. With this the cloth is finished.[28]

Today, the wide availability of industrial, chlorine bleach (known by its ubiquitous brand name, Eau de Javel) and commercial soaps enable artists to more easily remove the yellow tint of the n'gallama or n'tjankara dye.

### Bogolanfini's Patterns: A Language of Geometry

Like the cloth's manufacture, the iconography of bogolanfini is complex and distinctively Bamana. The rows of circles, crosses, zigzag lines, and other geometric elements that adorn bogolanfini carry messages for those trained in their interpretation. Bogolanfini symbols may refer to objects, historical events, mythological subjects, and proverbs. The designs have been likened to a written language, most notably by Brett-Smith, whose analysis of subtle irregularities in the patterns that adorn bogolanfini postulates that the artists deliberately obscure their designs in order to conceal knowledge, like encoded imperfections purposefully inserted into a written text.[29] The cloth's symbolic, linguistic functions have become important selling points as the cloth has entered the tourist art market. Ironically, the cloths sold in the tourist markets bear designs that have little or no relationship to bogolanfini's patterns.

Opinions vary concerning the size of the "bogolanfini-literate" population in Mali. According to Imperato and Shamir, the meaning of designs are "fairly well-known according to most adults in rural areas of Bamana country."[30] Brett-Smith, however, asserts that the cloths are "illegible to all but a few."[31] The question of bogolanfini's legibility has been complicated by the increased availability of information about the cloth's history and its functions, as a result of its increasing popularity among Malians and non-Malians. Students are taught the meaning of bogolanfini symbols at Bamako's only art school, the Institut National des Arts.[32] The symbols have also been elucidated for public consumption at art exhibitions and in tourist markets, where they become selling points for non-Malian consumers. Few of the artists currently making bogolan paintings and clothing learned the technique and its iconography as it has historically been taught; classrooms and publications provide the contemporary urban equivalent to apprenticeships.

Bogolanfini, like any foreign language, is a text that can be read if one learns its vocabulary. Many of the motifs have direct referents, including objects (drums, cushions, or houses), locations (streams, hills, and towns), animals, and historical events. Many designs have more complicated, historical or proverbial meanings beneath the basic identification of a motif's referent. According to Brett-Smith, "Medicinal knowledge, historical facts, and moral precepts for correct behavior are all coded into *Bogolanfini* designs."[33] She describes the deeper knowledge contained by the symbols in a discussion of the *sajume kama* motif (an **M** with a dot placed where the two middle lines meet in a **V**). Initially Brett-Smith's informants revealed only that the design represents the wing of a particular bird. Later, and without prompting, she was told that "the bird is the major ingredient in the cure for a disease which produces lower back pain and sterility in childbearing women between the ages of thirty and forty."[34] Thus, basic "literacy" provides only an introduction to the symbols, while fuller knowledge is reserved for experienced, expert women.

The examples illustrated here, all from the Beledougou region, include a number of well-known motifs.[35] The main motif in Plate 1 is *kalaka sen* (*kalaka* is a bamboo bed, *sen* means "foot"). The pattern refers to the bed of a newly married couple and, more broadly, to the union between man and wife. The top and left borders (finitay-oro and sokon bolo, respectively) are adorned with the dot pattern called *tiga farani* (peanut shells). Because women work a family's peanut fields, the symbol is associated with the female domain. According to one source, the portion of the pattern at the top, which wraps around the wearer's waist, also refers to the beads a woman may wear around her waist that are considered a very sensuous form of adornment.[36] Both interpretations stress the power and responsibilities of women.

Figure 4 features the popular motif *dan tigi mari. Danga* is a lake or river, *tigui* or *tigi* is a proprietor, and *mari* means "crocodile." Crocodiles, often associated with protective spirits, play important roles in Bamana mythology. Because towns and villages must always have a source of water, the crocodiles dwelling in that water become the guardians of both village residents and strangers who visit. Here, again, the top border is adorned with tiga farani. The right border (kenema bolo) repeats the dan tigi mari pattern. The left border consists of a pattern called *wosoko* or *woroso,* the "back of the sickle." Finally, the bottom (senkorola) is adorned with a historical theme—*Djosse kan kono.* Djosse is the name of a legendary Bamana warrior, and *kan kono* means "long neck," an attribute considered to be handsome. Djosse is also called Koumicolo Djosse, Koumicolo being the name of Djosse's village in the Beledougou region. Djosse was among the Beledougou Bamana warriors who resisted the imposition of French colonial rule early in the twentieth century and is famed for the moment of his death: when he knew his cause was lost, he committed suicide rather than suffer the indignity of

Figure 4. Bogolanfini wrap, artist and date unknown. Bogolan pigments on strip-woven cotton. 60″ × 35″ (152 × 89 cm). Collection of the University of Iowa Museum of Art, purchased with funds from Robert F. and Delores DeWilde Bina. Photograph by Steve Tatum.

*This wrap features the dan tigi mari motif, which refers to the role of crocodiles as protective spirits. Bogolanfini artists are admired for creating innovative combinations of motifs, selecting patterns whose symbolic meanings harmonize.*

French domination.[37] Bogolanfini's patterns contain a wealth of information about Bamana culture—history, mythology, daily life, morality—and myriad aspects of being Bamana are expressed by the cloths. Like its patterns, bogolanfini's functions penetrate deeply into the core of Bamana culture.

### Patterns in Use: Bogolanfini's Functions

Bogolanfini's functions are physical and spiritual, serving as both body covering and, in some circumstances, as a form of ritual protection in situations particularly rife with otherworldly dangers. In all of its forms, the cloth is used as clothing.[38] In its most common form, bogolanfini is worn by girls and women as a wrap, encircling the waist and extending to the midcalf. Bogolanfini is also worn by men either as shirts that consist of narrow cloths with a neck hole or more extensively tailored tunics.

Brett-Smith has researched the use of bogolanfini pagnes by women, focusing her study on the association of the cloth with excision (female circumcision) ceremonies.[39] Mali remains a country with high rates of excision, despite the efforts of several international organizations to eradicate this practice whose social and medical dangers have made it a major human rights issue. A study sponsored by the Population Council surveyed Malian health clinics in urban and rural areas, including Bamako, and found that 94 percent of the women who visited clinics had undergone some form of genital cutting—an extraordinarily high rate.[40] Excision remains prevalent in Mali as part of the rites by which young girls are transformed into socially "complete" women.

Bogolanfini wraps (basaie and *n'gale* styles in particular) are worn by girls and young women immediately following the excision ceremony. During the four weeks following the procedure, girls and women are confined to an enclosure with the *zeman,* an older woman who serves as their guardian and who may also wear bogolanfini. The cloths are worn and ritually washed each week until the end of the period of seclusion, when they are either given to the elderly female relative who cared for the girl during the excision or kept by the young woman to be worn when her marriage is consummated.[41] Brett-Smith asserts that the cloth's absorption of blood at moments of significant ritual transition—excision and first intercourse—indicates its role in the control of *nyama,*[42] the potentially dangerous spiritual power released at such moments:

> The porous Basaie cloths that ritually cover the girls and the blood of their wounds are able to absorb the nyama set free by excision. The painted cotton drinks in the girl's sweat and her blood as she heals, and these highly charged substances transmit not only the physical detritus of the operation to the cloth, but the incomprehensible forces of childhood, the unrestricted power of original nyama.[43]

Bogolan is, thus, intimately tied to a Bamana social practice central to the lives of women, bearing the immense weight of protection and healing at a moment of great consequence.

The cloth is also worn by Bamana hunters, men whose roles and significance extend far beyond the immediate tasks of tracking and killing animals (Plate 3).

Hunters must have extraordinary powers, for they face the dangers, both physical and otherworldly, of the untamed wilderness. They must possess physical, intellectual, and spiritual prowess to make their way successfully through a realm filled with dangerous animals, difficult terrain, and uncontrolled spirits. They are the stuff of legends; Bamana mythology and history is rife with stories of hunters as leaders, heroes, and adventurers. Hunters are considered extraordinary, existing outside the bounds of normal village and town life.

Patrick McNaughton's research on the arts associated with hunters confirms the importance of clothing, specifically bogolanfini tunics and shirts, as markers of the exceptional powers hunters control: "The shirts (*donson dlokiw*) in fact are symbols with a complex set of references, which ultimately include nearly every aspect of the hunters' abilities and their roles in traditional society."[44] His description of the shirts' powerful presence emphasizes the effectiveness of bogolanfini in creating an aura of mystery and drama:

> Old examples owned by expert hunters give the impression of having emerged full blown from the bush. They almost sting the eyes with large quantities of attachments, with horns and claws, strips of rawhide and skin-covered amulets. . . . Sometimes mud-dyed cloth called bogolanfini is used, and then the overlay of attachments is even more dramatic because it obliterates the complex pattern of off-white and black motifs.[45]

The association of bogolanfini with excision and with the powerful work of hunters places the cloth deep within the animist religious and social practices of Bamana society. The making of such spiritually charged cloth requires an experienced artist who knows how to negotiate its dangers. Freeman discusses the protective measures taken by one artist:

> One time when I was watching, Ntifè rinsed her mouth [with the water used to wash a finished bogolanfini cloth and] she looked up at me and laughed. She knew that I was just then understanding the import of her action. . . . This common part of the cloth-making routine, in which saliva is a key ingredient, is a protective measure against the general threat of sorcery that Ntifè's occupation entails.[46]

Freeman goes on to explain that work for individual gain, that which might set an artist apart from her neighbors, may attract the ill intentions of sorcerers, who are widely feared in the Beledougou region.[47] In addition, the making of a cloth that so powerfully embodies Bamana culture, using ordinary cotton, earth, and leaves, transforms these materials completely, imbuing them with power through that process. Involvement with this transformation can be dangerous: "The process of change is enacted by the hand of the artist, thus the artist takes precautions to protect herself from any of the energy (*nyama*) that may be released in the process."[48] The washing of hands, feet, and mouth and the use of incantations and other precautions taken by bogolanfini artists underscores the deep significance of the cloth.

The spiritual dimensions of bogolanfini, the culturally specific symbolism of its motifs, the use of local materials, the labor-intensive production process, and the division of labor into gender and age classifications all underscore its distinctly local character. All of bogolanfini's rural traits have an important effect on the patterns of its revitalization in Bamako, where the cloth has come to serve as a symbol of Bamana and of Malian identity. From small, rural villages to the crowded streets of Bamako and beyond, many of the traits that characterize bogolanfini are preserved, demonstrating the compatibility of a prototypically traditional art form with the swiftly changing demands of the contemporary, global marketplace.

# 3

# THE TOURIST ART MARKET

## Commerce in Authenticity

Tourist art is the
product of a careful,
anthropological study
of the material culture
and aesthetics of the
Western other by
Native artists and
craftspeople.
*Ruth B. Phillips, "Why
Not Tourist Art?"*

Bogolan is one of many textiles sold in Bamako's main tourist market, the
Grand Marché (see Map 3),[1] and in other tourist-oriented shops and stalls
throughout the city, in front of hotels, restaurants, and other businesses frequented by foreigners. Much of the bogolan sold in Bamako's tourist art markets
initially appears to be little more than quickly produced reproductions of "traditional" cloth; the brown, tan, black, and white hues of bogolanfini adorn cloths
with repetitive patterns, unevenly applied pigment, and stylized figures. The
cloth's deceptive simplicity, however, conceals its role in the complex systems by
which tourist art condenses, transforms, and reinvents Malian identity for non-
local audiences. This cloth also has a market among Malians, who use it to make
clothing and other items,[2] but because the cloth is produced with tourists and
other visitors as its intended market, the label "tourist market bogolan" describes
the cloth and its transformations.

The case of bogolan dramatically challenges Susan Vogel's statement that
"tourist art styles . . . don't evolve much."[3] Some styles, indeed, do not evolve—
Dogon figures and Bamana antelope headdresses are likely as popular today in
Malian markets as they were thirty years ago. To declare tourist art frozen in
time, however, much as "traditional" arts were long considered unchanging, is to
minimize the role of all artistic production as expressions of changing cultures,
shifting identities, and fluctuating demand in the world market. Tourist arts effectively express hybrid identities, created in response to the expectations and
perceptions of non-local audiences. Artists and merchants evaluate their markets
and work to create objects that fit consumers' preconceptions. As the expectations and preferences of tourists change, the artists and entrepreneurs of tourist
art markets work to develop new forms and discard those for which there is little
or no demand. Bogolan's adaptations to Bamako's tourist art market illustrate
such strategic, carefully considered responses to ever-changing consumers. Ruth
Phillips and Christopher Steiner have asserted that "neither the speed and acuity
with which indigenous artists responded to changes in taste and market nor the
dialogic nature of their creative activity has been adequately recognized."[4] The
analysis that follows might be viewed as a corrective to this observation.

## TOURIST ART IN BAMAKO

Bamako's active tourist art industry provides employment for many of the city's residents, as evidenced by the crowds of salespeople in the central market and in sites throughout the city where foreigners congregate, usually outside hotels, nightclubs, and restaurants. The visibility of the tourist art trade was, ironically, increased by the tragic burning of the main building of the Grand Marché in 1993. The conflagration forced merchants to relocate onto the downtown streets surrounding the burned structure. Moving through the market today can be a disorienting experience; stalls covered with plastic sheeting line makeshift alleyways that encircle the old market building, the narrow pathways snaking between piles of goods and crowds of shoppers.[5]

Another center for the tourist trade is the Maison des Artisans, commonly called the Artisanat (see Map 3), located across the street from the Institut National des Arts, five or six blocks from the Grand Marché. The Artisanat consists of two large rectangular buildings, each ringed by a series of small rooms that open onto a tiled walkway or loggia. In each room, or "boutique," male artisans work on their crafts; there are no women at work in the Artisanat, and few women have become involved at the management level. The media are grouped into categories; rows of boutiques for leather workers, jewelers, woodcarvers, and others ring the buildings. Wares are also for sale in each boutique, so tourists and others who purchase goods may see how the craftsmen work, wandering among the boutiques, watching the production process as they shop.

Whether in the old market, the Artisanat, or in the shops and stalls throughout the streets of downtown Bamako, merchants offer wares aimed to satisfy the expectations of tourists. The ubiquitous wooden figures (most frequently reproductions of Dogon sculpture),[6] ebony busts, and brass figurines crowded onto the shelves of stalls in markets and shops throughout the city attest to the initiative of producers and merchants. Alongside sculpture, textiles feature prominently in most tourist-oriented markets, including batiks, tie-dyed fabrics, wool blankets, and indigo-dyed cloth as well as bogolanfini-related fabrics (Plate 4).

Before the Grand Marché burned, the sale of textiles took place primarily in one section of the market's inner, covered area. Each stall, generally around ten to twelve square feet, was minimally furnished, with shelves, tables, and chairs. After the fire, the textile sellers who did not move to small shops or stalls on the streets surrounding the market fanned out through the streets downtown. They either sold their bogolan, Fulani blankets, and other distinctly Malian styles from small stocks of textiles they carried with them or approached tourists hoping to persuade them to visit their employers' shops, a strategy that had been in use before the 1993 fire. Here too all of the merchants were and remain men; women are the primary vendors of other types of textiles, including factory-produced cotton cloth adorned with large, brightly colored patterns.

The sale of textiles to tourists takes place in a variety of other venues throughout the city. Bamako's few large hotels—most notably the Hôtel Amitié, the Grand Hôtel, and the Hôtel Mande—have gift shops in their lobbies. At street stalls nearby, merchants not associated with the hotels seek to draw the attention of hotel guests as well. Restaurants, too, offer opportunities to target tourists. Along the heavily traveled Route de Koulikoro (see Map 3), which leads from the city's downtown to the Hippodrome neighborhood, home to a sizeable number of expatriates, several large restaurants and supermarkets cater to a non-Malian clientele.[7] Outside each establishment, stalls offer bogolan, batiks, wooden masks, baskets, and other products.

A great variety of textiles is sold in Bamako's tourist-oriented markets, from Saudi Arabian carpets made of synthetic fibers to mud-painted *korhogo* cloth from Côte d'Ivoire depicting masked dancers and fanciful animals. Textiles from Mali abound in the market, including brightly colored cotton blankets made in Mopti (a trading center north of Bamako, at the confluence of the Niger and Bani Rivers), wool Fulani wedding blankets, a variety of tie-dyed and batik fabrics, as well as bogolan. Beginning in the late 1980s, the amount of bogolan steadily began to increase; in the early 1990s it surpassed the trade in other Malian textiles. Wandering through the markets today, tourists and expatriates are likely to be approached by numerous vendors, all enticing them with the same question: "Vous cherchez le bogolan?" (You are looking for bogolan?).

## Authenticity: Defining the Indefinable

An exploration of the production and marketing of the bogolan sold in the tourist art market reveals the degree to which Ruth Phillips's incisive comment with which this chapter opens applies to the cloth's contemporary biography. The vast differences between the bogolan sold in tourist art markets and the bogolanfini made in villages for local use are the result of long experience and careful study by artists and art merchants in Bamako and other tourist centers. Through stylistic and technical modifications, bogolanfini has been reshaped and reinvented to suit the growing non-Malian, tourist-based market.

Alterations in bogolanfini and other art forms classified as "traditional" or "authentic" are intended to appeal to the tastes of foreigners, so many of the resultant objects are viewed by participants in and observers of the African art trade as corruptions, spurious reproductions of the "pure" originals. Already in 1926 Paul Guillaume and Thomas Munro were warning collectors of the wanton reproduction of "old and sacred" objects for profit:

> For the art had long been dead in Africa, and only the ancestral heirlooms, centuries old and sacred, were to be desired. But enterprising manufacturers, there and in Europe, began counterfeiting them, and reaped a harvest from directors of provincial museums. Everything negro, good or bad, real or false, found and still finds a ready market.[8]

The distinction between arts classified as "traditional" and those relegated to the category "tourist art" ("bad art" in Guillaume and Munro's view) is ambiguous at best; it is little wonder that the unfortunate provincial museums were left with "counterfeits." The same artists in Bamako and other Malian cities and villages who paint, carve, weave, and sculpt with tourists as their intended market also make objects for use in local, "traditional" contexts. The objects produced for these different markets cross-pollinate, producing art forms that are impossible to classify neatly. Similarly, Harry Silver's research among carvers in an Ashanti village in Ghana documented carvers producing for a variety of markets, from the tourist trade to local royalty. Their varied products, though stylistically and iconographically distinct, drew from a common pool of forms combined and recombined to "produce works which help to integrate tribal traditions with the new cultural demands of modern life."[9] Bamako's bogolan market serves a similar purpose, blending old and new to create cloth that serves constantly changing urban markets.

Artists and art merchants in Bamako are aware of the importance of the distinction between tourist art and "authentic" or "traditional" art and, of course, they recognize which is more highly coveted on the international art market. Their assessment of this distinction informs the stylistic modifications of sculpture and textiles such as bogolan to suit the expectations and desires of new, non-local markets, but stylistic changes are but one aspect of bogolan's modification to suit the tourist art market. Shifts in production and marketing also accompany these formal alterations. Each new element is carefully calculated to maximize the cloth's appeal to tourists and to facilitate production so that demand can be effectively met. Bogolan's prominence in the Grand Marché and in stalls near hotels and restaurants illustrates the complexity of tourist art, whose producers and merchants may skillfully manipulate the expectations of their intended customers while evading the derogatory classification "tourist art."

Tourist art's negative connotations in museum and collecting circles stem from its perceived lack of authenticity, a concept that is central to the classification of the many varieties of bogolan currently produced in Mali. Judgments concerning authenticity are not limited to works of art; peoples, cultures, and practices may also be deemed authentic or inauthentic. In examining bogolan's movements in and out of the realm of the authentic, we find that by implication the artists who make the cloth and the cultures out of which they emerge are similarly classified. Thus, questions of authenticity have broad ramifications.

Authenticity is a slippery concept, constantly negotiated and renegotiated by culture brokers and consumers. Brian Spooner, in his investigation of the Western appetite for Asian (or, in the parlance of the market, oriental) carpets, describes the concept's nebulous quality: "Authenticity is a form of cultural discrimination projected onto objects. But it does not in fact inhere in the object but derives from our concern with it."[10] The same object, thus, may be judged authentic in some contexts and inauthentic in others, a circumstance vividly described by Sidney Kasfir's varied sightings of Maasai jewelry in Nairobi's markets:

> Beginning at the ethnographic gallery of the National Museum in Nairobi, we may view Maasai or Samburu beadwork displayed as part of a standard "natural history" functionalist array with gourds, spears and the like. Near the front entrance, the museum shop does a brisk business in pastoralist jewelry, especially earrings, as souvenirs. At African Heritage we may see not only this same work being sold as aesthetic objects but also (on Tuesday mornings) the Maasai women selling it to the buyer and *at the same time wearing it themselves*. Or the artifacts may be seen on dancers performing at the Nairobi tourist village. . . . Fi-

nally, bookshops all over Nairobi sell Terilit Ole Saitoti and Carol Beckwith's *Maasai,* Mirella Ricciardi's *Vanishing Africa,* Angela Fisher's *Africa Adorned* . . . in which photographs of the same objects and their wearers are now recast as evocations of a vanishing "golden land."[11]

Similarly, bogolan and bogolan-derived products appear in multiple contexts, but always carrying connotations of "authenticity" and "tradition." Yet, despite its indeterminate nature, authenticity is the standard by which much non-Western art is judged. In the words of one prominent collector of African art, "[N]othing else matters if a piece is not authentic."[12]

African art is the subject of a complex system of connoisseurship, the domain of experts who evaluate objects, assigning high value to those deemed "authentic." Authenticity may be dependent upon an object's age, its conformity to the predetermined stylistic and iconographical attributes of specific ethnic groups and regions, and use patterns prior to its arrival on the art market. An object's manufacture, its medium, and the manner in which it is made also weigh heavily in determinations of authenticity. Scientific tests of an object's authenticity, such as x-ray and wood analysis, are predicated on the assumption that "non-authentic" African artists will deliberately produce art imitating the "authentic," artificially aging sculpture, adding patination and wear, or otherwise deceiving the consumer.[13] Such deception constitutes fakery or forgery, categories distinct from objects that are "inauthentic," which do not deliberately deceive the consumer. In practice, however, the threat of forgery makes all objects subject to suspicion.

Thus, authentic objects must reflect their local origins and their local use; they should be made of natural materials gathered and prepared locally, and they should be made by hand in a manner that requires skill rather than elaborate technological aids. As such, these objects serve as references to a pre-technological past. Spooner found that production techniques played a major role in oriental carpets' appeal as "authentic," "exotic" art:

> [T]he fact of their [the carpets'] being hand-made became a significant characteristic and . . . the survival of traditional relations of production became an additional factor [in their success on the international art market]—the rug was an exotic product made in its own exotic production process for its own exotic purpose.[14]

The fascination with handmade production is evident in many recent discussions of African art, such as *The Spirit of African Design,* a richly illustrated book by Sharne Algotsson and Denys Davis. The book's introduction, a broad description of the appeal of African textiles and sculpture as elements of home décor—the cover features a bogolan-patterned pillow made, ironically, of factory-produced cloth—clearly identifies manufacture as an important aspect of that appeal: "It [African art] evokes a time when fabric dyes were derived from plants, earth, and minerals; when cloth was produced from the pounding of tree bark; when wooden objects were carved with rudimentary tools."[15] This is the case with bogolan as well; the hand of the artist, the use of low-technology production techniques, and the imperfections that reflect the use of natural pigments and "rudimentary" tools are an important part of the appeal of African textiles in popular Western imagination.

Contextual information is also crucial to the production of authenticity in the tourist art market, usually in the form of descriptions of the use of objects in religious and spiritual practices. Observation of the interaction of merchants and consumers in Bamako's tourist markets confirms Steiner's assertion concerning the interest of tourists: "While collectors are interested in learning the path of objects from village to market, tourists in Africa are concerned with learning the traditional meanings and functions of African art."[16]

As prospective consumers file in and out of the stalls of the Grand Marché, salesmen supplement the visual appeal of bogolan and their other wares with elaborate information on their uses in Bamana or Dogon villages and their symbolic references to cosmology and mythology. In a sense, bogolan and other products made for the tourist art market serve as evidence not only of their owners' travels but also of the identities of their makers. Arjun Appadurai describes the particular nature of the tourist art trade as "a special commodity traffic in which the group identities of producers are tokens for the status politics of consumers."[17]

Information about an object's function prior to its transformation into a commodity—by implication presuming that the object was not made as a commodity—increases its value, augmenting its ability to serve as a marker of the "authentic" culture from which it emerged. As Susan Stewart notes, souvenirs do not "function without the supplementary narrative discourse that both attaches it to its origins and creates a myth with regard to those origins."[18] In their important role as suppliers of supplemental information, salespeople in the tourist market serve as "cultural brokers,"[19] translating an "exotic" culture into easily digestible components. Exegesis of sculpture, textiles, and other objects is condensed into a handful of key ideas: for example, *ci waraw* are symbols of fertility;[20] Dogon figures are prayers to ancestors; and bogolan is an encoded record of Bamana history and mythology. Thus, merchants offer abridged histories of the objects they sell, condensing complicated analysis into the few memorable anecdotes that consumers can take home with the object.

"Authenticity" may also be created out of thin air; a creative artist might invent a form, create a context for that form with or without the help of a cultural broker, and thus meet the expectations of his or her audience. For example, Madi Sissoko, a Senegalese sculptor working in Bamako's Artisanat, created a new art form that he called Tête de Tuareg (Tuareg Head), a mask based not on any preexisting forms but on the design of a logo for the Bamako-Dakar railroad.[21] In fact, the Tuareg, a traditionally nomadic ethnic group concentrated in Algeria, Libya, northern Mali, and Niger, have no tradition of masking; Sissoko chose the name for his creation in order to attract the attention of tourists, telling them that the mask was used in Tuareg ceremonies.[22] He met with some success, but eventually stopped making the mask, as it had a limited market. In this case, an "authenticity" acceptable to some audiences was created entirely anew, without a basis in preexisting facts. Thus, authenticity may be created by many routes.

The criteria for authenticity are perpetually in flux. In recent years, objects once considered inauthentic have found a place in the realm of the authentic; commemorative and other factory-printed cloth, Baule and Guro *colons* (figures representing African and European colonial officers), and Zulu earplugs made of vinyl, to name a few, are all art forms that have in recent years gained attention in venues reserved for "authentic" African art.[23] New regions, new media, new styles, and new types of objects shift in and out of fashion; recent years have seen the reemergence of African currency, textiles, weaponry, and pottery as important genres. In the past decade, the canon has begun to open further to admit contemporary studio arts.[24] Thus, the canon is not immutable, creating the possibility that a fortunate artist may create an innovative new form that will be favorably received by the tastemakers of the international art market.

### Authenticity: Implications of Reflexivity

The international art market's definition of an African object as "authentic" or "inauthentic" is more than an evaluation of the object's age, the identity of its maker, its conformity to a particular regional or ethnic style, or its function in its original context. Rather, these appraisals are each components of a single, larger characteristic by which authenticity is defined: reflexivity. This term refers to a sense of self-referentiality and, by implication, an awareness of the ways in which one is perceived by those outside oneself. The various characteristics of authenticity all provide the consumer with assurances that African artists create without awareness of the markets in which their work will circulate, uninfluenced by non-local techniques, materials, and iconography.

According to this logic, the consumer of "authentic" art is aware of both the international art market *and* the local market for a work of art, but the artist is aware only of the local market. There is nothing more disheartening to an eager tourist in Mali's art market than to find that the sculptor from whom one has purchased a wooden mask copied the object from a Western art book in an effort to cater to the consumer's taste.[25] Such intrusions of the art market into the pristine world of "authentic" art jolt the consumer, as if the actors in a play suddenly removed their costumes to reveal that they dwell in the same modern world as their audience.

Objects that are suspected of being made explicitly for sale, that is, catering to consumer tastes, are often presumed to be poorly made by observers who use Arnold Rubin's reasoning that "things which I make for myself, or my neighbor, are likely to get care and attention beyond that invested in work for a middleman and destined for an anonymous consumer in a distant market."[26] Yet, many of the objects designated "tourist art" are as skillfully made and imaginatively conceived as "authentic" art. In fact, the existence of specialists such as curators and art appraisers, whose duty is the policing of boundaries between tourist art and fine art or between forgery and authentic art, attests to the tension that surrounds the ambiguous territory that divides these categories. Steiner notes that the boundaries between "authentic" and "inauthentic" art "remain volatile because they are never objectively fixed or, in certain cases, even immediately distinguishable."[27]

Ultimately, what is at stake in the act of connoisseurship, in the selection of objects based upon belief in their authenticity, is control—control over the production of a highly valued commodity: fine art. Larry Shiner's observation of the non-Western art market summarizes this paradox:

> What is conceptually interesting about this situation is that carvings not intended to be Art in our sense but made primarily as functional objects are considered to be "authentic" Primitive or Traditional art, whereas carvings *intended* to be Art in our sense, i.e., made to be appreciated solely for their appearance, are called "fakes" and are reduced to the status of mere commercial craft.[28]

Deliberate, self-conscious art making is, thus, inherently suspect.

African artists who seek to earn a living on the art market face a dilemma, for their success depends upon the creation of an illusion: Objects created for sale to tourists must incorporate denials of their commodity status. Paradoxically, as Bennetta Jules-Rosette states, the creation of tourist art is a supremely reflexive act: "The tourist art system is based on a process of double reflection between the artist and the audience. The artists create images that are received and purchased by their audiences. Through this process, the artists present their perceptions of themselves and their works."[29] Thus, the tourist art offered for sale in non-Western locales the world over both represents a creative act and, as artists and merchants produce new forms and modify existing ones, a denial of that act, as these forms are sold with assurances of their long histories and their origins in villages far from the urban centers where they are sold. Implicit in these assurances is a denial that the objects offered for sale are the result of a self-conscious representation of "tradition" for a targeted audience.

### Authenticity: Reproductive and Mimetic Adaptations

Bogolan's immense popularity among the assortment of goods that compete for the attention of visitors to Mali is a recent phenomenon, placing the cloth amid an array of products in a variety of media. Artists and merchants who work in Bamako's tourist art market employ a wide range of strategies in their efforts to associate their wares with "authentic" Malian culture, concealing their awareness of the market in which they are sold. The bogolan produced for Mali's tourist art market incorporates all of the strategies by which artists and merchants in the tourist market trade seek to produce authenticity. Woodcarving is the medium most frequently employed by artists in the tourist market, so it will be used as an example of two strategies—the "reproductive" and "mimetic."

Tourist art markets abound with reproductions of sculptural forms that have become familiar to many Westerners as a result of their frequent reproduction and their long presence in Western art collections: Dogon doors and figures, Bamana ci waraw, Senufo and Bamana female figures. To describe the logic by which these objects communicate authenticity, the term *reproductive* will be used, a reference to their replication of extant art forms. These objects, however, are far from simple reproductions. Artists may alter various elements of the "traditional" forms that serve as their models; for exampe, the size, medium (from locally available woods to ebony, for example), and style may be changed to suit the perceived desires of consumers. Nelson Graburn, in his seminal work on tourist art, notes that miniaturization, giganticism, and general exaggeration often accompany the translation of extant artistic genres into commodities for the tourist art market.[30] Though altered in a variety of ways, each adjustment the result of efforts to meet the desires of consumers, these objects are clearly based on forms broadly recognized as "traditional."

Alternatively, woodcarvings aimed at the tourist market may depict Africa itself in scenery, animals, and people. This category of tourist art can be described as mimetic, for these objects are characterized by an ostensible basis in the depiction of objective Malian realities. These new forms serve as mementos, much as postcards do, providing a glimpse of an "exotic" locale and its inhabitants. The human figures these carvings portray are all engaged in stereotypically African activities, such as hoeing, playing the West African board game *wari* or *mankala,* and carrying loads on their heads. The animals are all "exotic"—elephants, hippos, giraffes—despite the fact that one is unlikely to see these animals in Mali today. Salespeople often use these anecdotal figures as points of departure for descriptions of traditional life. Such objects, carved in essentially naturalistic styles, represent a distinct but related approach to the problem of creating authenticity through works of art.

Mimetic art can be likened to Phillips's classification of some native North American souvenir arts that depict Native Americans and their environment as "anecdotal or narrative."[31] Her terminology is not adopted here, largely because she seeks to make a different type of distinction, separating narrative themes from the floral and vegetal motifs commonly used in other souvenir arts. The separation of reproductive from mimetic art in the present study is as much conceptual as it is literal: the former category borrows from an extant pool of forms altered to meet the demand for speedy production in new markets; the latter category consists of newly invented forms that borrow from several preexisting categories, in this case combining bogolan with postcard imagery, to create a new class of objects.

The distinction between reproductive and mimetic approaches to the creation of an aura of authenticity is evident in other media as well. In metalwork, for example, artists make reproductions of "traditional" forms, such as brass versions of Fulani gold earrings and aluminum alloy versions of bracelets customarily made of silver.[32] Other products are presented as images of Mali (or more broadly Africa) itself, including cast brass figurines of women carrying loads on their heads, farmers hoeing, and masked dancers.

The success of bogolan amid the tourist art market's diverse selection of sculpture and textiles may be partially explained by its adaptability to both the reproductive and mimetic characteristics by which tourist art marks the authentic. In brief, tourist market bogolan may be "reproductive," that is, made to resemble bogolanfini though modified to suit the perceived desires of consumers. Alternatively, it may be "mimetic," adorned with depictions of scenery, people, and animals engaged in "traditional" Malian activities, such as farming and masking. The two strains of tourist market bogolan are sold from the same shops and stalls, thus offering consumers two versions of "authentic" bogolan from which to choose. Each of the two types, which incorporate many substyles, reveals much about the elements out of which "authenticity" is constructed in the tourist art market.

Plate 1. (above) Bogolanfini wrap with geometric patterns, artist and date unknown. Bogolan pigments on strip-woven cotton. Approx. 60″ × 35″ (152 × 89 cm). Collection of the University of Iowa Museum of Art, purchased with funds from Robert F. and Delores DeWilde Bina. Photograph by Steve Tatum.

*The sharpness of lines, with clean edges separating the dark ground from the white motifs, is one mark of an accomplished bogolanfini artist. As a wrap, bogolanfini is worn around the waist and usually extends to midcalf.*

Plate 2. (left) Nakunte Diarra at work. Kolokani, Mali, 1993.

*Nakunte Diarra works seated on the ground with cloth she is painting draped over a calabash bowl on her lap. She is working on the hunter's tunic in Plate 3.*

Plate 3. (above) Hunter's shirt (*donson dloki*), Nakunte Diarra, 1993. Bogolan pigments on strip-woven cotton. 30" × 31" (78 × 80 cm). Collection of the University of Iowa Museum of Art, gift of Michael Annus. Photograph by Ecco Wang Hart.

*Bogolanfini protects hunters, who risk their lives encountering dangerous animals and other threats in the forest, just as wraps of the cloth protect young girls at vulnerable moments, following excision and childbirth.*

Plate 4. (right) Textile stall, Grand Marché. Bamako, 1993.

*This display of textiles is typical of those in the tourist art shops and stalls throughout Bamako's downtown. This stall includes various styles of bogolan, multi-colored batiks, and ko-rhogo cloth, which is associated with the Senufo of southern Mali and Côte d'Ivoire.*

Plate 5. (above) Bogolan made using stencils and in the yellow color associated with the Dogon region. Bogolan pigments on strip-woven cotton. Approx. 40″ × 24″ (102 × 61 cm). Collection of the University of Iowa Museum of Art, purchased with funds from Stanley Support for African Art Programs. Photograph by Ecco Wang Hart.

*Although the regional distinctions between bogolan styles have become increasingly blurred, the yellow bogolan sold in tourist art markets is identified with the pays Dogon (Dogon country), a popular tourist destination near Mopti.*

Plate 6. (above) Alou Traoré's bogolan displayed for sale, Marché Medine. Bamako, 1993. Photograph by Morna Foy.

*Alou Traoré's stenciled pagnes (right), boubous, and shirts are sold from a stall that also carries medicinal materials, partially visible at the lower left. Plain white shirts and white strip cloth are also displayed here. The shirts are standard wear for rural men, considered appropriate for work in the fields.*

Plate 7. (opposite above) Binde Traoré, son of Nakunte Diarra, at work. Kolokani, Mali, 1993.

*Unlike his mother, who draws designs freehand while seated on the ground with her cloth draped over a calabash bowl on her lap (see Plate 2), Binde Traoré spreads his cloth on a table and works with a ruler to create perfectly straight lines.*

Plate 8. (opposite below) Wares on display, Bamako, 1992.

*A variety of bogolan is offered for sale at the Centre Culturel Français alongside locally produced ceramics, basketry, and glass paintings.*

Plate 9. *Nyama*, Groupe
Bogolan Kasobane,
1989. Bogolan pigments
on strip-woven cotton.
89″ × 36″ (225 × 91
cm). Collection of Ann
Starck. Photograph by
Steve Tatum.

*This painting is a visuali-*
*zation of nyama, the en-*
*ergy that animates all liv-*
*ing things, connecting*
*human beings with every*
*aspect of the world*
*around them. It is fairly*
*typical of the Groupe Bo-*
*golan Kasobane's work in*
*its large size, its use of*
*every inch of the canvas,*
*and its subject matter,*
*which is rooted in Ba-*
*mana history, mythology,*
*and cosmology.*

Plate 10. *Nyòkala Sô,* Groupe Bogolan Kasobane, 1989. Bogolan pigments on strip-woven cotton. 65.5″ × 34″ (165 × 86 cm). Collection of Ann Starck. Photograph by Steve Tatum.

*Like many of the Groupe Bogolan Kasobane's paintings, this work has a message that is based in indigenous ethical precepts (though it is universal in its applicability). Nyòkala Sô, the tale of a man who rides a millet stalk though he thinks his mount is a fine steed, is a Malian version of the story of the emperor's new clothes. The dramatic composition, with its concentric rings of color, is an example of the group's innovative use of the medium.*

Plate 11. (right) *Foule de Mars* (Crowds of March), Ismaël Diabaté, 1999. Bogolan pigments on canvas. 59″ × 36″ (150 × 91 cm). Collection of William F. Blair. Photograph by Steve Tatum.

*Using a technique that has become one of his trademarks (much imitated by younger bogolan artists), Ismaël Diabaté dilutes his pigments to create watercolor-like washes. His application of colors creates a swirling sense of motion quite distinct from the careful control required of bogolanfini artists. This painting commemorates the bravery of the women who led demonstrations during the 1991 overthrow of Moussa Traoré.*

Plate 12. (opposite) *Géometrique Bogolan,* Ismaël Diabaté, 1995. Bogolan pigments on canvas. 36.5″ × 29″ (93 × 74 cm). Collection of the University of Iowa Museum of Art, purchased with funds from Stanley Support for African Art Programs. Photograph by Ecco Wang Hart.

*Using diluted washes of bogolan pigments, Ismaël Diabaté created a series of paintings that transform the geometry of bogolanfini into a mazelike series of interlocking forms. Some of the patterns in Diabaté's complex geometry duplicate bogolanfini's symbolic motifs, here placed in a very different context.*

Plate 13. *La Gaieté au Village*, Sidicki Traoré, 1997. Bogolan pigments on cotton strips. 63″ × 40″ (160 × 102 cm). Collection of the University of Iowa Museum of Art, purchased with funds from Stanley Support for African Art Programs. Photograph by Steve Tatum.

*Like several other artists employing bogolan, Sidicki Traoré has made use of the cotton strips that characterize indigenous cloth to create a distinctive, interlocking surface. The strips are adorned with calligraphic motifs, some of which resemble Komo ideograms.*

Plate 14. (top) Bogolan collage, Yacouba Koné, 1991. Pieced bogolan and other strip-woven fabrics.

*While working with the Chiffons de Samé artists, Yacouba Koné created meticulously stitched collages that combine bogolan with other fabrics, often adorned with blocks of color created by repetitive stitches of cotton thread.*

Plate 15. (bottom) *La Communication,* Atelier Jamana, 1996. Bogolan pigments on strip-woven cloth. 16″ × 21″ (41 × 53 cm). Collection of the University of Iowa Museum of Art, purchased with funds from Stanley Support for African Art Programs. Photograph by Ecco Wang Hart.

*The ideogram tló (ear), at the center of this image, is echoed by the ear that emerges from the right side of the symbol. Here, the artists equate the ear with the concept of communication, expressed in a modern idiom by the telephones that frame the image.*

Plate 16. (left) *Left to right,* Hama Guro, Rokiatou Sow, Boureima Diakité, three members of the Atelier Jamana. Bamako, 1993.

*Along with their paintings, the Atelier Jamana artists earn money through postcards and clothing, such as the hats and scarves they wear here. The garments are made quickly, using stencils to produce several at one time. The artists stand in front of two of their large, richly illustrated paintings.*

Plate 17. (below) A Chris Seydou ensemble, Dak'Art festival fashion show. Dakar, Senegal, 1992.

*Chris Seydou's bogolan ensembles are precisely tailored, often combining bogolan with undyed strip-woven cotton.*

Plate 18. (above) Movie still from *Guimba: Un Tyran, Une Epoque,* 1995, directed by Cheik Oumar Sissoko, with costume and set design by members of the Groupe Bogolan Kasobane. Courtesy of Kino International.

*In their award-winning designs, Baba Fallo Keita, Boubacar Doumbia, and Kandiora Coulibaly of the Groupe Bogolan Kasobane created distinctly modern variations on bogolan's geometric patterns.*

Plate 19. (left) Wedding participants wearing formal boubous. Bamako, 1993.

*These women wear boubous and headwraps in styles typical of contemporary Bamako. Back row, left to right: Maryam Sissoko, Assa Sissoko, and Mafy Sissoko.*

Plate 20. (above) Members of the Atelier Jamana wearing bogolan boubous that they designed, 1992. Photograph courtesy of the Atelier Jamana.

*These extraordinarily ornate boubous are, like the Groupe Bogolan Kasobane's robes, based on the embroidered boubous worn by Malians as formal attire. Because such garments are extremely labor intensive to produce, the group members have turned to simpler, more readily reproducible designs.*

Plate 21. (above) Man's shirt, Atelier Jamana, 1996–97. Collection of the University of Iowa Museum of Art, purchased with funds from Stanley Support for African Art Programs. Photograph by Ecco Wang Hart.

*Like many of the garments produced by the Atelier Jamana in recent years, this shirt combines splattered pigments with sharply delineated stencils, including paired ci wara figures.*

Plate 22. (opposite) Bogolan boubou, Alou Traoré, 1997. Collection of the University of Iowa Museum of Art, purchased with funds from Stanley Support for African Art Programs. Photograph by Ecco Wang Hart.

*This elaborate boubou includes ci wara and mask motifs, along with intricate stenciled floral patterns that are not based in pre-existing bogolan motifs.*

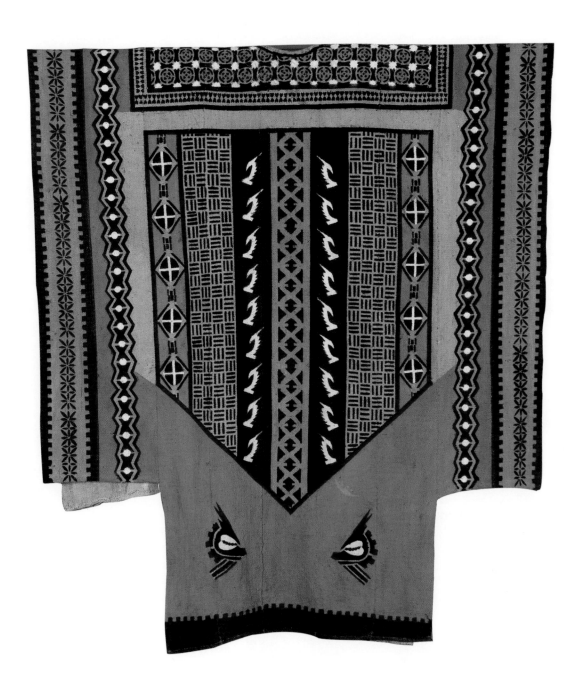

Plate 23. (left) Bogolan-patterned paper cups, plastic travel mug, and bags. Peet's Coffee and Tea Company, 1994.

*Peet's has adopted bo-golan-like patterns as its signature style, accurately noting the origins of the motifs on its products.*

Plate 24. (above) Malian hunter in the Marché Medine. Bamako, 1993.

*Two worlds of bogolan intersect in Bamako. A hunter wearing camou-flage-style bogolan, one of the cloth's distinctly rural uses, stands behind a non-Malian wearing a bogolan boubou (left foreground) in a contemporary style.*

# 4

# TOURIST MARKET BOGOLAN

## Changing Demands, Changing Forms

De nouveaux motifs, de nouvelles techniques découverts, la lutte contre le temps entraînant une production quantitative très remarquable ... pour donner bogolan de la zone du San que j'appellerai "la Nouvelle Ecole," un cachet particulièrement commercial. (New motifs, newly discovered techniques, the struggle against time brings with it production in very remarkable quantities ... giving the bogolan of the San region, which I will refer to as "the New School," a particularly commercial appeal.)

*Youssouf Kalilou Berthé and Abdoulaye Konaté, Un Mode de Teinture*

A closer examination of the bogolan that crowds the shelves of stalls, shops, and boutiques of Bamako's tourist centers reveals the complexity behind the cloth's apparent simplicity. Here, artists experiment with techniques and styles aimed at efficiently meeting the demands of their market, often pushing the limits of authenticity in their efforts to speed production while preserving the cloth's handmade character.

The bogolan sold in tourist markets is made of cloth locally woven on narrow single-heddle looms, the distinctly West African technology touched on in Chapter 2. This strip-woven cloth is immediately recognizable, the seams created where the narrow strips are sewn together and the rough surface of the hand-spun cotton setting it apart from the industrially produced textiles to which most visitors to Mali are accustomed. Thus, even without the addition of bogolan's distinctive colors and patterns, the cotton cloth is set apart as "authentic," thereby appealing to tourists. For this reason, most of the cloth sold in tourist art venues is strip woven, despite the ready availability of inexpensive cotton percale and other industrial cottons. In an adaptation to the exigencies of the tourist art market, the narrow strips of cotton cloth are today frequently sewn together using a sewing machine rather than by hand. This modification is but one among many, each a strategic effort to meet tourists' demands. In reviewing the two broad categories of innovation in the tourist art market—the reproductive and mimetic—we find bogolan has been skillfully adapted to both.

## CREATING AUTHENTICITY

### Reproductive Bogolan

Most of the bogolan crowded onto shelves and piled in storehouses in Mali is made of cotton strips sewn together to create wrap-sized cloths, dyed in hues of yellow, brown, black, and white and decorated with abstract patterns. This cloth, reproductive bogolan, is designed to resemble "authentic" bogolanfini yet remain clearly distinguishable from the labor-intensive, densely symbolic patterns that characterize the rural "traditional" cloth.

Among the most visible and recognizable traits of tourist market bogolan are the earth tone dyes, whose colors are particularly distinctive where the cloth is displayed among the vibrant blues of indigo-dyed textiles and the rainbow of brilliantly colored strip-woven blankets, batiks, and tie-dyed cloths whose colors

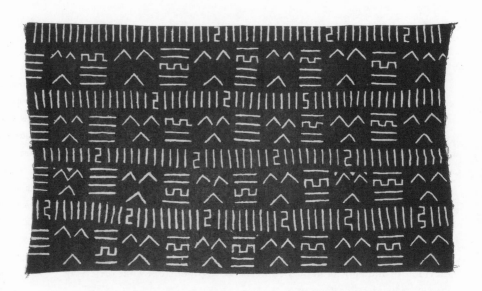

Figure 5. Bogolan in the
highly contrasting style
associated with San.
Bogolan pigments on
strip-woven cotton. 52″
× 35″ (132 × 89 cm).
Collection of the Uni-
versity of Iowa Mu-
seum of Art, purchased
with funds from Stanley
Support for African Art
Programs. Photograph
by Ecco Wang Hart.

*San, a city northeast of
Bamako, is known for its
volume of bogolan pro-
duction. The stark black-
and-white patterns are
made using industrial
bleach, removing the
dark pigment to expose
the white cloth beneath.*

are produced by synthetic, chemical pigments. Merchants in the markets provide information about the different colors and styles of bogolan, as each element is associated with specific places of production. For example, cloth from the city of San and
the surrounding region are distinguished by their stark, deep black color and their
highly contrasting bleached white designs (Figure 5). Bogolan from the Dogon villages of the Bandiagara region and surrounding areas is often yellow (Plate 5).[1] These
regional variations are, however, becoming increasingly blurred.

The patterns that adorn reproductive bogolan differ dramatically from bogolanfini's designs, yet an aura of authenticity is created through the retention of salient aspects of the techniques and patterns that mark "authenticity." Tourist market bogolan
is characterized by simplified patterns, often applied without a great deal of attention
to detail; fuzzy edges and splatters of mud are common (Figure 6). The bogolanfini
motifs that carry specific meanings appear rarely if at all. In the words of one young
man who produces bogolan for the tourist market and for the local clothing market,
"You don't find traditional-style bogolan in Bamako's markets."[2] Often, a single
motif, such as crosses or zigzag lines, covers the entire cloth (Figure 5; Plate 5). Such
repetition occurs rarely in bogolanfini, where combinations of several motifs are used
to create a coherent message. Although it does not carry references to specific historical events or proverbs as does bogolanfini, this bogolan's colors and patterns simply
and directly declare its relationship to its rural counterpart, and thus shares in its authenticity. Tourist market bogolan need only be an inexact reproduction, close
enough to associate itself with the cloth that is its inspiration.

Susan Stewart's discussion of souvenirs elucidates the repetitive, often minimal
patterns that adorn reproductive bogolan. In order to meet the desires of consumers,
tourist art, like other souvenirs, "retains its signifying capacity only in a generalized
sense, losing its specific referent and eventually pointing to an abstracted otherness."[3]
Paula Ben-Amos's characterization of tourist art as a "reduction in [the] semantic

level" of the traditional art forms on which it is based is apt here as well.[4] Using a linguistic metaphor, Ben-Amos discusses tourist art as the artistic equivalent to pidgin languages, developed in situations of contact between culturally distinct groups. Like pidgin languages, tourist art permits communication—in this case, communication of information about authentic culture—between two groups, though a great deal of subtlety is sacrificed. Thus, the minimally articulated designs communicate in a "generalized sense," relaying the essential information that the bogolan cloth offered for sale is an authentic, Malian art form.

In the case of bogolan produced for the tourist market, the pidgin language metaphor—with tourist art's reduction in semantic level—becomes quite literal, because the cloth, as stated above, is made without the symbolic motifs that adorn the bogolanfini, thus ceasing to communicate to "bogolanfini-literate" observers. Looking at examples of the mass-produced bogolan for which San is known, artist Nakunte Diarra declared, "They [pagnes from San] are . . . nonsense."[5] Significantly, however, this stylistic (and semantic) shift is deliberate and strategic, not the result of any lack of sophistication.

Just as bogolan's patterns have been strategically modified for the tourist market, so too have the techniques by which it is produced. Rather than the painstaking process by which the traditional cloth is made, one finds a variety of innovations. Frequently, mud is used to paint patterns directly onto the cloth, rather than to fill in the negative space around the designs. Thus, the brown or red of the n'gallama-dyed cotton serves as the ground, and the traces of the mud produce a pattern without the time-consuming outlining process that distinguishes the traditional cloth. In 1970, Pascal James Imperato and Marli Shamir noted the use of this technique in the Mopti and Djenne regions, northeast of Bamako.[6] This reversal—creating patterns out of

Figure 6. Bogolan made using stencils and showing blotchy, blurred patterns. Bogolan pigments on strip-woven cotton. 48″ × 70″ (123 × 177 cm). Private collection. Photograph by Steve Tatum.

*Much of the bogolan made for sale in Bamako's tourist markets is speedily produced, creating blotches of mud and blurred designs. In this example, stencils have been used to create patterns in both the dark brown or black of mud and the maroon of n'beku bark. Such cloth, while it does not conform to the clean, crisp lines of bogolanfini, preserves the colors and abstract patterns on which it is based.*

Figure 7. An apprentice to the Groupe Bogolan Kasobane stenciling a bogolan robe. Bamako, 1993.

positive instead of negative space—is now widespread, used in Bamako as well as San, Dogon country, the Beledougou region, and other bogolan-producing areas. Most of the artists in Bamako who have adapted bogolan techniques to the museum and gallery trade also use the pigments to create patterns and images in positive space, though to very different effect.[7] In the tourist art market, the goals of technical innovations are speed and efficiency.

Moving still further from bogolanfini techniques, the makers of tourist market bogolan were, in the 1990s and early 2000, using stencils with increasing frequency. The use of stencils in the production of bogolan is not a recent phenomenon, however; Patrick McNaughton saw stenciled cloth in San in 1978, and Barbara Frank documented metal stencils in Kolokani in 1983.[8] According to textile merchants and artists in Bamako today, the technique has been widely used only since around 1991–92, inspired by the flourishing bogolan market.[9]

The stenciled bogolan sold in Bamako's tourist markets preserves the essential elements of authenticity; it is made of locally woven cotton, prepared with n'gallama, and painted with the same type of mud that is used in the creation of non-stenciled cloth. The stencils cut from a variety of materials, including cardboard, recycled tires, and discarded plastic, are placed on the cloth, and mud is applied using a brush or sponge (Figure 7). Stenciled cloth is readily distinguishable from that painted by hand, in part because designs are often replicated with little variety, resulting in a monotonous cloth (Plate 5). Exceptions to this rule can be found, for some artists in this market have created innovative stencils and stenciling techniques. Stenciled patterns are often geometric and bear little or no resemblance to the motifs that characterize bogolanfini.

By simplifying the application of mud, producers of bogolan for the tourist market greatly reduce the amount of time required to create the cloth, enabling them to send cloth to the market in greater volume. According to one artist who produces and sells both stenciled and hand-drawn bogolan, it is possible to produce six or seven stenciled pagnes in the time it takes to make one without stencils.[10] Stenciling also permits the use of assistants or apprentices at nearly every step of the production process, because the skills required to apply mud to stencils are minimal.[11] Apprentices can be instructed to place particular patterns on a cloth, requiring little or no supervision from the artist or entrepreneur marketing the cloth. The stencil design is the most demanding step in the creative process.

Despite their distance from bogolanfini's labor-intensive production and deeply symbolic motifs, both the reproductive bogolan with designs drawn directly onto the cloth and that with stenciled designs retain all of the basic elements by which bogolanfini is defined: The color, the locally produced dyes and cotton cloth, the geometric motifs (even if modified), and the contextual information supplied by merchants all preserve the cloth's identity as bogolan and, by extension, as authentic.[12] For the tourists and others who purchase it, this speedily produced form of reproductive bogolan represents the rural, traditional Malian culture they seek.

## Mimetic Bogolan

Along with bogolan adorned with motifs that approximate bogolanfini's abstract, symbolic patterns, consumers may choose among cloths that feature depictions of Malian people, places, and activities—a weaver at work, villagers sitting around a meal, farmers hoeing, women pounding millet, to name but a few typical subjects. These scenes are painted in the mineral and vegetal pigments of bogolan though they do not incorporate geometric designs (Figure 8). Other themes include exotic wildlife, such as zebras and elephants, the famous mosque in Djenne, and idealized Malian women.[13]

Figure 8. Textile stall, Grand Marché. Bamako, 1993.

*Amid many examples of reproductive bogolan, including tailored jackets, this stall offers several types of mimetic bogolan, such as those (lower right) depicting a village scene and rabbits.*

This version of tourist market bogolan functions much as postcards do, depicting the sights a tourist might hope to see during a visit to Mali's "exotic" locales. In fact, mimetic bogolan has literally been made into postcards.[14] Mimetic bogolan does not incorporate depictions of Bamako's office buildings, people dressed in T-shirts and business suits, or taxicabs plying city streets. Such images do not represent the "authenticity" that tourists seek. The depictions of Malian culture presented by mimetic bogolan are not inaccurate—these images do not depict a "counterfeit" Mali for the benefit of tourists—but they do present a carefully edited version of reality. Such editing makes obvious those aspects of Malian culture generally considered to be "authentic," and "traditional." As Ruth Phillips notes, the use of such emblematic, or in a more negative reading, stereotypical, imagery enables mimetic bogolan to more efficiently communicate with its consumers: "The success of tourist art iconography derives from its employment of stereotypes precisely because such images can signify across cultural boundaries. They incorporate elements of objective 'truth' . . . while leaving out much else that would have painted a more complex and nuanced picture."[15]

Like reproductive bogolan, mimetic versions of the cloth preserve selected aspects of the rural bogolanfini that is its inspiration. The use of n'gallama and other bogolanfini pigments, and by extension the colors typical of the traditional cloth, link this bogolan to its rural roots. In a step away from bogolanfini, the makers of mimetic bogolan occasionally paint on industrially produced cotton cloth rather than on strip-woven cloth. The village scenes and figures often incorporate greater detail than the hand-painted or stenciled geometric patterns of reproductive bogolan, so the smooth surface of industrial cotton aides in efficiently producing the images. The makers of mimetic bogolan also increase their production through the use of stencils.

Among the most intriguing examples of mimetic bogolan are the many cloths sold in the tourist art market that themselves depict tourist art—a "doubling" of the strategies used to attract consumers. Most prominent in this category are cloths adorned with schematic depictions of ci waraw, Dogon dancers, and other motifs common in the tourist market (Figure 9). These cloths conflate popular genres of Malian tourist art from several media. Dogon masked dancers, a genre of performance popular with tourists, and wooden ci wara sculptures are both associated with "traditional" Mali. According to several salespeople, in 1992–93 the cloth stenciled with Dogon dancers sold well, while the ci wara cloth was of interest to a limited audience.[16]

The designers of these stencils aim to capitalize not only on the popularity of bogolan, but also on the popularity of other tourist arts, creating a sort of "super authenticity." Although all of the elements of these hybrid cloths are based in preexisting traditions—the wooden antelopes, the masked dances, and the bogolan technique—when they are combined an entirely non-tradi-

Figure 9. Mimetic bogolan with stenciled Dogon masked dancers. Textile stall, Grand Marché. Bamako, 1993.

*Dogon dancers, among the iconic images associated with Malian culture, are a popular motif for stenciled bogolan.*

tional product results. Yet, these super-authentic cloths conform perfectly to the logic of the tourist market: Surely if Dogon masked dances are popular, and if bogolan is popular, then bogolan decorated with Dogon dancers will be doubly popular. Through mimetic bogolan, the two are combined.

## CASE STUDIES

### The Atelier Jamana: Décor and Art

The artists of the Atelier Jamana (in English, "Country Workshop") are among Bamako's most prolific makers of bogolan paintings, stenciled cloth, and clothing. Since 1990 Boureima Diakité, Rokiatou Sow, Hama Guro, and Aly Dolo have been using stencils to create clothing and pagnes, the term group members use to refer to the wrap-sized cloth made for decorative purposes.[17]

The Atelier Jamana artists do not look to traditional bogolanfini for formal inspiration; their patterns bear little resemblance to bogolanfini's motifs. Guro told me that inspiration for his stencil designs come from a variety of sources, because the group's goal is not to re-create in an abbreviated form an already extant style of cloth. One of Guro's stencil motifs was, for example, inspired by the shape of an ant he watched crawling across the floor of the workroom.[18] The motifs carry no larger symbolic valences; they are first and foremost decorative. As Diakité explained, bogolanfini motifs would likely fail to communicate to contemporary audiences; judgments about the cloth are likely to be purely aesthetic: "In the city, if you use traditional motifs, nobody can understand; they buy it [the cloth] if it's pretty."[19] For the members of the Atelier Jamana, stenciled pagnes are explicitly decorative. In the words of Guro, "It is *décor* [decorative]. It isn't art."[20] Diakité used different terms to express the same dichotomy: "It isn't art. It's artisanal."[21]

The group's postcards and greeting cards are perhaps the epitome of its "artisanal" production. These are made using rows of identical stencils applied to industrial cotton cloth (see Figure 14). Each stenciled image, measuring approximately four by five inches (10 × 12.5 cm), is cut from the cloth and pasted onto a piece of white paper. At one point, the group received a commission for two thousand cards from Bamako's leading postcard merchant, whose stalls included a prominently placed display in front of the downtown post office. At the same time, they were working on a large bogolan card to be presented to the president's wife, Adam Bâ Konaré.[22]

Quite separate from these explicitly commercial portions of their oeuvre are the group's *tableaux,* or paintings, that are intended not as "décor" but as vehicles for personal expression, presented as aesthetic and social statements.[23] The diverse aspects of the group's work provide insight into the difference between fine art and tourist art, for they participate in both markets successfully. This distinction is apparent at numerous levels, from the production of cloth to its marketing.[24]

Pagnes are made quickly and are reproducible in large numbers. In the Atelier Jamana work space, it is not unusual to find up to a dozen pagnes in varied states of completion hanging from clotheslines, draped over tables, or lying on the ground. Using stencils, group members can produce dozens of cloths in a day. Guro, after initially making one pagne by hand a week, began using stencils. He could then produce one cloth in an hour, making the pursuit much more profitable.[25] In 1992–93, the Atelier Jamana was charging approximately 10,000 CFA per pagne, or about twelve dollars.

Paintings may take months to create, usually requiring several sketches as the group members negotiate the final form. The amount of time is, the artists hope, rewarded by the sale of paintings for upwards of three hundred dollars and by the recognition exhibitions bring them. Because the paintings are often large and densely painted, much time is expended in the application of several layers of mud, the number of layers varying with the intensity of the desired color. That the paintings are signed reflects the degree to which they are personal statements; the group's pagnes are essentially anonymous.[26]

"Décor" and "tableaux" continue to be separated as they enter the marketplace. Pagnes are sold at the Christmas bazaars held at the Canadian embassy and the Centre Culturel Français (see Map 3), at other art fairs, and at hotel shops. The group's paintings are sold only in galleries and by commission, a more rarified realm of marketing that sets this version of bogolan apart from the world of ordinary commerce. The Atelier Jamana offers an instructive example of the categorization of contemporary bogolan; even when made by the same artists, distinct types of bogolan live very different "lives" from their creation to their entry into the marketplace.

### Oumar Almani: Stencils as Brand Identifiers

Oumar Almani, a young man producing bogolan for the tourist market, has taken the commercialization of bogolan one step closer to the consumer readiness of modern mass production. He uses stencils to create labels, just as mass-produced clothing bears the label of its designer. Almani's bogolan cloth is stenciled on both sides, its faces adorned with stenciled patterns, the reverse sides stenciled with his name, the name of his workshop (BogoLafia, named for the neighborhood in which he lives and works—Lafiabougou), and his address. In the mid-1990s, his was the only cloth to be found in the tourist market that had incorporated this innovative use of stencils.

In 1992–93, Oumar Almani was a student at the Institut National des Arts, where he attended bogolan classes taught by members of the Groupe Bogolan Kasobane, who have also made use of stencils to label pillows and curtains sold in their gallery and at craft bazaars.[27] Almani's stencils serve more as brand markers than as resources for consumers to locate them, although each piece of bogolan Almani produces does bear the information a consumer needs should they wish to obtain more of his cloth. The labels can also serve as evidence of their owner's experience in Bamako, like a T-shirt imprinted with the name of a tourist resort, supplementing the stories and photographs travelers bring home with them.

### Alou Traoré: Stencil Techniques Elaborated

In 1992, when he was in his mid-thirties, Alou Traoré began producing bogolan for sale to tourists in Bamako. His business has since increased and broadened to include relationships with Malian entrepreneurs, providing him with a small but relatively reliable source of income. Like the Atelier Jamana, Traoré's work crosses boundaries; he creates work aimed at the tourist trade as well as clothing for sale to local consumers.[28]

Traoré's distinctive use of stencils sets his work apart from the rest of the bogolan made for sale to tourists. Traoré initially sought to sell his work in boutiques and shops, but he had difficulty finding a venue. He then presented his work to a variety of merchants, all of whom agreed that his stenciled pagnes and *boubous,* the West African robe worn by men and women, were expertly made and attractive. They found, however, that his labor-intensive technique made his production capacity too low and his costs too high. Traoré, therefore, chose to sell his cloth from a stall in the Marché Medine (Plate 6), a large market that marks the eastern edge of Bamako and caters primarily to local consumers rather than tourists (see Map 2); he relies on word of mouth to attract tourists to the market. By 1997, he had begun to sell his work at a street-side bogolan shop opened by Sidicki Traoré, a painter.[29] He had also begun to receive commissions from Malian and non-Malian entrepreneurs, producing bogolan for clothing designers and decorators.

Traoré's bogolan is made with carefully designed stencils cut from sheets of clear plastic that are often used in combination to create multihued motifs. Like the Atelier Jamana's stencils, Traoré's motifs are not based on traditional bogolanfini patterns. Traoré does not cite particular sources of inspiration but, like the Atelier Jamana artists, he draws inspiration from every aspect of his environment.[30] Some of the motifs are clearly recognizable, such as ci wara figures and cowrie shells; others resemble motifs from factory-printed textiles, which figure prominently in Bamako's visual landscape and would naturally provide a wealth of motifs for Traoré's work. One cloth Traoré created is adorned with a series of arabesques based on a motif from a French clothing catalogue.[31] This cloth was part of a commission from a Cameroonian clothing designer resident in Bamako who had contracted Traoré to do a good deal of work.

For "traditional" artists like Nakunte Diarra, Alou Traoré's appropriation of motifs associated with Western textiles constitutes a movement away from the sources of bogolanfini's designs.[32] Still, her work has much in common with the textiles Traoré creates, demonstrating the potential for sophisticated implementation of recent adaptations such as stencils. Though Traoré's technique and the motifs that adorn his cloth are only indirectly related to Diarra's bogolanfini, both employ complex, time-consuming techniques and work with local mineral and vegetal dyes. That is, despite the vast stylistic differences between the cloth produced by the two artists, both are working within a distinctly Malian tradition, working largely on commission for clients both local and non-local, responding to the demands of their markets, and making innovative cloth in response to those demands.

Traoré is assisted by his wife and several young men in a workshop setting, with each member of the group participating in the gathering of materials and the application of n'gallama, mud, and other vegetal pigments. Traoré, however, closely supervises every stage of the process. Although stencils are usually associated with speedy production, in Traoré's case the efficiency usually associated with the stencils is lost. He must carefully design the stencils to create interlocking patterns, and he works slowly with the intricate designs. To produce multicolored patterns, Traoré uses several "layers" of stencils, applying different vegetal and mineral dyes with each set of patterns. The resulting cloth is readily distinguishable from the hastily produced stenciled pieces that constitute the bulk of tourist market bogolan.

## PRODUCTION

### Shifts in Gender and Geography

In the above overview of producers of bogolan for the tourist market, only one female artist is mentioned—Rokiatou Sow of the Atelier Jamana—which is an accurate reflection of the dearth of female participants in Mali's tourist art markets. In 1997 among the more than one hundred stall owners and artists in Bamako's Artisanat, only one woman, the owner of a sculpture stall, was directly involved in sales and management.[33] By 1999 another woman had rented space, to sell bogolan, in the newly expanded Artisanat, though the difficulties in attempting to enter a male-dominated domain are daunting. The sale of bogolan in Bamako is the exclusive domain of men, who manage the shops and stalls and work as "runners" leading potential customers into shops in hopes of earning commissions if a purchase is made.

More surprising than male dominance over bogolan's sale is the near complete male monopolization of the cloth's production in Bamako, a dramatic shift from the patterns of rural bogolanfini production. The transformation of bogolan production from a female to a male art form is not limited to the tourist art market; the same shift is evident in bogolan production for the fine art and fashion realms. This dramatic twist in bogolan's biography may be traced to economic as well as broadly social factors.

One factor that surely has played a role in this "masculinization" of bogolan production is the changing economic situation of Bamako's students. Until the mid- to late 1980s, students received scholarships for their living expenses, and most expected to find employment in the ranks of the government's large bureaucracy after graduation. This situation changed as structural adjustment programs (referred to in Mali by the euphemism *disengagement de l'état*) led to increasing cutbacks in government spending.[34] The 1991 coup d'état that overthrew Moussa Traoré was, in fact, spearheaded by students whose frustration and anger led them into the streets to stage protests against the government.

Despite the change in government and the country's transition toward democracy, many students still found themselves in difficult economic circumstances.[35] Many recent graduates could not find employment, and though the government made efforts to restore scholarships, occasional student strikes continued to punctuate the school year well into the 1990s, indicating that discontent remained strong. Other Malians lost their jobs as a result of the reduction in government spending.[36] In their search for alternate funds, some young men began producing bogolan for sale in the tourist market and elsewhere. Many of these young bogolan producers are, not surprisingly, current or former students at the Institut National des Arts, where they learned the technique. Here, too, women are in the minority.[37]

According to custom, bogolanfini is the domain of women who observed their mothers and grandmothers at work, slowly acquiring the skills and knowledge of the iconography necessary to make the cloth themselves. Imperato and Shamir stress the intergenerational learning process in their discussion of the cloth: "The patterns used by artists have been handed down from previous generations and painstakingly learned through years of apprenticeship."[38] In villages where bogolanfini is made for local use, its production is the domain of elderly women who no longer work in the fields, such as Nakunte Diarra, and young women who find time for the activity during the dry season.

In Bamako, where mercantile and bureaucratic professions dominate, the opportunity to learn bogolanfini techniques and intricate symbolism through apprenticeships is limited at best. In rural settings, training in bogolanfini production is incorporated into domestic life, as young women learn from old with both remaining in the home to care for children and their husbands. In the city young children spend their days in school rather than at home, where they might observe older female relatives at work (in addition, many of these older relatives still live in villages, where young people visit them and occasionally stay with them for vacations). The extended apprenticeships by which bogolanfini skills are customarily acquired are, in short, impractical or impossible for Bamako residents to undertake.

The traditional, long apprenticeship of young girls to old women has been replaced in urban settings by brief, informal training sessions, often for the benefit of young men for whom bogolan represents the chance to earn money in the tourist market. Indeed, women in urban centers like Bamako have little opportunity to pursue training for entrepreneurial purposes outside the home. Although exceptions do exist, such as the two female-owned tourist art boutiques in Bamako's Artisanat, women in Bamako face overwhelmingly difficult barriers to entry into entrepreneurial activities beyond the socially sanctioned female domain of small-scale trading in cloth and food sales in markets and on street corners (in which male wholesalers earn huge profits). Lalla Tangara Touré, one of the female boutique owners, is struggling to find success as a bogolan merchant. With each step she faced difficulties, though she declares herself unusually fortunate in having a husband who is willing to allow her to pursue a business career. Negotiating the bureaucracy through which merchants receive business licenses, apply for loans and grants, and obtain shop rentals is particularly difficult, because many *functionaires* (bureaucrats) object in principle to women in business.[39]

The urban shift in the gender of bogolan producers has affected the rural women who make bogolanfini by creating new audiences for their expertise. Nakunte Diarra is one of the well-known bogolanfini producers who has come to serve as an informal instructor, teaching young men from Bamako who serve as her apprentices for days, weeks, or months. She is surprised at their desire to learn the technique, apparently bemused by the sudden male interest in what had for so long been a women's pursuit.[40] Although she enjoys teaching these young men, Diarra feels that bogolanfini is women's work; young men may see in it a temporary source of income, but they will eventually find other work.[41] One of the young men currently working with Diarra is her son, Binde Traoré, the only one of her children (including her daughters) interested in pursuing bogolan production. He has met with some success selling his cloth in Bamako, largely through Western researchers familiar with his mother's reputation and through Peace Corps contacts (Plate 7).

Other instances exist of gender shifts in artistic production that followed a similar path, with men taking up a skill as products gain popularity beyond local markets and they perceive a potential source of income. Richard Roberts describes the economic and political vicissitudes that transformed gender relations in the nineteenth-century textile industry of the Maraka, an ethnic group in the Bamana region.[42] As in bogolan's shifting fortunes, the expanding demand for Maraka indigo cloth—the work of women and a source of self-sufficiency in polygamous families—was a catalyst for change. The demand was spurred by regional political shifts involving the late-eighteenth-century establishment of the Segu Bambara state and the decades of stability that followed, providing larger markets through increased trade networks. Efforts to accelerate the production of indigo cloth led to the growing use of slaves, replacing the labor contributions of female family members. Their increased leisure time permitted wealthy families to seclude their female members in accordance with local interpretations of Muslim law, a sign of status that exacted a high price for women, who were prohibited from direct involvement in the commercial trading of the cloth. Their husbands and fathers took over management of production and traveled to market the cloth.

Peter Wollen notes a similar phenomenon in another part of the world where tourist art provides an important source of income for many residents. In his discussion of Australian Aboriginal acrylic "dreaming" paintings, Wollen observes that "originally, this painting was done by women, who still make up seventy percent of the Yuendumu artists. When the men saw that the women were able to buy a four-wheel drive truck with the funds that they had accumulated from painting, they joined in too."[43] In a European example of this phenomenon, Jane Schneider and Annette Weiner document the shift of female-to-male dominance in the seventeenth- and eighteenth-century linen industry as the cloth gained commodity status in increasingly wider markets.[44]

Thus, in many cultures the world over where men have greater contact with non-local markets, artistic production shifts from women to men as products become lucrative on a non-local level. The nearly complete transfer from female to male producers in Mali's contemporary bogolan market exemplifies this phenomenon. The dramatic shifts in style and format—including new forms of abstraction and figuration, new products, and new production techniques—may well have been facilitated by bogolan's transformation from a female- to a male-dominated art form.

Just as the identities of bogolan producers changed when the cloth reached the tourist market, so too did the locales of the cloth's manufacture, reflecting the new shape of the market. As increasing amounts of bogolan began to be produced for sale to tourists, production shifted to the urban areas frequented by tourists (Plate 8). Still, the merchants who sell the cloth preserve a sense of authenticity, for they provide consumers with information on the cloth's village-based production even when they purchase cloth made in Bamako.

Different colors and styles are associated with specific places of production. Within these varied bogolan "style areas," some regions have reputations for producing finer cloth than others. Increasingly, however, the correlations between style and geographic location of production are becoming a thing of the past. As bogolan has become more lucrative, a great many residents of Bamako have begun to produce the cloth. Often, students who come to Bamako to study earn money making and selling cloth in the style of their home region. This is also a frequent occurrence among young people from small towns who move to Bamako seeking employment.[45]

As noted earlier, the Beledougou region, north of Bamako, is particularly well-known for the production of bogolanfini.[46] Kolokani, the home of Nakunte Diarra, is located in the Beledougou. Because of its reputation as a historical center for bogolanfini production, Kolokani is often cited as the source of cloth in the tourist market regardless of whether it was actually produced there. For example, on discovering in the Grand Marché a piece of cloth that particularly resembled classic bogolanfini in its designs and its application of dyes, I was told not only that the cloth had been made in Kolokani, but I was also given the name of the woman who had made it, a certain Nyeleni. Further investigation revealed that Nyeleni resided in Bamako, where she made bogolan for the tourist market with the assistance of various family members.[47] Despite changes in production patterns as bogolanfini is modified to suit the tourist art market, some artists and merchants attempt to preserve the stylistic traits and contextual information necessary to maintain the cloth's association with "authentic" Mali.

### SUSTAINING SUPPLY, SATISFYING DEMAND

In contrast to the village setting in which women make cloth for the limited, seasonal demands of Bamana families, merchants in Bamako's tourist markets must maintain a constant stock of the cloth if they are to meet the demands of tourists. Brehima Konaté's shop in the Grand Marché dominates the tourist trade in bogolan. Situated behind rows of women offering factory cloth, batik, and tie-dye for sale, Konaté's shop offers one measure of the increased bogolan trade. The many rooms of his shop, which increased in size between 1993 and 1997 and grew still larger by 2000, epitomize the contemporary boom in bogolan production; every inch of space is covered with cloth either hanging, stacked, or rolled, and from inside the vestibule cloth spills out onto the walkway. The piles of cloth, which change constantly as items are purchased and new stock arrives, draw in potential consumers. As Bennetta Jules-Rosette notes in her study of tourist arts in several African countries, "Production of a surplus of items for informal 'advertising' purposes is an adaptation of Western marketing to the African setting."[48]

Konaté began selling bogolan in 1985. In 1992–93, he was the Grand Marché's primary bogolan supplier, selling in great volume directly to tourists as well as to the smaller merchants located throughout the market (that is, he sold both wholesale and retail). By 1997, Konaté had strengthened his position, with a network of small shops throughout the downtown area under his direct control and an ever-increasing number of clients for his wholesale and retail business. Although he sells a variety of textiles, including korhogo cloth from Côte d'Ivoire, a variety of batiks and indigo cloths, and woolen blankets associated with the Fulani of northern Mali, bogolan constitutes the bulk of his business. Konaté is also a key source for bogolan exported to other African countries, Europe, and the United States. Bogolan's transformation for Bamako's tourist art market set the stage for its diverse adaptations to North American markets. Export has become a major impetus for production. Although exact figures are impossible to obtain, merchants occasionally earn large commissions from exporters, who ship the cloth abroad in huge bales.[49]

In order to command the volume of cloth necessary to meet growing domestic and foreign demand, Konaté works with the producers of bogolan, supplying them with rolls of cotton strip-woven cloth, up to several hundred meters at a time. In his store Konaté has several young assistants who work measuring large piles of strip cloth for distribution. The cloth is woven in Bamako or in surrounding villages and towns and brought to the Grand Marché in immense bales either by a representative of the weavers or by one of Konaté's employees.[50] In Bamako, the sight of weavers alone or in groups seated at their strip looms is a common one. Some weave patterned fabrics to be assembled and sold as pagnes, but many of the weavers make un-patterned, undyed cotton cloth to be sold in strips, which is then sewn into cloths and dyed.

Commissioned by wholesalers like Konaté or by the middlemen and middle-women[51] with whom he contracts, weavers produce finimougou, plain strip cloth, on consignment. They are assured a market for their work, and Konaté is assured a ready source for cloth to meet the demands for bogolan production. Once measured and divided into smaller parcels, Konaté sends the white strip cloth out to villages or, in-creasingly, to bogolan producers in Bamako, San, and, occasionally, elsewhere, where groups—often entire families—produce bogolan pagnes. The finished cloth is sent back to Konaté's shop in Bamako, where he pays only for the labor.[52] He usually re-ceives the bogolan approximately fifteen days after sending out the strip cloth, en-abling him to react to shifting demand for the cloth in a timely manner. The speed of cloth production, however, may vary depending on the cloth's region of origin.

Throughout this system of production, control rests with Konaté, the urban mer-chant, rather than with the weavers and the dyers who create the cloth. He stands be-tween the cloth's producers, separating the weavers from the dyers. The two sets of producers cannot eliminate his role by working together directly, for few producers have access to the capital necessary to create their own production system.[53] Simulta-neously, he stands between the producers and the merchants who will eventually market the cloth. This type of commerce, distinguished by the middleman's control over production as well as distribution, is in economic terms a "putting-out" system. Ronald Waterbury's work on embroidered Mexican blouses and dresses, sold as "folk" garments in American and European boutiques, elucidates the characteristics of the system: "In a putting-out system, merchant-entrepreneurs mobilize labor to produce commodities without incurring much risk, and with a minimal investment in fixed capital."[54] Both of the prerequisites for the perpetuation of putting-out systems are clearly evident in Mali's bogolan trade: "One necessary condition for their [putting-out systems] survival or rebirth is sufficient consumer demand for handmade or quasi-handmade goods. Another is the presence of a population compelled by economic circumstances to sell its work cheaply."[55] As long as tourism in Mali continues to provide Konaté with consumers fascinated by bogolan's handmade appeal and its religious and spiritual associations, he will continue to find weavers and dyers willing to work for minimal compensation.

Much of Konaté's stock is produced in San, where bogolan production has become an important industry. In discussions of modern bogolan, *San* is used to exemplify commercialization; production is concentrated there to a greater degree than elsewhere in Mali. For Malians and foreigners who view bogolan as an aspect of "traditional" culture to be preserved, San represents an extreme that threatens to transform the cloth into little more than an economic product, completely separated from its original contexts. In 1977, two Malian employees of the Ministry of Culture submitted a report on bogolan stating, "In San, where bogolan has become a popular art, members of all generations joyfully devote themselves to this art form that here runs the risk of becoming purely commercial."[56] Imperato and Shamir also single out San as a source of bogolan in bulk and note, "The Bamana of San and Bla [a nearby town] enjoy a reputation for being skilled in making it [bogolan], but the quality of the work is poor compared to that of the artists from the Beledougou."[57]

For Nakunte Diarra, San is representative of all swiftly produced, non-traditional bogolan production: "Ours [the cloth of Kolokani] are ancient designs, they have *meaning*. . . . In San, people make [the] designs that they want."[58] More accurately, they make the designs the consumers in urban markets want. Diarra's views are not as distant as one might expect from the merchants in the tourist markets, who may highlight a cloth's origins in the Beledougou region or, more specifically, in Kolokani. Both recognize the importance of place as part of the identity of a piece of bogolan. San has come to stand not only for speedy production, but also for the use of inferior techniques, and the participation of non-traditional artists (that is, "members of all generations"). Kolokani represents (for its residents and for outsiders) the epitome of traditional bogolanfini, made in the labor-intensive manner that has been passed on for generations and is the exclusive domain of adult women.

The efficiency with which bogolan is produced in San is evident in the speed and volume in which the cloth reaches the market. Wali Mariko's experience is typical. Mariko is one of the many cloth retailers in the tourist-oriented, interior section of the Grand Marché, selling his wares from a stall typical of the market in size and layout. He purchases his stock of bogolan and other Malian textiles from Brehima Konaté. Mariko started selling bogolan in 1989, when he broadened the bead-selling business he inherited from his father to include textiles. His textile sales have increased every year since, with the amount of cloth from San growing more quickly than that from other regions.[59]

Discussing the relative qualities of cloth from varied sources, Mariko characterizes the bogolan from Kolokani as "very difficult" to produce, but the cloth from San is "very easy." He can order and sell in a week five hundred pagnes from San. The cloth from Kolokani, however, is much more difficult to acquire; he can only get two or three pagnes a week, but all of which he easily sells. Kolokani's bogolan is made by women in several families who create cloth in their spare time to earn extra money and who have not modified their laborious method of working. Clearly, the bogolan production for which San is renowned and, in some circles, notorious, represents the height of Malians' mobilization to meet the non-Malian demand for the cloth. By streamlining the production process, dyeing the cloth in stark, black-and-white designs, entrepreneurs can manage systems by which hundred of pagnes can be produced on short notice. The sophistication of this system indicates the degree to which tourist market bogolan has become an industry, providing work and a living (though too often a meager one) for Malians in both urban and rural areas.

The bogolan produced for the tourist art market clearly represents a strategic response to increased demand for the cloth from consumers whose location (in highly urban areas), expectations (to purchase the cloth on demand rather than on commission), and aesthetic preferences (not based on bogolanfini's symbolic motifs and painstaking manufacture) differ broadly from the rural, local demands in the Beledougou and other bogolanfini-producing regions. Skillfully assessing the new markets for the cloth, producers and merchants have created mimetic and reproductive bogolan, adapted stencils and labels to speed production and merchandising, and instituted geographically diverse production and marketing systems. Perhaps most importantly, despite all of these changes, modifications, and innovations, the bogolan produced for sale to tourists has managed to carefully maintain its ties to that all-important tool for success in the market: tradition. The cloth remains handwoven (with few exceptions), its distinctive colors are retained, and the stories of its rural origins remain paramount. In the fine art and fashion bogolan markets, the subjects of the chapters that follow, the notion of bogolan as "traditional" remains central, though the concept has distinctly different connotations in each context.

# 5

# FINE ART BOGOLAN

## Between Categories

"Contemporary art in India? There is no contemporary art in India." So an academic friend curtly reminded me a few years ago. How could an avant-garde exist anywhere in the "timeless" cultures of what we monolithically call Asia? If it did, it couldn't be any good. Too Western. Or too Asian. Or too little of one or the other.
*Holland Cotter,*
*"Brave New Face*
*of Art from the East"*

A great distance—stylistic, technical, and conceptual—separates tourist art bogolan from the bogolan of art galleries and museums. In some respects, however, the two realms of bogolan production share similar intentions and face similar resistance from international markets. Both are founded in the popularization of a local textile, both permit substantial divergence from the "traditional" forms of that textile, and both are based in and dependent upon the urban markets of Bamako. Both have also faced accusations of inauthenticity, though for very different reasons. The quotation with which this chapter opens, though it refers to contemporary Indian art, applies equally to the art of Africa today: "Too Western." "Too African." Throughout the world, contemporary artists from regions associated with "traditional" culture face paradoxical expectations from the international art market, while at the same time they often encounter a lack of local support.

Varied adaptations of bogolan are displayed and sold in venues quite distinct, conceptually as well as physically, from the Grand Marché and other tourist centers. This bogolan is not folded and stacked in market stalls, but stretched and hung on the walls of museums and galleries. It is not produced in great numbers using labor-saving techniques; on the contrary, each piece of this bogolan is unique, carefully designed to serve as an autonomous aesthetic statement rather than as a souvenir. The majority of artists who produce this bogolan are professionally trained, and they aim to compete in the same markets as professional Western artists, to vie for exposure in the same museums and galleries.

This manifestation of the bogolan revival, "fine art bogolan," is a relatively recent phenomenon, its place in Mali's art markets still ambiguous. The newness of this aspect of bogolan's revival has permitted direct observation of the development of the cloth's role in the fine art trade, rather than the documenting of an already integrated market. Artists' oeuvres and their success, or lack thereof, in the slowly growing market for fine art in Bamako reveal a great deal both concerning perceptions of fine art in urban Mali and perceptions of contemporary African art in Europe and North America.[1]

Although each of the participants in the fine art bogolan movement works in a distinctive style, commonalities among the artists do permit broad generalizations concerning the parameters of the movement. All share the same basic format, using bogolan's characteristic vegetal and mineral pigments to paint on factory-made or strip-woven cloth. The size of the paintings varies widely; some are stretched and framed, but others are too large for such treatment and are simply suspended directly from museum or gallery walls. Most of the artists involved in this market have in common methods of manipulating their bogolan pigments—applying the vegetal and mineral dyes with paint brushes and quills, varying the concentration of pigments to create a wide range of tones, and intensifying colors by applying several coats (as do makers of bogolanfini). Most also experiment with new colors, blending vegetal and mineral dyes long used by bogolanfini makers, as well as experimenting with entirely new leaves, roots, minerals, and methods of preparation. A minority of these artists incorporate other, non-local media, such as inks and synthetic pigments.

Stylistically, most of the bogolan paintings displayed in museums and galleries initially appear to be direct translations of Western artistic idioms into a Malian medium; the artists employ perspectival realism and expressionistic abstraction familiar in Western media such as oil painting or printmaking. However, closer examination reveals that bogolan paintings have emerged out of a range of innovative fusions of Western and Malian artistic traditions.

## THE DISTINCTIVENESS OF FINE ART BOGOLAN

The melding of disparate elements in fine art bogolan is not accomplished without friction; the conflict between modernity and tradition is a defining element of many contemporary Malian artists' work. Thus far, discussions related here with artists, patrons, and merchants who participate in the making and marketing of fine art bogolan have centered on what these paintings are not, or on the distinctions between fine art bogolan and the three artistic traditions to which it is most closely related: "traditional" bogolanfini, tourist market versions of the cloth, and modern Western art. Rather they examine the tensions between these various categories—between tourist art and traditional art and fine art, between Western art and Malian art. These tensions are characteristic of contemporary bogolan painting, a reflection of the efforts of Malian artists and other members of the artistic community to make space for themselves in Bamako's tightly circumscribed art markets, dominated by tourist art and "traditional" art.

It is in the relationship to and often the tension between what these artists consider to be Western and what they consider to be Malian that many contemporary bogolan artists define themselves. Often this Malian–Western dichotomy is translated into another, parallel opposition: traditional–modern. Although the tensions between these categories are evident in much contemporary non-Western artistic production, the use of bogolan by Malian artists places these contrasts in high relief. Such dichotomies figure, implicitly or explicitly, in the work of artists in Bamako, particularly as they negotiate the complex, often unstable territory between Western and non-Western art.

The distinctions between these realms might best be characterized as a conflict between divergent concepts of authenticity, proponents of "traditional" and "modern" art measuring authenticity against an idealized conception of the other. For many Malians, visitors to galleries, museums, and cultural centers, "authentic modern art" must be "Western" in style—abstract, expressionistic, clearly distinct from past Malian artistic practices. Western art patrons, conversely, seek paintings and sculpture that suit their preconceived notions of "traditional art": figurative, not centered on individual expression, clearly distinct from Western artistic practice. For each, in other words, authenticity lies in the cultural practices of the other. Christopher Steiner describes this quest for the authentic, in which this highly valued trait is perpetually located outside of oneself: "Just as the Western buyer looks to Africa for authentic symbols of a 'primitive' lifestyle, the African buyer looks to the West for authentic symbols of a modern lifestyle."[2]

An inherent internal tension exists in the production of bogolan paintings as modern art intended for display in museum contexts. The identification of these paintings as modern art is predicated upon their adaptation of formats and styles associated with Western painting, including stretched canvases, perspectival space, and gestural abstraction. For bogolan artists, however, the use of a distinctly Malian medium is the single most important factor in the production of authentically Malian art. The fine art bogolan movement is rooted in a celebration of bogolan's uniquely Malian origins and, as importantly, in its distance from Western media. Thus, despite the many ways in which fine art bogolan resembles Western painting, and despite its adaptation by many artists who intend to make a place for bogolan in Western galleries and museums, the movement also constitutes a rejection of Western artistic traditions, creating work in a uniquely Malian medium as an alternative rather than as an addition to the Western-dominated international art market.

Artists such as Ismaël Diabaté and Sidicki Traoré who have worked in other media find in bogolan a means by which to make a statement of pride in their Malian identity.[3] Distant as they may seem from one another, the tourists who purchase bogolan in Bamako's Grand Marché as a souvenir of their visit to an "exotic" locale and the artists who adapt bogolan as a statement of pride in their heritage share a fundamental response to the cloth: for both, bogolan represents a pure distillation of Malian culture. Significantly, however, two very distinct conceptions of Mali are evoked by the use of bogolan in these two separate markets, an indication of the cloth's particularly rich capacity to serve as a multivalent cultural symbol.

As discussed in Chapters 3 and 4, the bogolan sold in the tourist art market is associated with "traditional" Mali, making reference to bogolanfini through stylistic resemblance and through accompanying contextual information. In contrast, for many fine art bogolan artists the use of the medium to reproduce traditional forms is antithetical to their intentions. Just as they seek to distinguish their work from Western models, these artists also reject reliance upon preexisting local forms, feeling the need to move beyond the masks and sculptures that represent Mali in Western museums. In 1991, President Alpha Oumar Konaré spoke of this resistance to the restrictive reliance on the past, symbolized by masks and other traditional arts: "There will be no economic development and no real political evolution in African countries if they don't recognize the importance of their national products in the field of art and culture, if they can't go beyond a nostalgia for masks."[4]

Konaré's characterization of the force that holds Africans back in efforts to achieve economic and political development as "a nostalgia for masks" succinctly expresses a frustration that permeates much social discourse in contemporary Mali. Many Malians express pride in their country's indigenous cultures—the artistic, philosophical, economic, political, and religious systems characterized as traditional. Conversely, however, they also speak with equal pride of their nation's modernity, symbolized by a variety of traits, including the multicultural, multinational population of the capital, the availability of foreign products through international trade and mass media, and the nation's technological development.[5] To non-local eyes, this simultaneous pride in modernity and pride in tradition appear to be contradictory. In fact, as the contemporary markets for bogolan demonstrate, modernity and tradition are by no means mutually exclusive.

The conscious effort to retain an affiliation with the traditional while moving beyond the boundaries of that category has led bogolan artists to select carefully which of the cloth's attributes they will adopt. Such selection is reflected in the striking fact that none of the artists currently creating bogolan paintings makes use of the abstract designs associated with bogolanfini, laden with symbolic references to Bamana history and culture. Instead, bogolan paintings made for the gallery trade often depict figures, landscapes,[6] and abstractions unrelated to bogolanfini. Those artists who do incorporate dense, geometric designs reminiscent of bogolanfini's motifs employ them as borders and backgrounds rather than as central elements.

Just as the artists participating in the museum and gallery trade in bogolan seek to distinguish their work from traditional forms of the cloth, they also seek distance from the bogolan sold in tourist art markets. In one clear distinction, the tourist market cloth is produced as quickly as possible to meet the high-volume demand, while fine art bogolan is extremely labor intensive, each painting the result of several stages of production, from preliminary sketches to the application of dyes in multiple layers. Works are signed by the artists, clearly marking them as expressions of an individual's artistic vision. The prices of the paintings also dramatically distinguish them from the cloths of the tourist market. Artists routinely price their work at 100,000 to 300,000 CFA (in 1993, between three hundred and a thousand dollars),[7] while tourist market bogolan costs between 2,000 and 4,000 CFA (between six and thirteen dollars) per pagne. The value of bogolan paintings is partially located in the investment of time required for their creation, from the conception of a work's theme and iconography to the painstaking application of pigments.

### Self-Definition and Shaping Malian Modernity

Paradoxically, for many of the artists participating in the fine art bogolan market, the Western model of modernity is simultaneously a trap to be evaded and an ideal to be attained. Artists in Mali today who aim to create art in a modern idiom face a virtually irresolvable quandary: how does one produce modern Malian art, distinct from that of Western artists, from within a contemporary art system dominated by Western museums, galleries, and critics? Writing of African literary criticism, Anthony Appiah expresses this paradox faced by many African artists: "The pose of repudiation actually presupposes the cultural institutions of the West and the ideological matrix in which they, in turn, are imbricated."[8]

In the same discussion of the frustrations of contemporary artists and writers in Africa, Appiah employs a sartorial analogy particularly germane to the subject at hand, for many of the artists active in the fine art bogolan market also create bogolan fashion: "The Western emperor has ordered the natives to exchange their robes for trousers; their act of defiance is to insist on tailoring them from homespun material."[9] Like the emperor's subjects, many bogolan artists have sought to exempt themselves from the control imposed by Western classificatory systems by adopting a local medium. Instead, they find themselves firmly locked within the same system, the medium only serving to further exoticize them, trapping them in a new set of expectations.

The use of bogolan by Malian artists is variously employed in this West–non-West opposition. For those artists who define themselves as apart from Western artistic tradition, bogolan represents a refusal to participate in the Western artistic establishment, working instead within a Malian artistic tradition. For artists who seek to participate in the Western market, bogolan provides a means by which to distinguish themselves from Western artists, thereby clearing a space for themselves in the Western market. Thus, paradoxically, bogolan has been adapted by some Malian artists as a means of rejecting Western influence, and by others as a means of gaining entry into the Western market.

Ironically, artists in Bamako increasingly find that they must adopt bogolan techniques if they are to find a market for their work. One artist who does not use bogolan, Mamadou Diarra, who was in the early 1990s an official government painter, revealed the degree to which bogolan's success has created a new form of external (generally Western) control over Malian art markets. Diarra prefers Western media—he works primarily in oil paints—but, as he angrily explained, because he does not use bogolan he is unable to exhibit or sell his work.[10] In such circumstances, one wonders if the bogolan revival has succeeded all too well, becoming a requirement for legitimacy instead of a means by which Malian artists wield control over their own forms of legitimacy.

The fact that bogolan paintings are made to be hung on gallery walls rather than worn or employed in some other clearly utilitarian manner is their most distinctively "Western" characteristic. The distinction between art made as art, or "art for art's sake," and that made primarily to serve other functions, only later to be recognized as art, has often been cited as central to the distinction between traditional and modern African art. Paula Ben-Amos, in her thorough historiography of African art history, succinctly described this truism: "In the 1950s and 1960s a number of scholars were drawn to what they perceived as the core difference between Western and African art: utility."[11] The focus on African art's utilitarian nature, a focus rare in discussions of Western art, continues to be a fundamental aspect of African art studies. One case in point is the central role of utility in the production of "authenticity" for the tourist art market, where objects made to be sold as art are stigmatized.[12] The separation of objects from utility is key in the production of authenticity in the fine art bogolan market as well. Like Western fine art, bogolan paintings are made primarily as objects of visual contemplation.[13]

The language used by artists who participate in this movement exemplifies the degree to which modern Western classificatory systems shape the bogolan revival.[14] The language of the varied bogolan markets also reveals much concerning the complex relationships between the varied manifestations of the bogolan revival. My use of the term *fine art* reflects local classificatory systems, an approximate translation of *l'art modern, les arts plastiques* (loosely translated, "studio art"), or simply *l'art,* all terms Malian artists have used to describe their work. The terms are used to distinguish the paintings displayed in galleries from objects sold in the tourist market or those made in villages for local use, designated by the terms *l'art traditionnel, l'artisanat,* and *les arts decoratifs* (traditional art, tourist art, and crafts or decorative arts, respectively). The semantic marking of these distinctions among Malian art markets is as important to the artists as the marking of differences between Malian and Western art.

Anne-Marie Willis and Tony Fry, in their discussion of the international art market's treatment of art by Aboriginal artists, assert that "any cultural or political self-determination must include the freedom to name, to classify."[15] African artists have long recognized that the language used to describe art has great potential to affect the perception and, in turn, the reception of contemporary African art. At a 1966 colloquium on the state of the arts in Africa, held in conjunction with the first Festival Mondial des Arts Nègres (Dakar, April 1–24, 1966), the well-known Nigerian sculptor Ben Enwonwu, among the first African artists to gain international fame,[16] spoke of the insidious effect of Western-imposed vocabulary: "What we call Art in the Western sense of the word has no relationship to Art in the African sense."[17] By way of example, he describes the term *nka,* the closest equivalent in the Ibo language to the Western concept of art, concluding that the Western term lacks the spiritual resonances of the Ibo word. For Enwonwu, rejection of Western terms entirely is a means of combating the strong Western influence over African artists, encouraging instead a return to local languages as sources for aesthetic vocabulary.

Just as many African artists today seek to distinguish their work from modern Western art, so too do they work to distance themselves from tourist art. The revival of bogolan demonstrates both the many features that distinguish fine art from tourist art versions of a single art form, and the many points at which these two manifestations intersect. Both versions of bogolan are the products of uniquely urban circumstances in which local traditions and international markets converge. Even as they disparage the quickly produced, stenciled cloth of the tourist market and place high value on paintings made for display in galleries and museums, many artists make both types of bogolan.[18] Artists who create bogolan for both markets acknowledge the economic necessity of producing readily salable, inexpensive items in addition to the labor-intensive paintings whose high cost places them beyond the reach of most Malians.

Another important similarity between the two types of bogolan is the identity of their consumers; like tourist market bogolan, fine art bogolan's primary customers are non-Malian. Unlike the merchants of the tourist market whose intended audience is non-Malian, however, most of the artists in the fine art bogolan market deliberately seek to develop a local market for their work. The absence of a local market for the work of contemporary African artists is a problem lamented by artists, merchants, and scholars throughout the continent.

## BEING AFRICAN AND BEING MODERN

The tension between tradition and modernity, between Malian identity and Western identity, has produced a situation in which many artists feel that they are accepted nowhere. The long history of Western involvement in the production of modern, urban African art has made accusations of "inauthenticity" virtually inevitable; the same artists are as likely to be condemned for not being Western enough as they are for being too Western. Charges of inauthenticity may result from an artist's use of Western media or adoption of styles perceived to be Western, which might include anything from realism to abstraction. Ironically, at the same time Westernization may be signaled by working in a deliberately African, "traditional" manner, for such returns to tradition are often encouraged by Western mentors and Western markets.

Ghanaian cultural critic Kofi Awoonor cites one major source of Western involvement in the development of African arts: "The greatest influence on the artistic world in Africa has been exerted by single-minded European missionary artists."[19] Two European impresarios offer dramatic examples of the pressure placed on African artists to accentuate their African "traditions." The two took very distinct directions stylistically and technically, reflecting the range of art forms classifiable, in varied contexts, as "African." In 1944, Father Pierre Romain-Desfossés founded Le Hangar, an informal artists' workshop, in Elizabethville, Belgian Congo (now Lubumbashi, Democratic Republic of Congo). Romain-Desfossés's philosophy, revolutionary at the time, was to avoid imposing Western styles and subject matter on his students, instead supplying them with materials and allowing them to devise their own modes of expression.[20] Despite the fact that his students were using the oil paints and canvases he provided rather than local media, students at Le Hangar were presented in Africa and abroad as purely "African."[21] Of course, by urging his students to avoid Western subjects and styles, Romain-Desfossés was asking them to close their eyes to what was by mid-century the thoroughly colonial culture of Elizabethville. As V. Y. Mudimbe notes, Romain-Desfossés's teaching produced not the "pure" art he claimed but rather something new, "an *original* texture and style, situated as they [the artists] were at the intersection of local traditions and the artistic modernity of Romain-Desfossés."[22]

Two decades later, in the early 1960s, Frank McEwen founded a workshop in Salisbury, Rhodesia (now Harare, Zimbabwe). Rather than painting, McEwen supplied tools and materials for the sculpting of soft stones such as serpentine. He established a workshop at the national museum, where he was serving as director. Like Romain-Desfossés, McEwen sought to guard the artists he sponsored against Western influences, which he saw as contamination. He fervently believed in the existence of an inherently African creative force that needed only the encouragement to rise "from the bowels of Africa."[23] McEwen participated in the same 1966 colloquium on African art as Ben Enwonwu, where he advocated the elimination of Western-style art education, calling it "the major agent of destruction of African talent."[24] Like Romain-Desfossés, McEwen was convinced that African artists would, in the face of Western influence, lose their "African-ness." This view is, according to Clémentine Deliss, perpetuated in the preference for identifiably "African" artists in the international art market today: "The international visibility of the various African avant-gardes has been overshadowed by a potentially racist view of African artists as being unable to construct themselves vis-à-vis their work and dangerously derivative of Europe if exposed to its art systems and, in particular, its academies."[25]

Among the best-known instances of Western encouragement of deliberately "Africanized" art is the work of Suzanne Wenger and Uli and Georgina Beier at the Mbari

Mbayo center in Oshogbo, Nigeria. As Marshall Mount describes, the center's first teacher, Denis Williams, encouraged his students to "select images that he considered genuine and pure, and to reject those he considered false and derivative."[26] On her marriage to center founder Uli in 1964, Georgina Beier became a permanent artist-in-residence and teacher at the center, continuing Williams's policy of encouraging the expression of "native" talent. Wenger, Beier's first wife, took over the management of the center after Uli and Georgina's departure and continued to encourage the production of modern art based in the artists' traditional heritage. Twins Seven Seven and his popular paintings of Yoruba mythological and cosmological subjects, Jimoh Buraimoh and his assemblages of beads depicting similar subjects, and the many sculptors and painters who followed all continued the Oshogbo tradition of developing subject matter, iconography, and media identified as traditional, reviving local artistic practices to create a new art.

Though the artworks that emerged from the Oshogbo, Elizabethville, and Salisbury schools differ widely, in style as well as in medium, all emerge out of a similar enforcement of "tradition." Foreign sponsors who might earlier have demanded an acceptance of Western styles instead demanded a return to a "pure" past, a step toward recognizing the value inherent in African artistic expression yet still a selective vision of what constitutes African art. Artist and critic Everlyn Nicodemus succinctly describes the continued impact of these schools:

> Painting workshops for unscholared and "untouched" Africans were put up by European dilettante art tutors such as Pierre Desfossés, Pierre Lods with his Poto-Poto school in the Congo, Ulli Beier with his Oshogbo in Nigeria and Frank McEwen with his Shona construct in Zimbabwe. They helped each other to market their products as the genuinely African contemporary art. Paradoxically, they managed to dominate the scene for decades.[27]

Although they have not achieved the fame of their better-known counterparts, Mali has its own history of Western artistic impresarios and sponsors, including two who were involved with the revitalization of bogolan. For these Europeans as for many Malians, bogolan represented an opportunity to celebrate a uniquely local medium, emphasizing the artists' Malian identities. During the late 1980s Roland de Livry, a French businessman who lived in Bamako, sponsored a group of artists in Samé, a village that has become a suburb of Bamako. He encouraged artists to experiment with textile collages, creating an artistic movement known as Chiffons de Samé (*chiffon* means "rag" or "scrap"). When one of these artists, Yacouba Koné, introduced bogolan to the group, de Livry encouraged him and others to adopt the medium in order to make their work more clearly Malian.[28]

In another example of Western promotion of Malian "traditional" art, Sidicki Traoré was led to the use of bogolan by another French resident of Bamako. Traoré had been struggling to earn money through the sale of pencil drawings on paper and cardboard. He told me of a French man, probably an international development worker, who on seeing Traoré's work suggested that he abandon pen and pencil in favor of bogolan, advising him that for Europeans bogolan would hold more appeal. In the five years since he initially took up the medium, Traoré has found success as a painter, a clothing designer, and a retailer, running a shop outside his family's home in Bamako, using bogolan in all of these efforts.[29]

## THE DANGER OF LABELS

Many African artists have recognized the way in which Western insistence upon African identity may segregate them within the international art market, to be exhibited as "African artists" rather than simply as "artists." African (and other non-Western) artists are increasingly outspoken in their rejection of such segregation, refusing to be classified as "African." Some have refused to create art that makes reference to art of the past ("traditional" art), for to do so would be to provide Western audiences with what they expect of African artists, encouraging Western preconceptions about African art. This view was powerfully expressed by Senegalese artist Iba N'Diaye in 1970: "Certain Europeans, seeking exotic thrills, expect me to serve them folklore. I refuse to do it—otherwise I would only exist as a function of their segregationist ideas of the African artist."[30] Ghanaian sculptor Kofi Antubam, writing in 1962, was equally defiant in his rejection of Western pressure to perpetuate the "traditional":

> It will therefore be illogical for the Ghanaian in the twentieth century to be expected to go and produce the grave and ethnological museum pieces of his ancestors. The argument that he should continue to do so because of the unfortunate influence of African traditional art on the meaningless abstractionists' modern art of Europe is not sufficient to dupe him into complacency.[31]

The painter Ouattara, arguably the most successful African artist of the past decade, deliberately evades attempts by Western curators and critics to classify his work as "African." In his words, "I am not an African artist. I define myself as a painter from Africa."[32] His determination to discourage categorization is dramatically evident in his evasiveness regarding his ethnic background during an interview with cultural critic Thomas McEvilley when he states, "I could have been born in Russia, in Canada or in Africa."[33] He was, in fact, born in Côte d'Ivoire.

The same refusal to accept labels is evident in ethnic communities in former colonial metropoles such as London and Paris. In Paris, clothing designer Ly Dumas initially declined to reveal where she was born (Cameroon), articulating a reluctance to be classified much like Ouattara.[34] In London, South African artists Nicholas Serota and Gavin Jantjes wrote of their frustration with ethnic labels, which "can be used to diminish, or at least to question, the standing of art."[35] James Clifford, writing of the systems by which objects are transformed into art, notes that non-Western art carries cultural or ethnic identity in a way that non-Western art does not:

> For example Haitian "primitive" painting . . . has moved fully into the art-culture circuit. Significantly this work entered the art market . . . becoming valued as the work not simply of individual artists but of Haitians. . . . [T]he aura of "cultural" production attaches to them much more than, say, to Picasso, who is not in any essential way valued as a "Spanish artist."[36]

African artists are, thus, too often presumed to be limited to "traditional" parameters in their aesthetic sensibilities.[37]

### Creating New African Art

Many Malian artists have expressed frustration at the insistence that their work be exhibited as "African" or "Malian," denying them the opportunity to be judged by the same, ostensibly international standards as European and American artists. Recent exhibitions of contemporary African art, most notably the 1989 Centre George Pompidou exhibition *Magiciens de la Terre*,[38] have been the subject of much controversy, being accused of selecting works that conform to preconceived Western expectations of African art. Clémentine Deliss, organizer of a 1995 exhibition of contemporary African art, writes of the biases of earlier presentations: "*Magiciens de la Terre* and its offshoot, *Out of Africa*, brought to the fore artists such as Cyprien Toukoudagba and Esther Mahlangu, whose 'African' iconography was unmistakable and showed no contamination from European modernist sources that might have been received from the African art college system."[39] Little wonder, then, that many of the urbane, professionally trained artists in Bamako and other African urban centers seek to distance themselves from the "traditional" arts that provide reinforcement for the segregation of African art and artists.

As they work toward acceptance in the international art market, many African artists have adopted aspects of the prototypically Western art world. dele jegede catalogued some of these characteristics in his description of contemporary African art: "[A] new art has emerged that extols individualism against collectivism, spontaneity as opposed to conservatism, identification in place of anonymity, nationhood over tribality, and spirited expressiveness instead of sanctioned patterns of artistic engagement."[40] Similarly, Nigerian journalist Emma Ejiogu recently described popular conceptions of contemporary African arts: "While traditional art is graceful and seeks deep rooting in the most important social concerns, the Western model is for the most part preoccupied with form, thus leading to a high experimental tone devoid of social meaning."[41]

Contemporary African art is, according to such formulations, precisely what "traditional" African art is not. Thus, while "traditional" African art reflects "universal values of human expression . . . today the [contemporary] artist's urban consciousness has largely replaced the religious-sacral nature of the old culture."[42] Sidney Kasfir describes the broad generalizations current in both Western and African attitudes toward African art: "In contemporary Western culture, with its emphasis on individual achievement, innovation is considered the sine qua non of serious art. Conversely, African cultural values reinforce the stability of collective aesthetic norms."[43] The degree to which "traditional" arts are actually religious, conservative, and collective in nature and the degree to which "contemporary" arts are actually secular, spontaneous, and individualistic are less important than the *perception* that such generalizations are accurate. Perception alone, the cultural currency of beliefs and assumptions, often has an important impact on the system it concerns, in this case the African art market.

Taking their cues from culturally current beliefs concerning "traditional" (that is, African) art and "contemporary" (that is, Western) art, African artists may take up the traits that they perceive to be characteristic of Western, modern art, rejecting those traits they perceive to be African and traditional. For example, although in the West the general perception of African art focuses on anonymity, work for the society not the individual, in Bamako many artists focus on the artist-as-individual—a stereotypically modern trait. These artists tend to conceive of their work as a personal expression, often consisting of commentary on political and social issues, or as a form of purely emotional catharsis. Technically, their work is often experimental, another much-heralded trait of modern art, with individual artists claiming particular innovations as their own.

One cannot attribute to Western influence such tendencies toward self-expression and individual innovation, for to do so would be to accept long-standing generalizations about African art that scholarship in the field continues to combat and refute—that African artists are anonymous, working only for the benefit of the group, that they simply reproduce preexisting forms. These notions are not, of course, supportable in light of research by increasing numbers of scholars.[44] Recognition of the effect these Western-generated misconceptions have had on the self-perception of African artists is, however, crucial. Although many art historians and others concerned with art are moving beyond past generalizations, for many Africans, particularly for artists and art students, the impact of past truisms concerning African and Western art remains a constant source of pressure, a foil against which to shape their careers.

The effect of past (and current) preconceptions about African art on the lives of Malian artists today was vividly evident at a public lecture by André Magnin held in the Centre Culturel Français in Bamako on April 1, 1993.[45] The numerous artists who attended the lecture, including bogolan artists, repeatedly challenged Magnin's selection of artists for the *Magiciens de la Terre* exhibition, accusing him of perpetuating stereotypes by selecting only untrained artists. The tension in the lecture hall was perceptible, the artists in the audience eager to express their frustration at Magnin, a representative of the Western art establishment too often responsible for the segregation of African art from the mainstream of contemporary art. In an earlier interview, the artist Ismaël Diabaté had angrily noted that *Magiciens de la Terre* had not included any bogolan paintings in spite of the fact that the cloth is literally made of earth (*terre*).[46] This meeting, an unusual collision of local, African artists and the tastemakers of the contemporary international art market, provided an outlet for the deeply felt frustrations shared by many artists in Bamako.

One issue that encapsulates the complex relationship between "traditional" and "modern" art in Africa is abstraction, a defining characteristic of both traditional African art and modern Western art. The two are directly related, for European and U.S. artists were famously inspired by the abstraction of African and other non-Western art, a historical moment exhaustively documented in the Museum of Modern Art's exhibition and catalogue *"Primitivism" in Twentieth Century Art: Affinity of the Tribal and the Modern*.[47] Modernist artists like Picasso and Gauguin have become thoroughly associated with the quest for liberation from the classical Western tradition via African and other non-Western art, so that now, paradoxically, their work has become a route to appreciation for African art, as described by cultural critic Michelle Wallace: "For instance, my mother, Faith Ringgold [a contemporary African-American artist] saw in Picasso a place where she, as a black artist produced by the West, could think about her African heritage."[48]

Although abstraction may in the West be viewed as evidence of the influence of non-Western art, attitudes toward the abstraction of modern art are often very different in Africa. In a reversal of historical European conceptions, abstraction in Africa is often viewed as purely European and, therefore, foreign. For some African critics, abstraction is thoroughly Western, its use alienating for African audiences. The following are excerpted from the writings of African art critics concerning artistic abstraction:

[I]f an artist pre-occupies himself with transient configurations of formal assembly, in the name of abstraction . . . he could be described as professionally hedonistic, culturally insensitive.[49]

An artist must speak a language which people understand. A symbol that cannot be interpreted defeats its own end.[50]

An increasing number of African artists are receiving formal training outside their immediate environments, in Europe and other parts of the world. The consequence is the emergence of new artistic forms and styles which are . . . invariably so abstract that people . . . find them incomprehensible.[51]

Discussions and observations at art openings and related events in Bamako revealed the prevalence of similar attitudes in Mali today. Many of the attendees expressed frustration with the incomprehensibility of artists who worked in abstract styles associated with Western art. Malian artists too spoke of their frustration at the unwillingness of audiences to work toward acceptance of non-representational art. Thus, ironically, the abstraction that was the hallmark of "traditional" African art returns to the African fine art movement via Europe, becoming "Western" in the eyes of many artists, critics, and members of the art-viewing public.[52]

As Pakistani artist and cultural critic Rasheed Araeen discerns, one can scarcely expect African and non-Western art students and artists to quickly absorb and respond to the international art establishment's changing attitudes toward non-Western art:

The models which were the basis of art education in the colonies were often outmoded, conservative, and backward. When European artists were revolting against and overthrowing the whole tradition of Graeco-Roman classicism early this century, as part of their search for new modes of expression that would represent the spirit of modern times, art students in the colonies were being taught how to draw faces from Graeco-Roman casts imported from Europe.[53]

### Art Education in Mali

Araeen's description of art education in the then-colonial possessions of European powers leads us to an examination of Mali's art education system, which has played a crucial role in the revival of bogolan. Any attempt to comprehend the contemporary, professional (in the Western sense of the term) practice of art in Mali today must include an examination of the country's only art school, the Institut National des Arts, because most of the artists producing art for the museum and gallery trade have attended the school. Many have continued their study abroad. One may, therefore, reasonably assume that the school's curriculum has had an important effect on the character of the contemporary art scene in Mali.

At the Institut National des Arts, "fine art" is clearly defined as a discipline separate from the utilitarian, referred to as "crafts" or as "artisanal pursuits." This distinction is evident in the two divisions of visual art studies at the school: *metiers des arts* (art trades) and arts plastiques. The aim of the former division is carefully detailed in the introduction to the school's *Programmes Officielles* of 1988: "the final objective being . . . the training . . . of producers capable of promoting modern artisanal production, designing and implementing small projects . . . and rationally managing production."[54]

In the same catalogue, the description of the arts plastiques division centers on a single concept: "The introduction of perspective is the most important new addition to this section."[55] Perspectival realism is an artistic innovation closely associated with the Italian Renaissance and, more broadly, with Western scientific rationalism. Frederick Hartt, author of a survey text used in countless undergraduate art history courses, typifies the equation of perspective with Western cultural advancement as he extrapolates from the creation of perspectival realism to great voyages of exploration: "The investigation of perspective, one of his [the Renaissance artist's] great delights, was closely allied to the exploration of *actual* space, which culminated in the late fifteenth and the sixteenth centuries in the voyages of the great discoverers and the revolutionary theories of the astronomers and cosmographers."[56] That the study of perspective constitutes the most notable feature of the arts plastiques section at the Institut National des Arts, vividly indicates the division's Western orientation. The fact that until 1973 the Institut National des Arts had no Malian professors certainly played a role in the replication of the Western art–craft dichotomy in Mali's art education system.[57]

The media taught in the arts plastiques and the metiers des arts divisions further elucidate the sections' different orientations, one toward Western artistic media and styles, the other toward utilitarian pursuits. Until recently, only Western media were taught in the arts plastiques division. Students sculpted in clay, painted in oils, gouache, watercolors, and drew in pencil, charcoal, and ink. Demy Thera, a former professor at the school and a practicing sculptor in Bamako, uses marble to sculpt, not wood.[58] The use of marble is a particularly striking example of the adaptation of Western media, for although carving in soapstone or steatite and granite has a long history in some regions, nowhere in sub-Saharan Africa is the carving of marble practiced in an indigenous context.[59]

The metiers des arts section, by contrast, includes metalwork, leatherwork, weaving, and woodcarving, all media used by artists who sell their work in the tourist market rather than in galleries and museums. Projects listed in metiers des arts sample course syllabi include the making of small masks, statuettes, and busts—all items sold in the tourist market—and the training of students includes a visit to "authentic traditional sculptors" to learn more about masks.[60]

Clearly, the designers of Mali's art education system drew a stark distinction between art and craft, creating two separate realms of artistic education and production. The separation of these spheres reflects the influence of Western models (primarily French, the colonial power under whose auspices the Malian education system was created). In light of the preceding synopsis of the two divisions that comprise the art department at the Institut National des Arts, one would expect to find bogolan included in the metiers des arts division. Bogolan is a distinctively Malian technique, long used to produce cloth for local use, quite unlike the oil painting and life drawing offered to arts plastiques students. Yet, bogolan classes are offered as part of the arts plastiques curriculum. The Institut National des Arts and the government agencies that support the school are encouraging the same students who study oil painting to acquire proficiency in this local, distinctly Malian medium.

Bogolan's addition to the arts plastiques curriculum at the Institut National des Arts is part of recent official attention to the fine arts, marked by particular support for the production of bogolan. In 1978, when he was minister of youth, sports, arts, and culture, Alpha Oumar Konaré amended the school's official objectives to include encouragement of Malian modern art.[61] The curriculum now emphasizes the training of artists for participation in the museum and gallery trade in art, an option that did not exist during the institute's early years. Several of the artists now central to the revival of bogolan benefited directly from this official encouragement, learning the technique as part of their educational training. In his doctoral thesis on modern Malian art, Baba Moussulu Touré, a professor at the Institut National des Arts, wrote of the shift toward valorization of traditional arts, making particular note of the importance of bogolan in this shift: "During the period from 1975–1985, the first real efforts were made to revalorize, spread and make use of traditional forms and motifs. . . . This period saw the successful development of a decorative and graphic art form (bocolan) [sic] which includes traditional motifs and symbols ('ideograms')."[62]

The bogolan class I attended at the Institut National des Arts was taught by two members of the Groupe Bogolan Kasobane, Néné Thiam and Souleyman Guro. Another group member, Klétigui Dembélé, also taught bogolan classes at the school. The class provided, in several of its characteristics, a microcosmic view of Bamako's bogolan revival. The student body of approximately thirty students included only one female. In its dramatically skewed gender ratio, the class reflects the fine art bogolan field as a whole. Much as in the tourist art market, the production of bogolan paintings is almost exclusively a male pursuit. The only two female painters currently working in Bamako are members of cooperative groups (the Groupe Bogolan Kasobane and the Atelier Jamana).

The paintings the students created in class were also characteristic of much contemporary bogolan production. None adopted the abstract motifs associated with bogolanfini, laden with historical, mythological, and proverbial signification. Indeed, none of the students' compositions were abstractions. Instead, students used the bogolan medium to create elaborate figurative designs, most of which were centered on subjects that signify Malian (or more broadly African) culture for foreign consumption—drums, female figures, masks, and the like. These symbols of Malian identity as souvenirs, tokens of an exotic experience, are staples of the tourist art market. Here, however, Malian students working not for the tourist trade but in an educational setting—students did not sell the results of their class work—make use of the same iconography.

In much of the fine art bogolan market, as in the school where artists receive their training, "tradition" and "modernity" and national identity and international markets commingle and combine in a multiethnic, multicultural urban environment. Such circumstances create opportunities as well as obstacles for artists who seek audiences for their work. For many, the adaptation of bogolan provides a route to these audiences, both Malian and foreign.

# 6

# THE FINE ART MARKET

## From Bogolan to Le Bogolan

La teinture au bogolan, practiquée par les femmes durant la saison sèche, période de répit, devient "Le Bogolan." (Bogolan dyeing, the work of women during the dry season, a time of rest, has become "Bogolan.")
*Marie-Françoise Becchetti-Laure, "Aperçu de la Jeune Peintre à Bamako"*

Bamako is home to several of Mali's most prominent visual artists as well as many young artists determined to make their way in the increasingly crowded bogolan art market. These artists and artists' groups strive to create their own distinctive styles, adapting a variety of technical and stylistic innovations. All preserve some aspects of the bogolanfini in which the bogolan revival is based, speaking of their work as founded in Malian traditional arts, while simultaneously all are self-consciously modern in their intentions.

Because the bogolan revival in Bamako is a relatively recent phenomenon, gaining momentum in the late 1980s, the experiences of many of the artists at work today provide insight into the creation of the movement. Pinpointing the origins of the bogolan revival is impossible, because the movement emerged out of broad cultural shifts in attitudes toward tradition and Malian identity. Additionally, it is not possible to identify individual artists who first began to use the medium to produce paintings for sale in galleries, for the movement had several separate inceptions, with a number of artists, working independently, making use of bogolan to produce painting and clothing in contemporary styles.[1] The movement's multiple origins indicate that bogolan's revival is most accurately viewed as the manifestation of a broad cultural undercurrent rather than the work of a single innovator.

Although it is not a factor frequently discussed by critics of African art (or of any other art for that matter), the market in which artists produce, sell, or fail to sell their work has an important effect on the work they produce. John Povey succinctly describes this rarely acknowledged aspect of the field: "Much as our purists might object, artists do prefer to eat, and for that they need markets."[2] The drive to find markets is a central aspect of the revival of bogolan in the context of Bamako's fine art bogolan movement. The motivations of artists to adopt bogolan can be illuminated by an awareness of the economic boundaries within which these artists work and by an examination of the market for contemporary art in Bamako.

In many instances, artists have arrived at the use of bogolan in response to pragmatic financial needs. Basic materials used by artists, such as oil paints, brushes, canvas, and the like, are, if available in Mali, prohibitively expensive. Very few shops in Bamako sell art supplies, and even at the art school oil paints and other materials are in short supply. Many artists rely on contacts—friends or family members who travel abroad—for supplies of such materials.[3] Bogolan, of course, eliminates this reliance on imported supplies, as it is made from local materials. Many artists gather n'gallama leaves themselves from trees growing in Bamako and surrounding areas. All prepare their own mud, often according to their own particular "recipes."

For an artist, the lack of materials is a serious difficulty, but the absence of a market in which to sell one's work is an even more effective barrier to success. Like artists throughout Africa (and elsewhere) who seek to make and sell art that is not "traditional" according to the canons established by Western collectors and museums, Malian bogolan artists are scarcely supported by local art markets, and they have limited access to the Western art market. Bogolan continues to be adopted by artists in an attempt to make space for themselves in one or both of these markets. They have met with mixed success.

### BUILDING A MOVEMENT

Although several of the artists currently working in Bamako are credited with the popularization of bogolan as a contemporary, urban artistic medium, these artists have several little-known predecessors. Discussion here of the chronology of fine art bogolan begins with two artists whose work has never received significant attention but whose careers as teachers had an important impact, instilling an interest in bogolan in young people in the early 1980s. Several of their former students are today active artists in Bamako. Both worked as *animateurs,* government-employed cultural promoters who led workshops and organized exhibitions. Lamine Sidibe was an animateur in the Bamako region (Commune IV) during the early 1980s. His experimentation with bogolan was an important influence on several bogolan artists. Sidibe worked with Ismaël Diabaté, Yacouba Koné, and Djelemakan Sacko, and several members of the Groupe Bogolan Kasobane acknowledge Sidibe's early influence on their work.[4]

The resemblance of Sidibe's paintings to the work of many current artists in terms of format, style, and iconography points to Sidibe's direct influence on the bogolan revival. Artists he worked with, however, perceive his presence as more diffuse. Surprisingly, the work of the three bogolan artists he worked with most directly—Diabaté, Koné, and Sacko—bears little resemblance to Sidibe's work. According to all three, Sidibe provided important inspiration, demonstrating the potential of a medium they had encountered only in village contexts.[5]

Sidibe's paintings do, however, resemble those of the Groupe Bogolan Kasobane and their many followers. His subject matter is also characteristic of many artists currently participating in the movement—figurative and stylized with copious references to "traditional" forms, such as Bamana masks, drummers, and women wearing local hairstyles and garments. The paintings are large, figurative, and richly hued, using bogolan in varied intensities to create subtle chiaroscuro, all traits that separate the work of Sidibe and other creators of "fine art" bogolan from the artists who aim for the tourist art market.

Sidibe did not, however, incorporate abstract patterns as borders and backgrounds, as do the members of the Groupe Bogolan Kasobane and many of their followers. Such patterns, according to the artists who use them in their work, constitute a reference to bogolanfini's richly symbolic motifs. The absence of abstract, geometric patterns indicates the distance between Sidibe's work and the more direct bogolan-fini-inspired paintings of later artists. That is, he adapted the medium but not the iconography. Bogolan artists at work today range widely in their stylistic relationships to bogolanfini's characteristic patterns, some incorporating specific symbolic patterns, others creating their own forms of abstraction, or, like Sidibe, working in a purely figurative style.

Another animateur, an M. Berthé, has also been identified by several artists as a source of inspiration. Known as Solitaire Solitaire, Berthé worked at Bamako's Maison de Jeunesse, a cultural center for youths where he taught bogolan techniques, introducing numerous young people to the medium.[6] He was said to have then moved to Sikasso, a city south of Bamako, where he had a business making leather goods. Information on his background and his whereabouts was vague, though it is clear that he studied at the Institut National des Arts.

Other Malians credited with initiating bogolan's revival in the fine art market are not themselves painters. In 1975 Maryam Thiam, a former schoolteacher in Markala, a town near the city of Segou in the important bogolan-producing region of Beledougou, began a project aimed at providing Markala's female population with a source of income. Working with the American Field Service, a Quaker development organization, Thiam organized a group of elderly women to teach bogolanfini production to young women. Without Thiam's organization, which ensures that the women will have a market for their cloth, many of Markala's women would not have learned bogolan skills. By commissioning cloth, which she sells in Bamako in a shop called La Paysanne (The Peasant), Thiam offers a source of income for the women while providing incentive for the preservation of a local textile technique. La Paysanne is a source for bogolan products for a primarily expatriate audience.[7]

Another Malian who early began to champion recognition of bogolan's value as a uniquely Malian art form was the clothing designer Chris Seydou.[8] Because he was making use of the cloth in his garments beginning in the mid-1970s, Seydou is mentioned here along with Lamine Sidibe, Solitaire Solitaire, and Maryam Thiam as one of the founders of the modern bogolan movement. His position as an early and influential innovator also indicates the diversity of bogolan's revival, with manifestations in fashion as well as in the fine arts. The existence of several early innovators also supports the theory that the inception of the bogolan revival is best viewed as a broad movement and not the work of a single artist or entrepreneur.

### The Groupe Bogolan Kasobane: "Les Pioneers"

The Groupe Bogolan Kasobane looms large in any discussion of bogolan's revival in Bamako because of their high visibility in Mali and abroad and because of their influence on younger artists. The members of the group view themselves as the originators of the bogolan revival; according to Néné Thiam, one of the group's five members, "We are the pioneers."[9] Indeed, the Groupe Bogolan Kasobane did much to popularize bogolan's use as a fine art medium, regardless of whether they were actually the first to make use of the technique to create paintings for sale in galleries.

The members of the group—Kandiora Coulibaly, Klétigui Dembélé, Souleyman Guro, Boubacar Doumbia, Néné Thiam (the sole female member of the group), and Baba Fallo Keita—are in their mid-forties to early fifties. "Kasobane" is a combination of five group members' names: KA (Kandiora and Klétigui), SO (Souleyman), BA (Boubacar), NE (Néné). The word is also a close approximation of a Bamana phrase that might be loosely translated as "an end to imprisonment." In an exegesis of the term, group members said their work represents freedom from past strictures that prevented artists from fully expressing their identities.[10]

The members of the group met in 1974 while students at the Institut National des Arts, where they were enrolled in the arts plastiques program. In 1978, Coulibaly wrote his thesis on bogolan, calling attention to the medium at a time when it was not generally discussed at the school.[11] Coulibaly began making bogolan in 1972, after learning the technique while traveling in bogolan-producing regions with his uncle.[12] His earliest success was in the realm of clothing rather than painting. According to Coulibaly, "I made and wore a lot of bogolan clothing between 1974 and 1978, and every year I sold everything I made."[13]

The other members of the group came to bogolan by various routes, one learning the technique from family members (Guro), another only learning the technique as she began to work professionally as an artist in Bamako (Thiam). The group began exhibiting bogolan paintings in 1978 although they had worked together before that time, making bogolan uniforms for social groups called *grin*.[14] Their first exhibition, in September 1978, was not held in Bamako but at the Maison de Jeunesse in Segou. Nearby, in Markala, the group established its first studio.

Coulibaly said that the group has, from its earliest exhibitions, shown clothing along with paintings.[15] A description by a student in the Institut National des Arts newsletter of the Groupe Bogolan Kasobane exhibition at the 1989 Semaine Artistique et Culturelle[16] indicates the importance of the cloth's role as clothing as well as a fine art medium:

> A surprise awaited visitors in the first room. A statue of a woman, dressed in two pagnes of bogolan and holding in her arms a baby she is nursing, welcomes those who enter. This is an original way to introduce the cloth's colors, because this hall is reserved for the display of bogolan. . . . This was the work of the Groupe Bogolan, a group of young artists . . . each of whom has studied the bogolan techniques of their own regions.[17]

In installing their paintings along with a mannequin wearing bogolan pagnes, the Groupe Bogolan Kasobane drew visitors into the gallery with a reference to the cloth's customary function as clothing in rural contexts. Thus, they ensured that viewers would associate the figurative, elaborately worked paintings inside the gallery with the more familiar use of the cloth as a garment on display as they entered.

The group's paintings are generally large, up to seven feet in width or height, representational and elaborately worked, covering every inch of the cotton canvas with intricate patterns. Their cooperative working method may have a role in the size of their paintings, for the size permits all group members to work simultaneously on separate sections of the canvas. Bogolanfini motifs, when they appear, are confined to borders and backgrounds, minimizing their visual impact. Among several of the group's paintings in 1997, many had no borders and made no use of bogolanfini-like designs, eliminating any direct iconographical reference to the abstract representations that characterize the traditional cloth. In response to inquiries concerning the reason for the lack of border and background designs, Baba Fallo Keita replied that the composition was the result of purely aesthetic considerations.[18]

Beyond aesthetic motivations, one might hypothesize that the elimination of the bogolanfini-based designs reflects the growing acceptance of bogolan as an artistic medium in and of itself, without necessitating reference to the cloth with which the pigments used were originally associated. The Groupe Bogolan Kasobane might be expected to be among the last bogolan artists to relinquish the direct reference to bogolanfini, as they were among the earliest to transform the technique into a fine art. When the technique was first adapted to paintings, audiences required sufficient similarity between the bogolanfini they associated with rural use and the paintings in modern styles in order to appreciate the artists' intentions.

In their choice of subject matter, the Groupe Bogolan Kasobane typify many contemporary Malian artists, reflecting a preference for "typical" Malian subjects. They incorporate a plethora of referents to "traditional" Mali—ci waraw, n'tomo (a mask worn at young men's initiations) and other Bamana mask types, the Djenne mosque, and drummers and dancers, among other motifs. The iconography of the group's paintings also includes motifs more broadly associated with African culture. One painting, *An Bo Sira,* or *L'Art Africain à Travers l'Histoire* (African Art through History), incorporates a wide-ranging assortment of African icons—rock paintings, Malian masks, drummers and dancers, the mosque at Djenne, and Egyptian sphinxes and pyramids. According to the didactic label that accompanied the painting in a Paris exhibition, the painting symbolizes Africa's breadth of artistic history with the aim of increasing awareness of that history.[19] Other paintings make reference to proverbs. *Nimisa* (Regret), a depiction of figures locked in combat, alludes to the proverb "After the dispute, regret," a cautionary commentary on the effect of aggressive behavior on social cohesion.[20] The painting *Nyama* refers to the interconnectedness of all living things, a concept group member Keita described as an aspect of Bamana cosmology (Plate 9).[21] In the written commentary that accompanied the painting's sale, the group members describe the subject as "the relationship between man and animals, between man and nature, between men themselves." They note that this force is "called 'Nyama' in Bambara and Karma among the Hindus."[22] Another painting, *Nyòkala Sô* (Millet Stalk Horse) provides a commentary on the futility of overconfidence in scientific solutions to life's problems (Plate 10):

> Man is in the midst of running and to move faster he uses scientific means. But in reality it is man himself who is being used and used up even as he apparently thinks that he is satisfied. This is like a child in Africa who uses a stalk of millet as a horse, he gallops and runs with it, he waters and feeds it, but in reality it is he himself who is running and ends up exhausted.[23]

Thus, using distinctly local imagery—the stalk of millet, the powerful symbolism of nyama—the Groupe Bogolan Kasobane's paintings communicate messages that speak broadly to viewers of all cultural backgrounds. Some of their other paintings feature commentary on environmental degradation, the important role of women in Bamana society, and the plight of victims of drought and war.[24]

The Groupe Bogolan Kasobane have had a distinguished career, both in Mali and abroad. In 1983, they were awarded first prize at the prestigious Lauréat du Concours de Peinture BIAO,[25] at the time among the only domestic competitions available to aspiring artists, an indication of the scarcity of opportunities for Malian artists to exhibit their work. In 1986, they received a special mention at the Deuxième Biennale de la Havane in Cuba. In 1984, the Groupe Bogolan Kasobane became the only Malian artists to be featured in a solo exhibition at the Musée des Arts Africains et Océaniens in Paris. The exhibition, *Bogolan et Arts Graphiques du Mali,* had a small accompanying catalogue, which was until 1995 the only published reference devoted to contemporary bogolan.[26] The Groupe Bogolan Kasobane were also the only Malian artists illustrated in *Africa Explores: Twentieth Century African Art,* arguably the most ambitious, influential, and controversial American publication on contemporary African art to date.[27]

The Groupe Bogolan Kasobane's work epitomizes the efforts of many contemporary bogolan artists to preserve, share, and disseminate this uniquely Malian art form, seeking to increase awareness of bogolan not only through their paintings and clothing but also by exporting the medium itself. An interview with the group in the popular Malian magazine *Jamana* (published by the Association Jamana) features a step-by-step "how-to" description of bogolan production, complete with advice on avoiding common mistakes (for example, "The colors are very fluid. Use them with prudence and care.").[28] According to Néné Thiam, the group members have been offered grants to move elsewhere to teach bogolan techniques abroad, but they prefer to stay in Mali, working to "change the mentality" of Malians so that bogolan will become a symbol of national pride.[29] Kandiora Coulibaly speaks of bogolan as a part of the essence of the country itself: "Bogolan is in fact a mosaic of fantasy and reality, around a proverb, a legend or a major topic or real situation. Bogolan is a technique that our ancestors have left us."[30]

The Groupe Bogolan Kasobane's members have already begun teaching the medium to non-Malians who will, the group hopes, discover similar mineral and vegetal dyes where they live. In a report submitted to the Institut National des Arts following six months of study, a student from Benin named Arouna Mouniratou wrote of her hopes to "create a bogolan workshop on my return to my country."[31] Her professors, Souleyman Guro, Néné Thiam, and Klétigui Dembélé, actively supported her efforts. Rather than working to prevent other artists from entering the bogolan painting market, the group members encourage the spread of bogolan techniques, which they view as a source of pride in their national identity rather than as a source of income to be closely guarded.

In addition to teaching bogolan techniques to others, both Malian and foreign, the members of the Groupe Bogolan Kasobane conduct research themselves, visiting villages and small towns in the regions where bogolan is made. Although they are motivated to seek new information by a desire to broaden their repertoire of dyes and techniques, they also record information so that bogolan-producing skills will be preserved. For Kandiora Coulibaly, whose research provided the foundation of the group's activities, investigation of bogolan's history and its geographical variations began with his dissatisfaction with the Western-style techniques he learned as a student at the Institut National des Arts in the early 1970s. Frustrated by the expensive, scarce oil paints and inks he was expected to master, Coulibaly sought to prove that he could do the same things with bogolan, that in fact bogolan, the "colors of [my] own country, are . . . richer in possibilities than European oils or inks."[32]

The Groupe Bogolan Kasobane's research among rural bogolan producers may initially appear to resemble the "salvage" efforts[33] of anthropologists or art historians (usually Western) who carefully document a practice, a society, an art form, or any other identifiable subject for research. Dembélé, in describing the advantages of being Malian in conducting research on bogolan, explained that the group members are able to interact with their informants in a more fluid, natural manner than foreign researchers.[34] Beginning in the Segou areas, the members of the Groupe Bogolan Kasobane traveled extensively in bogolan-producing regions, such as Kolokani and Markala as well as other towns and villages nearby. Their research extends into other forms of artistic expression as well. Coulibaly, for example, is researching embroidery styles in the Djenne region.[35]

The Groupe Bogolan Kasobane's use of the information they gather might be best viewed as recycling rather than salvaging. In lieu of preserving information on bogolan in a static form, as in a book or research journal, separated wholly from its "living" context, the group members "activate" the information they gather by translating the medium into new forms. James Clifford's conception of authenticity as a contemporary, postcolonial concept might be fruitfully applied to the Groupe Bogolan Kasobane's work, in which "authenticity is reconceived as a hybrid, creative activity in a local present-becoming-future."[36] The Groupe Bogolan Kasobane, like the other artists combining bogolan with new formats, styles, and media, are reformulating an "authentic," "traditional" art form in response to their own urban, multiethnic, and international experiences.

The broad ethnic profile of the group members perhaps helps explain their interest in increasing bogolan's appeal and synthesizing its varied regional styles. The group's members are Bamana, Dogon, Malinke, Minianka, and Soninké—a broad representation of Malian ethnic groups.[37] The group members indicated that the fusion of their varied ethnic backgrounds was not a deliberate decision, but rather a reflection of the multiethnic character of Bamako.[38] Thus, bogolan's transformation from an exclusively female, rural activity to a male-dominated, urban pursuit has a parallel in the shifting ethnic profile of producers. Bogolan has moved from an overwhelmingly Bamana art form to an essentially pan-ethnic activity.[39] Even traditions that discourage the production of bogolan by members of particular ethnic groups have had little effect on the young urban artists now taking up the technique.[40] The Groupe Bogolan Kasobane's membership exemplifies the blending of ethnicities in the contemporary bogolan market.

The group's working method ensures that all members have the opportunity to bring their own technical and stylistic experience to the collective enterprise. Discussions of the group have consistently made note of its communal nature, describing the emergence of paintings out of a collective vision. For example, "Each artist takes possession of a corner of the immense, stretched canvas and draws with a duck feather, responding to his or her own inspiration fed by each other's ideas,"[41] and, "The artists share their sources of inspiration, elaborating a composition together, but leaving responsibility for the entire or partial completion of the work to the group member who best grasps the theme at hand."[42] Both of the above observations hint at the idealized, seamless unification of artistic visions, and the catalogue that accompanied the group's solo exhibition in Paris goes a step further, interpreting the collaborative work as an erasure of individual identity: "With their cooperative production, the artists in the group move beyond individualism, subjectivism and the Western 'me.'"[43] In his review of the *Africa Explores* exhibition, Francesco Pellizzi makes note of the "trans-individual Bogolan Kasobane group,"[44] reflecting the presentation of the artists as a seamless unit.

Such assertions concerning the group's working methods bring to the fore common past (and, in some quarters, present) misconceptions concerning African artistic traditions, which have long been considered the work of anonymous artists reproducing the art forms of their ancestors. My own interactions with group members indicate no such effacing of the self, intentional or otherwise. Although the Groupe Bogolan Kasobane members work as a group, each painting can be clearly identified as a single artist's conception, style, or subject. Néné Thiam expressed great pride in the fact that perceptive viewers have been able to distinguish the hands of the separate artists in their large paintings. Klétigui Dembélé revealed that the artists are very rarely all in the same place at the same time, for each has a full-time job—some teach, one works at the Musée National du Mali, another works at the national film agency—and all travel frequently to exhibitions, conferences, and workshops. The group is genuinely cooperative, making business as well as artistic decisions collaboratively, yet each artist also retains his or her individuality. Working together, they have both individually and collectively achieved great success. [45]

The members of the Groupe Bogolan Kasobane were not the first to utilize bogolan in the context of fine art, but they are exceptional in their perception of the medium's potential. They discerned bogolan's distinctive appeal as a uniquely Malian art form, viewing it as a means of artistic expression and as a source of profit. The group has created a veritable bogolan empire, diversifying their adaptation of the technique to create a huge variety of products, including pillows, curtains, clothing, and upholstery as well as paintings.[46] Coulibaly has led the group into the realm of theatrical costuming and set design,[47] and they have opened a boutique to market their clothing and home décor products.

Like other artists who adapt bogolan to a variety of markets, the members of the Groupe Bogolan Kasobane clearly hold their paintings in much higher esteem than their "utilitarian" products. As noted in Chapter 3, many bogolan artists find that paintings do not provide a viable living, so they turn to quickly produced, readily salable products to supplement their incomes. Bogolan's appeal in all of these forms permits artists to move from market to market with relative ease. The applicability of bogolan to varied markets can, however, pose difficulties; artists who produce bogolan for more than one market risk becoming associated with one genre of cloth to the exclusion of another. Some members of the Groupe Bogolan Kasobane, as well as several of their critics, assert that their association with housewares and clothing has compromised their reputation as producers of fine art. Group member Baba Fallo Keita expressed his concern that any exhibition or publication of the group's work clearly distinguish between the varied aspects of their oeuvre, placing particular emphasis on their paintings.[48]

Their insistence on the primacy of their paintings reflects the Groupe Bogolan Kasobane's conviction that their paintings should serve as tools for education, not only as aesthetic statements or decorative objects. Just as their use of bogolan is rooted in a desire to celebrate and to preserve the technique, so too is their choice of subject matter an effort to create works of art that serve society through the preservation of "traditional" beliefs, the communication of historical information, and the depiction of proper moral behavior.

Criticism of the Groupe Bogolan Kasobane in Bamako's artistic community is focused largely on the lack of a clear distinction between their fine art and their artisanal production. Mansour Ciss, a Senegalese sculptor living in Bamako in the mid-1990s who had displayed his work at the Musée National and at numerous foreign venues, is highly influential in Bamako's artistic circles. In Ciss's opinion, the Groupe Bogolan Kasobane's paintings might be considered contemporary in subject matter, but not in style. For him, their work is not avant-garde, but artisanal—in his words, they represent "l'artisanat de l'art" ("the artisanat of art")—created to sell rather than to express any philosophical or aesthetic ideas.[49] A prominent employee of the Musée National who would likely prefer to remain anonymous on this point expressed similar ambivalence, indicating that the group's production has great decorative appeal but lacks the seriousness that distinguishes the work of important artists.[50] Such judgments are a matter of personal taste and might be expected in a market as competitive as that for bogolan paintings in Bamako. Still, none of their detractors can deny the importance of the Groupe Bogolan Kasobane in the revitalization of bogolan, for their high profile has led many young artists to adopt the medium, taking it in seemingly infinite directions.

### Ismaël Diabaté: Bogolan for National Pride and for Profit

Two artists—Ismaël Diabaté and Sidicki Traoré—epitomize the bogolan movement's diversity of style, motivation, and background. One of these artists had formal artistic training and a long professional career before adopting bogolan, using the medium as a political statement to reflect his rejection of Western artistic traditions. The other, who has had no formal training, views bogolan as a means of gaining access to the lucrative contemporary art market. Both have encountered the difficulties inherent in the marketing of bogolan paintings—a lack of exhibition venues, domestic consumers, and access to foreign markets. Their responses to these difficulties, however, have differed broadly.

Ismaël Diabaté, one of Mali's best-known contemporary artists, graduated from the Institut National des Arts in 1968, a member of the school's second graduating class. He is proud of the fact that, unlike most professional artists in Mali, he was not educated abroad. From 1968 to 1991 Diabaté taught art at high schools in and around Bamako. He founded the Association Nationale des Artistes du Mali, and in 1991 he received a Médaille d'Argente du Mérite National (Silver Medal of National Merit) in recognition of his many contributions to Malian cultural life. Diabaté's list of exhibitions is long, including several shows in European museums and galleries.[51] In *Africa Explores: Twentieth Century African Art,* Susan Vogel makes note of Ismaël Diabaté as an extraordinary example of success against the odds: "The fifth poorest country in the world, it has not yet formed a university; in this context, the personal histories of two independent artists [Diabaté and Abdoulaye Konaté, a painter who also creates multimedia installations] . . . show a surprising level of activity."[52] In 1991, Diabaté ceased teaching and began supporting himself solely as an artist, though he must exhibit and sell abroad in order to survive, a fact he regrets.[53]

Throughout his career, Diabaté has worked in a variety of media, including oils, acrylics, monotypes, and, beginning in the early 1980s, bogolan. Since 1991, however, he has focused solely on bogolan, working in widely diverse styles. The range of Diabaté's bogolan paintings, from intricate geometric abstractions to painterly canvases built of washes of vegetal dyes, dramatically demonstrates the medium's applicability to a spectrum of styles as broad as that of any of the media he used before turning to bogolan. Why, he reasons, should a Malian artist continue to employ media that Westerners have already exploited, particularly when he might employ a medium unique to his homeland? In Diabaté's words, "It's not worth the trouble to use what Europe has already used."[54]

Diabaté holds a strong conviction that art by Malian artists should be for a Malian audience, not for expatriate patrons in-country nor for foreign collectors.[55] Many artists in Bamako express frustration, even resentment, at the domination of the domestic market in contemporary art by non-Malian patrons, but Diabaté is the only artist who has made a personal statement of protest against this non-local control. Diabaté desires to work entirely for local markets, and in 1992 declared his intention to decline all offers to exhibit in Europe—an immense sacrifice for a Malian artist who has an active career outside Mali.[56] Diabaté's conviction that Malians should control their own markets and communicate directly with their compatriots is reflected in his support of the *n'ko* writing system, which has been labeled "the militant alphabet"[57] and was invented in 1949 by Souleyman Kanté, a Muslim cleric dismayed by the abandonment of African languages by Africans themselves. In an effort to assert the relevance and sophistication of African languages, Kanté set out to create an alphabet that could be used to transcribe numerous African languages.[58] *N'ko,* which means "I say" in Malinke (Kanté's first language) and in Bamanakan, has been championed by Diabaté and other prominent Malian cultural figures. His involvement with the *n'ko* movement is of a piece with his artistic focus on bogolan.

In 1983, motivated by his desire to create distinctly Malian art, Diabaté began to investigate bogolan's potential as an artistic medium. To study the medium, he apprenticed himself to the Groupe Bogolan Kasobane.[59] Later, working independently, he experimented with new pigments and new methods of application. Using a technique he employed in his printmaking, Diabaté applied bogolan pigments in a freeform, manner. According to Pauline Duponchel, "he has evolved toward a freer, more abstract style of working . . . not dissimilar to the 'dripping' of J[ackson] Pollock."[60] Much like Pollock's action-painting technique, Diabaté's energetic application of mineral and vegetal pigment creates a sense of vitality quite distinct from the methodically applied, highly controlled works of the Groupe Bogolan Kasobane. Diabaté's images emerge out of the drips and stains created by the pigment, skillfully making use of the bogolan dyes' variations on browns and tans to create effects reminiscent of chiaroscuro. Diabaté's *Foule de Mars* (Crowds of March) exemplifies this drip technique (Plate 11). Diabaté views the work, which he has revisited in several versions, as seminal in his efforts to make of bogolan a versatile medium for contemporary artistic expressions.[61] The painting makes reference to the bravery of women, who were in the forefront of protests during the March 1991 overthrow of the government. The figures of five women emerge out of the churning colors, a dramatic representation of the strength many women in Bamako exhibited in the face of the military's efforts to stifle the demonstrations.

Diabaté's technique might also be compared with a Malian form of "gestural" painting in use long before Pollock's abstract expressionism—the splattered, stained bogolan worn by hunters at work in the bush, where the mottled cloth serves as camouflage (see Plate 24). Diabaté's study of the cloth likely brought him into contact with this type of bogolan, which is not as well known in art historical circles as the elaborately and intricately decorated bogolan, with its geometric motifs. Diabaté himself did not identify the camouflage-style bogolan as his source of inspiration for his gestural material, instead describing it as a personal innovation employed as a means of self-expression.

Diabaté also uses bogolan to create paintings whose hard edges and meticulously controlled application places them at the opposite end of the stylistic spectrum from the splattered canvases. This series of works, which Diabaté calls "géometriques," are painted not on strip-woven cloth but on industrially produced cotton canvas, the smooth surface permitting the fine detail of Diabaté's intricate lines (Plate 12). Although he leaves behind the strips of cotton that mark handwoven cloth in Mali, his medium (bogolan) and iconography (symbolic motifs associated with Bamana culture) preserve the work's close connections to local culture.

Among Diabaté's most remarkable innovations is his development of an aerosol-type application of bogolan's vegetal dyes, creating washes of subtly modulated tones. He also creates distinctive effects by emphasizing the narrow cotton strips of cotton that are the support for his bogolan pigments, stretching the strips to create delicate, angular canvases. Thus, the voids between the strips become part of the work's composition. Many of his paintings in the mid-1990s also incorporated assemblage, with small packets made of cloth or leather attached to the surface of the canvas. These he refers to as his *gris-gris* paintings, a reference to the amulets and other powerful spiritual objects used by diviners, hunters, and others to contain the augmented power they require to combat negative forces in the dangerous realms where they dwell.

## On Innovation, Ideograms, and Secrecy

Diabaté, like most of the artists at work in the highly competitive bogolan art market, carefully guards his "recipes" for specific vegetal dyes and his other innovations. He in particular has expressed great frustration at the speed with which young artists take up each of his technical and stylistic innovations, flooding the art market with their versions of his aerosol paintings, his strip paintings, and, most recently, his attachment of leather and cloth amulets to the surface of his paintings. Artists rarely reveal the details of their leaf, root, and mineral combinations or their techniques for preparing, blending, and applying colors; their technical innovations are a source of great pride. Among the artists who have revealed their techniques are Yacouba Koné, Mamadou Diarra, and Brehima Koné, whose innovations involved the addition of specific materials to the water in which the mud mixture is fermented, to the dye bath of n'gallama leaves, as well as the use of diverse plant materials to create new colors.[62]

Concealment of the knowledge by which artists and merchants operate in complex, contentious contemporary bogolan markets may be viewed as a modern, urban manifestation of the central role of secrecy in much "traditional" African art. Objects and the rituals by which they are utilized may serve as containers for information and power—and the two are often inextricably connected—accessible only to "insiders," that is, initiates, elders, hunters, sorcerers, rulers, women, or innumerable other subgroups. In her introduction to *Secrecy: African Art That Conceals and Reveals,* Mary Nooter describes the operation of secrecy in artistic forms as "a means of ordering knowledge, regulating power, and demarcating differences between genders, classes, titles and professions. Secrecy is a channel of communication and commentary; a social and political boundary marker; and a medium of property and power."[63] In the tourist art and fine art markets for bogolan in Bamako, secret technical and commercial information separates professionals from students, innovators from imitators, power brokers from power seekers.

Diabaté's bogolan paintings manipulate a more familiar form of secrecy—the use of encoded symbols. Like most of the artists in the contemporary bogolan market, Diabaté deliberately selects subject matter that, like his technique, is specifically Malian. His early work, in the late 1970s and early 1980s, evoked Malian culture through the same subjects utilized by most artists: "traditional" village life, picturesque scenes, and the like.[64] His work in bogolan explores particularly esoteric (and specifically Bamana) symbols of Malian culture. By 1992, Diabaté had begun to focus his bogolan paintings on a system of graphic symbols or ideograms associated with a powerful Bamana secret society. Diabaté had used the ideograms in other media, including monoprints. In bogolan, however, the symbols became a consistent aspect of his oeuvre.

Bamana ideograms are a series of two hundred sixty-six signs that constitute, according to Germaine Dieterlen and Youssouf Cissé, the foundation of knowledge for the most powerful Bamana secret order, the Komo society.[65] As Patrick McNaughton describes it, the Komo society is "the most potent of all power associations. . . . It involves itself in nearly every realm of community and inter-community affairs."[66] He notes elsewhere, "The komo association is owned by [black]smiths."[67] Those initiated into the powerful Komo association learn how to interpret the ideograms, which re-

Figure 10. *Si-Kólómá*, Ismaël Diabaté, 1993. Bogolan pigments on canvas. 28.5″ × 22″ (72 × 56 cm). Collection of the National Museum of Natural History, Smithsonian Institution, Department of Anthropology, cat. no. 99-21092. Washington, D.C.

*Ismaël Diabaté had worked with Komo ideograms in other media before adopting bogolan as his primary medium. Diabaté applies soft layers of color by using an aerosol spray applicator. The ideogram at the center of this evocative bogolan landscape is called si-kólómá, which translates literally as "brown." Germaine Dieterlen and Youssouf Cissé, in Les Fondements de la Société d'Initiation du Komo, describe the sign's deeper meaning as one "associated with persons who are said to be 'neither white, nor black, nor red,' that is, people who have not yet been ontologically defined, such as the uncircumcised, called bilakorow" (p. 108).*

count the seven stages of Earth's creation.[68] Diabaté, though he is not actively involved with the Komo society himself, is the son of a blacksmith from the Kayes region, making him particularly sensitive to the symbols' significance. In 1974, when Diabaté encountered Dieterlen and Cissé's 1972 publication on the Komo society, he began to utilize their "lexography" of ideograms, incorporating the signs into paintings and prints.[69] In the early 1990s, he began producing a series of bogolan paintings, each centered on a single ideogram (Figure 10).

Diabaté's series of aerosol-sprayed canvases, each with an ideogram at its center, resemble cubistic landscapes, creating planes of pictorial space in modulated tones of brown and tan. His geometric paintings are less explicit in their references to specific ideograms, and the surfaces are worked with intricate linear patterns. Within these weblike constructions, Diabaté incorporates ideograms, difficult to identify yet readily visible to patient viewers willing to study the geometric landscapes. These paintings also occasionally incorporate bogolanfini's symbolic motifs, blending the two systems of meaning. Although he has not been explicit about the parallels between the secretive nature of the symbols and his stylistic replication of the notion of concealment, Diabaté has spoken of the importance of ideograms as containers for culturally specific information that remains strictly veiled to all but those skilled in their interpretation.[70]

In light of his interest in ideograms as containers for secret knowledge, museum and gallery displays of Diabaté's ideogram-centered paintings take surprising forms. The paintings are identified by title and date, but also on the wall next to each piece are photocopied excerpts from Dieterlen and Cissé's book on Komo ideograms explicating the symbols. By accompanying the images with written exegesis, Diabaté implicitly acknowledges that a significant proportion of viewers would otherwise be unable to interpret the images. In exhibitions abroad, one would, of course, expect that few viewers would be skilled in the motifs' interpretation. In the brochure that accompanied *Monochromies Sacrées: Ouverture sur la Mythologie Bamana* (Sacred Monochromes: Introduction to Bamana Mythology),[71] a 1992 exhibition of ideogram-centered paintings in Marseille, France, Diabaté reproduced text from Dieterlen and Cissé's book to explain the symbols he used and their cultural context.

In his Malian exhibitions, too, Diabaté labels each painting with a photocopied excerpt from Dieterlen and Cissé. In Bamako, as in Marseille, the artist does not presume that his audience is versed in the interpretation of the symbols. Here, like the Groupe Bogolan Kasobane, Diabaté works through his art to introduce Malians to aspects of their culture. Unlike the Groupe Bogolan Kasobane, however, whose members are explicitly concerned with public education, Diabaté does not speak of his work's educative role. In fact, he regrets the necessity of having to supply such explicatory information to his compatriots.[72]

The fact that Diabaté, who is particularly alert to the imposition of Western cultural models onto Malian practices, uses a Western format—the scholarly publication—to provide an exegesis of Komo symbols reveals new layers of complexity in the contemporary bogolan market. Diabaté's use of Western-style scholarship[73] points to the willingness of Malian artists to combine Western and Malian elements in their work. Taking this notion further, Diabaté's photocopied excerpts might also be viewed as an illustration of the inextricable presence of the West in Mali's perception of itself. Like many contemporary African artists, Diabaté struggles to define his identity within a system dominated by Western markets and Western institutions.

The use of Bamana ideograms by Diabaté and other contemporary Malian artists is also germane to the discussion of abstraction as it functions in contemporary Malian art (see Chapter 5). For Diabaté, part of the appeal of ideograms is their multivalence, for they are, in his words, "abstract and at the same time figurative."[74] That is, non-Malian art collectors can appreciate ideograms without interpreting them or recognizing them as anything other than abstract designs. For viewers familiar with the signs' significance, however, the designs are references to Bamana philosophical and religious thought. Diabaté's *Flani* (Twins), for example, is centered on an ideogram that Dieterlen and Cissé explicate as a symbol of the creation of the cosmos, the moment at which the Earth and sky are united. Separating the symbol into three parts, they describe first a horizontal line (the vast emptiness that precedes creation), a triangular projection above the line (the masculine element associated with the sky), and a hooklike projection below (the feminine element associated with Earth).[75] A single ideogram, thus, may communicate a great deal about Bamana mythology and symbology. For Diabaté, ideograms provide a means by which to communicate directly with his fellow Malians while maintaining his market among non-Malians and among Malians unfamilar with the symbols' meanings, many of whom are intrigued to find that the designs have symbolic meanings even if they do not comprehend those meanings.

Many other artists using bogolan in Bamako today make use of ideograms, including the members of the Groupe Bogolan Kasobane. Members of the Atelier Jamana also use ideograms, as do Sénou Fofana and Abdoul Karim Ouedraogo, all successful artists in Bamako whose primary medium is bogolan. These artists, like Diabaté, seek to communicate with Malian audiences; the frequent appearance of ideograms, a visual language unique to Bamana culture, is one manifestation of this desire. Through the revived bogolan tradition, an entirely new system of communication is created with the combining of ideograms that previously existed in a wholly different context. Significantly, the context of Komo ideograms was that of an exclusively male domain prior to their adaptation by Diabaté and other contemporary artists; women are strictly excluded from the ceremonies and initiatory knowledge of the Komo society. Conversely, bogolanfini's symbolic motifs are associated with the world of women, passed from mother to daughter and laden with information of relevance to women. The shift in bogolán iconography reflects the changing identities of artists, following the cloth's movement from a female- to a male-dominated art form. Thus, in the hands of these artists, bogolan retains its Malian identity in both medium and imagery, and yet it resembles only obliquely the art form on which it is based.

Unlike art forms that have come to be closely associated with Mali, for example, sculpture such as ci waraw and Dogon figures, ideograms imply the need, or at least the potential, for interpretation beyond visual recognition. Ci waraw and Dogon sculptures have become familiar sights in many contexts—in exhibitions, collections, and publications on African art, tourist art markets, and even African-oriented shops and catalogues in the United States. Although these works of art certainly make reference to complex cultural information—ci waraw symbolize the fertility of land and people, Dogon figures play crucial roles in the interaction between people and the ancestors that ensure their survival—they do not necessitate such interpretation. Ideograms, because of their textual nature, contain the potential for decoding in their very form. Many viewers may appreciate their formal qualities even as they are aware that they cannot fully comprehend their meaning. Others appreciate the ideograms' specific denotations in their original contexts. Komo ideograms, thus, offer Malian artists the opportunity to attract multiple audiences.

Like bogolan itself, separated from bogolanfini's forms and functions, Komo ideograms are in this context completely separated from their original purpose—to teach initiates into power their associations. In Bamako, they are transformed into subject matter for artists whose work is displayed in public galleries and museums. A more dramatic movement from secrecy to visibility is difficult to imagine. Despite dramatic changes in the manner and the contexts in which they appear, Komo ideograms, like bogolan, remain relevant to contemporary Malian artistic endeavors.

### Sidicki Traoré: Bogolan Entrepreneur

Sidicki Traoré's use of bogolan to create paintings is motivated by forces very different from those that drive Ismaël Diabaté's work. In 1992, Traoré was a young artist selling bogolan paintings and clothing on a street corner outside his family's home in Bamako's Missira neighborhood. Unlike Diabaté, he has had no formal artistic training;

Figure 11. *Untitled,*
Sidicki Traoré, 1997.
Bogolan pigments and
acrylic paint on strip-
woven cloth. Approx.
22″ × 22″ (56 × 56 cm).
Courtesy of Sidicki
Traoré.

*Using dark, thick outlines,*
*Sidicki Traoré depicts sin-*
*uous figures and masks,*
*neither of which are*
*specifically Malian in*
*style. Here he also com-*
*bines bogolan's mineral*
*and vegetal pigments*
*with synthetic paints and*
*incorporates graphic ele-*
*ments reminiscent of*
*Komo ideograms and*
*Arabic script.*

early in his career he worked outside the circle of artists trained at the Institut National des Arts who display their work in the city's few exhibition spaces and tend to
know each other well. Traoré began to draw and paint in the late 1980s, on his return
from several difficult years of living in Paris.[76] Traoré told me that he initially used
drawing as a means of cathartic self-expression, only later attempting to sell his
work.[77] He used pens and colored pencils to draw on paper and cardboard, offering
to sell the results to friends and, whenever he encountered them, to expatriates; he
met with very limited success. As noted above, Traoré began to work with bogolan
after a French acquaintance who had expressed interest in his work suggested that he
translate his style into a more distinctly Malian medium.[78] In ensuing months, he
made contacts with other non-Malians who, he found, preferred bogolan to other
artistic media.

Although his family came to Bamako from San, the center of bogolan production
for the tourist art markets of Bamako, Traoré did not learn the technique from relatives or friends in San. Instead, he traveled to a village near San in November 1992 to
observe and learn from bogolan producers there. Informal apprenticeships with rural
women are a common means by which young men acquire the expertise they need to
enter the bogolan market. Traoré said that in a week he had sufficiently mastered the
technique and returned to Bamako, where he began to produce his own bogolan
paintings and continued to learn and modify his style as he worked.[79]

Unlike Diabaté, Traoré does not focus on Malian subject matter or style. Traoré paints sinuous human figures, animals, and vegetation, using strip-woven cotton cloth as his support. His style is strongly linear, with pictorial elements bounded by prominent, crisp outlines often painted in the deep black of earth-based pigment; his colors are contiguous but rarely blend. Traoré's bogolan paintings are also characterized by his depiction of interlacing figurative and landscape elements, using sinuously curved lines to create fantastic beings whose rubbery limbs echo the trees and animals that surround them (Figure 11).

Using the same curvilinear forms, Traoré often adds ideogrammatic elements to his canvases, graphic symbols that resemble linguistic elements, or, more rarely, words in French. In some cases, these graphic elements refer to Komo ideograms, though they are approximations that capture the general form of the symbols rather than actual ideograms. Like the transformation of bogolanfini into paintings for display in galleries and museums, retaining the medium but transforming the iconography, Traoré preserves the style of Komo ideograms without retaining their literal meanings. In the 1997 painting *La Gaieté au Village* (Joy in the Village), Traoré experimented with the use of strips to create a woven grid, each strip painted with distinct patterns in bogolan pigments (Plate 13). Traoré did not create this technique.[80] The strips are painted with ideogrammatic motifs, making vague reference to the symbols and their secretive significance.

Occasionally, Traoré depicts masked figures that may refer to Bamana masking traditions, though in interviews he did not stress the Malian roots of his subject matter. Unlike Diabaté, for whom bogolan provides a means of potentially subverting the Western-dominated art market, Traoré's attraction to the medium is founded in its potential to create a demand for his work in that market—in his words, "I want to Westernize it [bogolan] a bit."[81] Bogolan is a convenient medium for him, both because of the availability and affordability of its materials and because Western clients prefer it to his drawings.

Traoré's increasingly frequent use of synthetic inks and pigments along with bogolan dyes—his use of acrylic and other paints was more frequent in 1997 than in 1992–93—is part of his effort to Westernize the uniquely Malian medium (see Figure 11). To an inquiry concerning his increased use of synthetic pigments, Traoré spoke of his interest in the color combinations these materials enable him to create, a tacit acknowledgment of his interest in modernizing the traditional rather than preserving its "purity."[82] In balancing the two media by using the synthetic paints to complement the browns and tans of bogolan dyes, Traoré aims to "harmoniously unite the two techniques."[83]

Malian interest in Traoré's paintings is limited at best. Like most Malian artists, his work is purchased primarily by non-Malian tourists and expatriates. In 1993, Traoré spoke of the sole Malian who had purchased several of his paintings. When Traoré, surprised by her purchase, inquired about her interest in his work, the woman explained that she intended to give them to Western friends as gifts.[84] Because he sells his paintings from a neighborhood street corner rather than a stall in the tourist market, Malian passersby have ample opportunity to see Traoré's work and to offer their comments (Figure 12). In 1993, Traoré reported that most were perplexed; they could not imagine

why he painted with bogolan. Some still do not even recognize the paintings as bogolan until closer examination convinces them. Traoré described the typical response to encounters with his street display: "Malians say, 'It's pretty but what is it?'"[85] Traoré continues to produce his paintings, and by 1997 had sent some abroad with German sponsors, who have been successfully selling them in Germany. Traoré is currently living in France. Like so many Malian artists, Sidicki Traoré has had his greatest success among those most distant from his homeland. Malians may appreciate his efforts, but not his art.

Figure 12. Sidicki Traoré's shop outside his home. Bamako, 1997.

*Traoré's family lives on a well-traveled corner in the Missira neighborhood near downtown Bamako. When he began selling bogolan in 1992, Traoré hung his paintings on the exterior wall of his family's compound, hoping to attract passersby. By 1996–97, he and his family had constructed a small shop, stocked with Traoré's paintings as well as bogolan pagnes and clothing purchased in villages or sold on consignment for local artists (including Alou Traoré).*

## THE DEARTH OF OUTLETS

Ismaël Diabaté and Sidicki Traoré, though their work and their careers differ vastly, both face the challenges created by Mali's lack of a local market for contemporary art. Marie-Françoise Becchetti-Laure, in her 1990 thesis on the art scene in Bamako, characterized the situation succinctly, if perhaps too absolutely: "The contemporary art market does not exist."[86] Two common solutions to the problem are reliance on patrons and exhibitions outside the country and the creation of bogolan for more than one market, avoiding dependence on the limited "fine art" trade. Many who take the latter route create bogolan clothing or other inexpensive items that find a more ready market with both Malian and non-Malian audiences than do expensive paintings.

Diabaté and Traoré represent two distinct approaches to the problem of selling art in Mali's limited art market, each strategizing to reach the consumers he wishes to attract, yet neither finding the success he seeks. Ironically, while Diabaté seeks a local market, working to separate himself from Western art through the use of bogolan, he has instead attracted attention from Europeans and Americans, who remain his major patrons. Traoré, whose aim is to find non-Malian patrons, has received little attention from that market, due to his lack of access to the galleries where he might gain visibility. He has sought to circumvent the gallery and museum system by selling from his own shop at the front gates of his family's compound. With no money to invest and no access to the gallery trade, few artists find the relative success that Traoré enjoyed in the late 1990s, before he moved to Paris.

Most Malian artists complain of the predicament of their location between two categories—too "modern" for Western markets and too "Western" for Malian markets. They also bemoan the lack of an indigenous patronage system for their work, the type of system that supported the artistic production of generations of artists before them and many rural artists today. The sculptors who carve ci waraw and the women who create bogolanfini pagnes for local markets are meeting a need, providing the objects necessary for the successful realization of crucial societal practices—the celebration of fertility and the initiation of young women. Bogolan paintings, like other artistic production created as part of the international "studio art" trade, exist outside such systems of necessity.

Many Malian artists, frustrated by their compatriots' lack of support for their efforts, complain of the inability of most Malians to comprehend their work and of the Malian public's lack of taste. Diabaté, for example, feels that Malian taste has been deformed by colonialism; Malians no longer feel an affinity for their traditional arts, nor do they have sufficient understanding of Western arts.[87] Djelemakan Sacko, a young artist in the early 1990s who was finding a growing expatriate market for his bogolan clothing, complained that Malians do not understand the value of bogolan.[88] Another artist who uses bogolan along with other media, Moussa Koné, bemoaned the lack of appreciation for the quality and workmanship he devotes to his paintings, complaining that they judge the value of bogolan by its size rather than its aesthetic value.[89] Habib Ballo, a drawing professor at the Institut National des Arts and the former president of the Union Malienne des Artistes Plasticiennes (Union of Malian Studio Artists), expressed the same sentiments, adding that Malians do not appreciate the art displayed in galleries and museums, because they are accustomed to objects whose functions are clearly evident.[90]

When questioned further concerning their frustration with the lack of Malian art collectors, artists have conceded that their predicament is as much economic as it is cultural. The Malian public can no more afford the cost of fine art than Malian artists can afford to buy expensive, imported materials. Furthermore, fine art is not a status symbol in Mali. Malians are likely to spend discretionary income on a car, a VCR, or an expensive article of clothing rather than a painting. Among Malians, paintings are not a common form of decoration. Instead, home decor generally consists of family photographs, pictures cut from magazines and newspapers, and religious images, such as depictions of Mecca. Most Malians have little opportunity to view the contemporary paintings, sculpture, and, most recently, conceptual art being produced by Malian artists.[91]

Fine art exists in a rarified atmosphere—confined to the museum, the city's few galleries, and the homes of foreigners—far from the lives of most of Bamako's residents. Artists in Bamako have a limited number of venues for the exhibition of their work. Most of the exhibition space at the Musée National is devoted to a permanent installation of traditional arts accompanied by didactic labels describing their functions in the societies that produced them. One portion of the museum is devoted to temporary exhibitions. Here contemporary work by Malian artists may be displayed and sold. Because Malian patronage of the Musée National is sparse at best, it is not a likely forum for the development of Malian interest in contemporary art.[92]

According to Samuel Sidibe, Musée National director since 1987, the Malian public is generally interested in traditional art, which is familiar to them. Contemporary art, on the other hand, many find either decorative ("pretty") or incomprehensible.[93] In recent years, the Musée National has exhibited the work of many artists residing in Bamako, including French, Senegalese, and Ghanaian, as well as Malian artists. Sidibe has tried to reach out to the museum's potential audience through exhibitions on topics such as daily life in different parts of Mali and urban dyeing industries.[94] All of these topics concern, in Sidibe's words, "the contemporary, but not just contemporary art."[95] These, he says, have been the museum's most popular exhibitions.

Contemporary Malian art is also exhibited and sold at the Centre Culturel Français, which was established in 1982. Denis Decraene, director during the early 1990s, focused the center's activities on contemporary art. It is one of the most vital art spaces in Bamako, sponsoring exhibitions, conferences, films, and performances by musicians and theater and dance troupes from all over Africa and beyond. The center's library is for many Malians an important source of books, journals, and newspapers. Although relatively few artists have the opportunity to exhibit their work there, because the center has only one gallery, the gallery's history clearly indicates the growing popularity of bogolan as a fine art medium. From 1989 to 1991, the Centre Culturel Français sponsored seven exhibitions of bogolan artists, both individually and in groups.[96]

In the early 1990s, several additions to Bamako's art scene indicated an increased interest in contemporary art among Malian businesspeople and supporters of the arts. The Galerie Tatou was founded in 1990 and is largely funded by the Centre Culturel Français.[97] The center also sponsored exhibitions at Le Yanga, a popular nightclub unfortunately destroyed by fire in 1992. Work by contemporary artists is also exhibited and sold at shops that cater to the expatriate population, including the Galerie Indigo (open since 1991) and gift stores at the two major, long-established hotels—the Hôtel Amitié and the Grand Hôtel—as well as the Hôtel Mande (open since 1992). According to salespeople, tourists and expatriates are the chief consumers of the bogolan paintings displayed at these locations, but the exhibitions and related events, such as openings and advertisements, are likely increasing local, Malian awareness of contemporary painting. During the early to mid-1990s, bogolan was taken up by ever-increasing numbers of artists, some of whom were former art students or professional artists, and others who were self-taught.

### BREHIMA KONÉ AND YACOUBA KONÉ: CHIFFONS DE SAMÉ

Brehima Koné and Yacouba Koné (no relation) are both former members of a group of artists in Samé, a community just outside of Bamako. Yacouba Koné has had an affinity for drawing and painting since his childhood, but he has never had any formal training. From 1980 until 1983 he studied bogolan with Lamine Sidibe and briefly with Solitaire Solitaire, the animateurs who had an influence on numerous bogolan artists. He worked with bogolan for several years, primarily making clothing for European clients, such as the Association Française des Voluntaires de Progrès (a French equivalent to the Peace Corps), for whom he made bogolan shirts that served as uniforms. The shirts sold for 4,000 to 6,000 CFA in 1993 (twelve to eighteen dollars), prices too high for most Malians yet not expensive enough for Koné to support his family on the earnings. According to Koné, he sold bogolan only to expatriates and tourists: "Malians like my work but they don't have the money to buy it."[98]

In 1987, Yacouba Koné met Roland de Livry, who was living in Samé.[99] De Livry encouraged and provided studio space for a group of Malian artists to experiment with a variety of media, including collage. The group became a recognized part of Bamako's art scene in 1989 with a self-titled exhibition at the Centre Culturel Français,

*Les Chiffons de Samé* (The Samé Scraps), a reference to the use of fabric scraps for the creation of collages.[100] The next year, Koné had a solo exhibition at the Centre Culturel Français featuring his bogolan-based collages.[101]

Yacouba Koné was already familiar with bogolan when he joined the Samé group, so he applied the technique to his textile collages along with other scraps of fabric (Plate 14). His collages tend to be based in figurative forms, the canvases constructed using irregular scraps of fabric often with linear elements added by sewing the pieces together with thick stitches that remain visible in the finished piece. Less frequently, Koné paints canvases in bogolan, varying the concentration of the vegetal dyes to use them in a manner not unlike watercolors. He carefully applies layers of bogolan pigment, allowing the thinly applied colors to soak into the cotton, creating a sense of shading as tones fade at the edges of forms.

Koné also adapted the synthetic dyeing techniques that the other artists in the group employed, combining chemical dyes with bogolan work.[102] He quickly found success with European clients; in 1988, he went to Paris and sold all of the paintings he brought with him.[103] Koné's use of bogolan dyes in combination with synthetic paints distinguishes his work from that of Ismaël Diabaté and the Groupe Bogolan Kasobane, for whom use of bogolan is a matter of principle in addition to an aesthetic choice, not to be compromised by the use of European media.

Brehima Koné also worked with the Samé group in the late 1980s. Before his involvement with de Livry and the Samé artists, he studied at the Institut National des Arts from 1982 to 1986, when he first encountered bogolan techniques.[104] His work with Yacouba Koné and the other Samé artists provided an opportunity to develop his facility with bogolan dyes. In 1989 he left the Samé group to pursue a solo career, beginning with a 1991 exhibition at the Centre Culturel Français. A 1992 exhibition at Le Yanga featured textile collages, some of which incorporated bogolan.[105] His subject matter included a masked dance from Kongola, his home village, marriage celebrations, and commentaries on city life.

Koné has developed his own bogolan dyes, including a deep black made by combining concentrated mud with iron and lemon juice that he uses to produce rich chiaroscuro effects. His work also includes gestural abstractions, using dyes applied with brushes in combination with staining techniques. Inspired by Ismaël Diabaté, Koné has also applied pigments with an aerosol applicator. Koné deliberately experiments with forms, media, and methods of application. His most distinctive innovation is his use of bogolan dyes to create prints, applying the mineral and vegetal pigments to leaves and other materials, which he then presses onto the canvas (Figure 13). Using his deep black bogolan pigment, this printing or stamping technique creates a sense of depth, the modulated tones of the pigment fading at the edges of each leaf. Koné's oeuvre does not

Figure 13. *Zantiguéba,* Brehima Koné, 1992. Bogolan pigments on strip-woven cloth. Approx. 27″ × 18″ (68 × 45 cm). Destroyed in 1993 by fire at Le Yanga nightclub, Bamako.

*Brehima Koné, who worked with the Chiffons de Samé group, used leaves dipped in bogolan pigment to create this depiction of a leaf-dancer, a style of masquerade he recalled from his childhood. Leaf masquerades are associated with Burkina Faso's Bwa ethnic group, whose heartland is located near the border with Mali.*

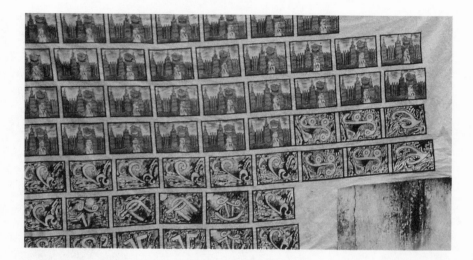

Figure 14. Sheet of stenciled images for postcards, Atelier Jamana, 1993.

*Using stencils that they retouch by hand, adding additional colors, the members of the Atelier Jamana earn a small income selling bogolan postcards. Each image is cut and glued onto a folded piece of paper.*

consist solely of bogolan paintings; he also uses watercolors and oil paints. He prefers bogolan, however, because of its affordability and accessibility and, like numerous other artists, he takes pride in the medium because "it [bogolan] is part of our tradition."[106]

### The Atelier Jamana: Collaboration and Innovation

The oeuvre and the careers of the members of the Atelier Jamana—Boureima Diakité, Aly Dolo, Hama Guro, and Rokiatou Sow—closely parallel that of the Groupe Bogolan Kasobane.[107] The group members, who produce bogolan paintings and clothing, have experimented with vegetal and mineral dyes to produce new colors, and they are currently working with bleaching agents to lighten the hues produced by various vegetal dyes. They likely have the widest range of products of all of Bamako's bogolan artists, applying bogolan dyes to wooden picture frames and plaques and using stencils to create decorative fabrics, clothing, and bogolan postcards (Figure 14), which are sold at Bamako's main post office.[108]

The Atelier Jamana was founded by (and continues to be supported by) the Association Jamana, a cultural center and publishing house established by Alpha Oumar Konaré in 1981, when he was minister of arts and culture in the regime of Moussa Traoré. The organization was created to promote Malian culture, encouraging Malians to become more aware of their country's patrimony and protect it against "the (invasion) of decadent aspects of foreign cultures."[109] The Atelier Jamana embodies the organization's aims in the realm of the visual arts.

When the Atelier Jamana was founded in 1988, it was not conceived of as a workshop for the production of bogolan. Instead, it was intended to serve Malian artists in all media. The Association Jamana invited all interested artists to join the atelier with the stipulation that a percentage of all of their sales would be returned to the association. In return, they received studio space. According to the current members of the Atelier Jamana, only the bogolan artists found enough of a market to survive, so by default the Atelier Jamana essentially became a small artists' cooperative that produces a wide range of bogolan products.

The members of the group, all in their mid-twenties in the mid-1990s, are in many ways typical of the bogolan artists of the generation following the Groupe Bogolan Kasobane. They studied bogolan techniques at the Institut National des Arts, where a three-month bogolan internship was required of all arts plastiques students in their fourth year.[110] The Groupe Bogolan Kasobane began their professional careers with an exhibition in Segou before finding success in the capital. The Atelier Jamana, working after the initial acceptance of bogolan painting, found audiences immediately and gained access to a range of venues for the display and sale of their work in Bamako. Since 1989, the Atelier Jamana has exhibited at least twice a year, in Bamako and abroad.[111] Group members have received governmental assistance to participate in international craft fairs in Washington, D.C., and Los Angeles.[112]

The Atelier Jamana's paintings bear clear resemblance to those of their Groupe Bogolan Kasobane mentors.[113] Both groups favor large formats, elaborately worked compositions, and specifically Malian themes that often contain elements of social commentary. They also make extensive use of ideograms, the symbols' presence announcing the artists' Malian identities while also serving as compositional elements. Unlike Ismaël Diabaté, who discovered ideograms through a European publication, the Atelier Jamana artists were provided with information on the symbols and their meanings as a part of their education at the Institut National des Arts.[114] Accompanied by exegesis in the works' titles or on wall labels, the ideogram-centered paintings often refer to aspects of traditional Bamana life. Music, farming occupations, and polygamy are among the themes these paintings address.

The Atelier Jamana's paintings do not incorporate the motifs associated with bogolanfini. As with the Groupe Bogolan Kasobane, and Ismaël Diabaté, Komo ideograms are the favored source of abstract symbols. According to Hama Guro, the motifs are popular in Bamako primarily because they are "pretty." He explained that "in the city [Bamako] people don't understand the motifs. They buy if the work is pretty."[115]

The Atelier Jamana's paintings often combine ideograms with figurative elements to create hybrid forms, the two elements communicating complementary ideas. In *La Communication,* a Komo ideogram that refers to the idea of communication, the exchange of ideas, is combined with a telephone, a contemporary international symbol for the same concept (Plate 15). Another painting features an ideogram for "music" combined with a stylized *kora,* a harplike instrument associated with traditional Malian music that is used by professional griots and recording artists. The ideograms permit this type of multilayered communication, combining varied systems of signification. Using these distinct "languages," the group members create paintings that depict the continued relevance of "traditional" knowledge to contemporary lives.[116]

The members of the Atelier Jamana have experimented extensively with supports for bogolan dyes. In the early 1990s, they began working with the application of the dyes to wood. Initially, they limited this experimentation to the creation of picture frames, which were dyed to match the stretched canvases they enclosed. Later, they began to create bogolan plaques of plywood images cut to form the outline of an ideogram (Figure 15). In 1997, group members said that their bogolan paintings on wood continued to be popular and that, in fact, they were planning to lead a workshop on the technique.[117]

The Atelier Jamana cleanly separate their paintings and other fine arts from other elements of their oeuvre, such as postcards and clothing (Plate 16). The former are their primary source of pride and reputation, while the latter are simply sources of income. Speaking about their clothing and fabrics, Boureima Diakité spoke deprecatingly of the purely utilitarian nature of the group's postcards, hats, and other inexpensive items: "It's decor. It isn't art."[118] Only the paintings and plaques are signed and sold in galleries, while other items are sold at holiday bazaars and fairs.

### Sénou Fofana: From Apprentice to Artist

The career and work of Sénou Fofana indicate the changed atmosphere in which young artists work today. His education and his training have provided him with ample opportunity to hone his skills in Bamako without traveling to the rural areas where bogolan is made in its traditional forms. Fofana's success is partially the result of his close association with the members of the Groupe Bogolan Kasobane, with whom he studied at the Institut National des Arts and who helped him to find exhibitions and professional contacts. After his graduation, Fofana worked in the group's workshop preparing paintings for exhibitions. He sold his own work as well as that of the Groupe Bogolan Kasobane at the Centre Culturel Français. Like most artists who sell their work at bazaars, Fofana displayed only his garments, pillows, and scarves in this venue, reserving his paintings for display and sale in galleries and museums.

Fofana learned bogolan techniques at the age of fifteen in his home village of Toukoto, in the Kayes region northwest of Bamako. There he met a woman from Sikasso who earned money by making bogolan paintings for sale to tourists and visitors.[119] Toukoto is one of many small towns along the route of the Bamako–Dakar railway, an important travel artery constructed by the French colonial government to connect their two major administrative centers. Many of the towns along the railway's west-northwest route have benefited from tourists, business travelers, and other passengers. Because she was the only bogolan producer in Toukoto, the woman taught Fofana the skills he needed to take part in the trade with her. Initially, he sketched the images she would transform into bogolan; later, he began to work in bogolan as well.[120] Fofana took the skills he acquired from her with him when he moved to Bamako to attend school.

From 1983 to 1987 Fofana attended the Institut National des Arts, earning a degree in the arts plastiques program. He studied with Néné Thiam and Souleyman Guro, both members of the Groupe Bogolan Kasobane, and augmented his classroom studies with work in the group's studio. Like many young artists today making bogolan paintings and clothing, Fofana gained experience preparing dye baths, applying stenciled designs, and otherwise assisting the group members. Fofana's paintings show the influence of the Groupe Bogolan Kasobane in their focus on figures, with abstract designs and

Figure 15. Bogolan-dyed wooden plaque, Atelier Jamana, ca. 1993. Approx. 24" × 22" (61 × 56 cm).

*The Atelier Jamana were the first to use bogolan to dye wood, creating plaques and picture frames. The symbol at the center of this plaque is the ideogram sánú (gold). Dieterlen and Cissé, in Fondements, describe the motif as a symbol associated with the divine and with human moral purity (p. 84).*

Figure 16. *Réunion des Ancèstres*, Sénou Fofana, 1991–92. Exhibition at the Centre Culturel Français. Bamako, 1993.

*Covering every inch of his strip-woven canvas, Sénou Fofana combines abstract decorative motifs with figurative elements. Some of his paintings incorporate bogolanfini's symbolic motifs, used as borders and backgrounds.*

symbolic motifs appearing as secondary elements, in their heavily worked surfaces, and in their distinctly Malian subject matter. Fofana's academic training at the Institut National des Arts, which as noted in Chapter 4 would have included lessons in perspectival realism and the use of chiaroscuro, is also clearly evident. He works on a smaller scale than the Groupe Bogolan Kasobane, whose large, richly detailed canvases require the hand of several artists. Whatever the size of his canvas, Fofana fills every inch with carefully worked figures, landscape elements, and geometric patterns (Figure 16).

Fofana uses dark, sharply delineated outlines, creating in some paintings an effect reminiscent of brown-hued stained glass. Figures are abstracted, assembled of geometric elements to create iconic, schematic images. Human figures are composed of spherical heads with wide, oval eyes and linear mouths. The dark outlines that surround each geometric element emphasize their use as building blocks of which both image and background are constructed, linking the representational elements of each painting to the geometric patterns that surround each image. Though he did not describe his use of geometric elements as a deliberate decision aimed at unifying the varied compositional elements of his paintings, Fofana's skillful manipulation of the intricate, interlocking forms is a hallmark of his style.

Since 1992–93, many young artists have taken up bogolan as a fine art medium. As bogolan moves into its second decade as a tool for the production of art for museum and gallery exhibitions, the number of artists and exhibitions focused on bogolan paintings indicates the depth and the impact of the movement. Artists still have few outlets for their work in Bamako, and the lack of local support for the fine art trade remains a challenge for artists who seek local recognition. Bogolan paintings, adaptations of a local technique and iconography to the museum and gallery trade, stand between the expectations of Malians and non-Malians, challenging the preconceptions of both. Like the bogolan produced for the tourist art market, bogolan paintings represent the wide-ranging adjustments Malian artists have made to a "traditional" medium to suit Bamako's urban, heterogeneous, globalized environment.

7

# CULTURE THROUGH CLOTHING

## Bogolan as Fashion

Visual forms are essential in the realization of ethnic identity both on political and personal levels. In the arts the forms may include anything from architecture to dress.
*Esther Pasztory, "Identity and Difference"*

Whether conventional, collusive or rebellious, clothing ultimately enables us to be ourselves with and among other people— sometimes the same as them, sometimes not. Clothing is the bearer of our, and society's, image of ourselves, of our desires and impulses.
*Aminata Dramane Traoré, "African Fashion"*

Bogolan fashions are displayed on the runways of elite fashion shows in Paris, Dakar, and Abidjan, sold in exclusive boutiques, and featured in fashion magazines such as *Elite Madame* and *Femme d'Afrique*.[1] They also appear in the classrooms of Bamako *lyceés* (high schools), on the dance floors of neighborhood discotheques, and on the shelves of inexpensive shops near the Grand Marché. In no other form has bogolan crossed so many markets, achieved such popularity, and gained such visibility, and in none of its many sartorial permutations does bogolan completely shed its associations with "tradition" (though the concept carries varied connotations in these distinct clothing markets).

Bogolan fashion combines aspects of both tourist market and fine art bogolan, making it an appropriate subject for the final set of paired chapters in this study. Bogolan vests, hats, shirts, scarves, and other items are sold in tourist art markets as well as in expensive boutiques and galleries, the prices of garments ranging from the widely affordable to the exclusive. Bogolan clothing traverses boundaries in other manners as well; much bogolan clothing is made by artists who also create paintings, and some is made by artists who also produce cloth for the tourist art market. Bogolan garments embody many of the same stylistic and conceptual principles as the bogolan paintings and pagnes made for other markets.

In addition to its applicability to the markets elucidated in previous chapters, bogolan's adaptation to garments brings issues specific to the study of attire to this investigation. Bogolan clothing is a dramatic and widely acknowledged part of Bamako's visual environment, commanding attention as neither the cloth produced for the tourist market nor that produced for the fine art market have done, despite the efforts of their producers and merchants. Clothing is embroiled in questions of identity and modes of communication quite distinct from those of bogolan paintings or tourist art.

Bogolan clothing's primarily Malian market also distinguishes it from other bogolan products. This market is not monolithic, encompassing Bamako residents of all ethnic backgrounds, economic levels, political convictions, and geographical origins. On the streets of Bamako, in the pages of magazines, and on television, bogolan clothing is widely visible, worn by residents ranging from teenagers and professional musicians to government officials and wealthy expatriates. Another striking peculiarity that sets bogolan fashion apart from the cloth's other recent incarnations is its simultaneous popularity in Mali and abroad. In other African countries, in Europe, and particularly in the United States, bogolan clothing (and clothing made of bogolan-patterned fabrics) can be seen on city streets, in fashionable catalogues, and in department stores.[2]

By wearing bogolan clothing, consumers make the cloth a part of themselves, a direct visual statement inseparable from their personal presence. The transformation of cloth into clothing "activates" it, making of cloth a highly effective form of communication, immediately accessible for visual analysis and responsive to manipulation by the wearer. Clothing is a very public form of artistic expression, its communicative potential shared by both the artist who creates a garment and the consumer who wears it. Juliet Ash and Elizabeth Wilson describe the democratic nature of fashion production: "The skills required for the making of fashion are not necessarily specialized; it is made in abundance by all people who put together fabrics and colors."[3]

In addition to its visibility and accessibility, the temporality of clothing, the chronological dimension that transforms garments into fashion, adds to its effectiveness as a tool for communication. The notion of high fashion, however, has only in the past decade been applied to the study of African cultures, and African fashion designers are only recently receiving attention in mainstream European and U.S. contexts.[4] Like modern or contemporary art, fashion is often associated with the Western, industrial capitalist world. In Western popular imagination, Africa is closely associated with authenticity and adherence to tradition, concepts diametrically opposed to the ephemerality of fashion. The present study, one of a small but growing number of contributions in the field, demonstrates the rich potential of fashion studies in contemporary African cultures.[5]

Analyses of African clothing as fashion are few, but there is no dearth of scholarship concerning African dress, textiles (the building blocks of much fashion), and other body adornments. Numerous publications elucidate the social significance of garments and the cloth of which they are made.[6] Many are concerned with documentation of the use of clothing and adornment in ceremonial and ritual contexts, an important project, though one that differs from the task here. Others have focused on weaving and dyeing technologies and on the iconography of textile adornment. Although many of these past studies have made note of shifts and adaptations in clothing styles, the changes that mark fashion, these shifts are rarely the focus of study.[7]

African fashion is the subject of a number of periodicals published in Africa and in centers of the African diaspora. Magazines aimed at women in Africa and in African communities abroad—for example, *Afrique Elite, Amina, Elite Madame,* and *Makiss Mode* (published in Paris, Dakar, and Abidjan)—provide extensive photographic documentation of contemporary fashion by African and non-African designers. Several other popular African periodicals regularly feature articles on and photographic documentation of current fashion trends, including *Afrique Magazine, Balafon,* and *Jeune Afrique.* Although these publications provide invaluable insight into the variety and the cosmopolitan nature of African fashion, their aim is popular and celebratory rather than analytical. The present examination of bogolan fashion seeks to combine the rich scholarship on African clothing as a document of cultural practices with the popular journals' acknowledgment of and fascination with constant changes in style.

Walking the streets, visiting the nightclubs, and shopping in the clothing markets of

Bamako in the past decade, one could see bogolan adapted for use in widely varied and surprising contexts—bogolan suitcoats worn by government representatives at an arts ministry conference, bogolan curtains in the waiting rooms of the U.S. embassy, a car interior with bogolan upholstery. The cloth's varied purposes and multiple significations were perhaps epitomized by its appearance at an exhibition opening at the Musée National du Mali. There, a dance troupe wearing bogolan costumes cut in local clothing styles—wide drawstring pants for men, pagnes wrapped around the waists for women—performed before an enthusiastic audience, which included a European tourist wearing a bogolan blazer. The "traditional" costumes and the "Western" blazer might have been cut from the same cloth, yet their significations differed dramatically. As bogolan clothing moves the cloth from art galleries, boutiques, and tourist markets into the streets, it acquires new significations and broader visibility, and it becomes embroiled in the identity politics that characterize fashion the world over.

## HOW CLOTHING COMMUNICATES

In recent years, an increasing number of theoretical analyses have addressed the anthropology or cultural history of dress, examining the political, historical, and economic determinants that affect personal comportment, including styles of dress and other body adornment. Within this broad field, I have particularly focused on the theorization of fashion, which itself encompasses widely varied subject matter and theoretical models from semiotic to qualitative analysis.[8] Fashion, as distinguished from clothing or attire, incorporates its own obsolescence through change. Dulali Nag defines the term in her discussion of fashion and gender in contemporary India: "The word *fashion* is commonly taken to mean styles of dressing that come to be accepted as desirable in a particular period. Defined thus, fashion embodies change; it is itself only by being forever transient."[9] Jennifer Craik describes popular conceptions of fashion as similarly focused on its temporal, transient nature, to which she adds a description of the engine that according to common conceptions of fashion propels the perpetual changes: "Thus, the hallmark of fashion is said to be change: a continual and arbitrary succession of new styles and modes that render previous fashions obsolete. Fashion is conceived as an authoritarian process driven by a recognised elite core of designers dictating the fashion behavior of the majority."[10]

Fashion has been associated with the development of capitalism, the social, economic, and political system most closely associated with Western societies. The socioeconomic assumptions embedded in that association are succinctly described by Jane Schneider and Annette Weiner in *Cloth and Human Experience,* a valuable addition to the corpus of literature on cloth and clothing:

> Capitalist production and its associated cultural values reordered the symbolic potential of cloth in two interrelated ways. First, altering the process of manufacture, capitalism eliminated the opportunity for weavers and dyers to infuse their product with spiritual value and to reflect and pronounce on analogies between reproduction and production. Second, by encouraging the growth of fashion—a consumption system of high-velocity turnover and endless, ever-changing variation—capitalist entrepreneurs vastly inflated dress and adornment as a domain for expression through cloth.[11]

In short, capitalism and its attendant mass production of goods replaces the spiritual with the novel; traditional culture becomes fashion culture. Bogolan clothing, however, even amid the high-velocity changes of contemporary fashion, retains in many instances its associations with spiritual or more broadly cultural practices, though these associations are generalized and objectified.

Because it is, by its very nature, mutable and mercurial, fashion appears to be a poor vehicle for the transmission of tradition, that prototypically stable and reliable element of culture. Yet, in the form of bogolan garments, fashion serves just that purpose, encouraging the production and utilization of an art form that has been identified by both cultural insiders and outsiders as "traditional." In this role, bogolan clothing complicates prevalent conceptions of both "fashion" and "tradition." As these two seemingly incompatible realms—one quintessentially stable and the other quintessentially ephemeral—are melded in a single art form, other, related, issues are inevitably implicated in the mix.[12]

Because clothing is a mutable, easily altered aspect of self-presentation and because it is highly visible, many analyses have centered on its potential to shift in response to the communicative requirements of the wearer. The role of clothing as a form of visual language has been the focus of much recent scholarship in the field. In *Fashion, Culture and Identity,* Fred Davis provides the basis of the treatment of clothing as language: "Obviously, because clothing . . . comprises what is most closely attached to the corporeal self—it frames much of what we see when we see another—it quite naturally acquires a special capacity to, speaking somewhat loosely, 'say things' about the self."[13] Davis's work focuses on clothing as a communicator of identity, particularly in places and times of unusually swift changes in identity, in his estimation typified by highly technological Western societies.

Craik's wide-ranging investigation of the cultures of fashion also has at its core the presupposition that clothing is a form of communication: "[F]ashion can be considered as an elaborated body technique through which a range of personal and social statements can be articulated."[14] In their introduction to *Dress and Gender,* Ruth Barnes and Joanne Eicher base their approach to the topic on the same principle: "Textiles or skins as dress may be fundamentally protective, but they also have social meaning. . . . A cultural identity is thus expressed, and visual communication is established before verbal interaction even transmits whether such a verbal exchange is possible or desirable."[15] Clothing can carry messages in a subtle manner; it is elastic in meaning, allowing for multiple interpretations by different populations and individuals within a given community. The artists who make and the consumers who wear bogolan clothing take advantage of all these potentialities.

### Recognizing African Fashion

Popular conceptions of fashion have long focused on Western, "modern" cultures to the exclusion of "traditional" societies, one aspect of the reluctance to place African and other non-Western societies within the same present time as Western cultures.[16] Observations of changing styles of dress in non-Western cultures have long been held up as evidence of the demise of "tradition" in the face of overpowering "modernity."

Much as the artists discussed in the previous chapter risked condemnation for adapting Western-associated media and styles, so too has the incorporation of Western-associated garments, fabrics, and technologies into African dress prompted cries of protest (primarily from Western quarters). According to this logic, the African adaptation of non-local (Western) styles of dress is evidence of the loss of tradition, signaling the absorption of local societies into the global culture dominated by the Western juggernaut.

In the introduction to *Africa Adorned*, a lavishly illustrated, widely distributed book that may be taken as representative of mainstream Western conceptions of Africa, photographer and author Angela Fisher writes with dismay of the influx of Western-style attire:

> During seven years of traveling in Africa to research this book, I was constantly aware that many traditions—including some outstanding styles of jewelry and dress—were rapidly becoming rarer or had already disappeared. . . . That this should be so is tragic but understandable. . . . On successive visits to the isolated Dinka people in the Nile swamps of southern Sudan, I noticed that in a matter of months these proud nomads, traditionally naked except for a covering of ash and body beads, had, like many others on the continent, begun to wear synthetic headscarves, motif T-shirts, and even platform-heel shoes.[17]

Fisher admires the few, isolated peoples whose "cultural and moral framework is still strong, who guard their traditional beliefs."[18] The use of verbs such as *guard* and *disappearing*, common in such rhetoric, imply that the adaptation of Western-style garb constitutes a failure, a breach in the vigilance of "traditional" peoples.

The currency of such equations of Western-style dress with Western cultural dominance in academic discourse is also indicated in a recent analysis of fashion in another part of the world, the Maya regions of Latin America, which, like the Africa of Western imagination, is closely associated with tradition. Barbara Brodman's essay in a volume of fashion studies decries the loss of cultural integrity marked by the adaptation of Western dress: "Adoption of Western dress is part of an on-going process of Western colonialism that began almost five centuries ago, and it may signify the demise of cultures that have existed and thrived for millennia."[19] Further still, Brodman asserts that "the imposition of Western fashion . . . is no less than a subtle form of genocide."[20]

Although Brodman's condemnation is somewhat more extreme than most criticisms of the spread of Western attire, it does exemplify the degree to which clothing is tied to its wearer's cultural integrity, so that changes in clothing style may be interpreted as changes in identity. Far from viewing the blending of traditional and Western attire as creative adaptations or bricolage, Brodman views such changes as evidence of cultural defeat at the hands of Western commodity culture. The economic and political domination of many African and Latin American societies by North America and other global powers is undoubtedly manifested in cultural spheres such as clothing. Yet to simplify the interaction between local and non-local modes of dress into an opposition between "victor" and "vanquished" denies Dinka nomads, Mayan villagers, and countless others any agency in the blending of styles of dress.

Several recent analyses of fashion in Africa and the African diaspora focus on this agency. These studies acknowledge that situations of cultural interaction are not transparent; what appears to be capitulation to the impact of a non-local culture may in fact be a subtle form of subversion, a celebration of one's own culture in the face of a dominant power, or simply playful transformation of one's style. In some instances, clothing is embroiled in political movements, becoming a symbol of partisanship. In other cases, including the present revival of bogolan clothing, fashion is less a specific political stance than an assertion of ethnic or national identity—an assertion that in some cases may carry significant political weight.

Phyllis Martin's analysis of the melding of local and non-local fashions in colonial Brazzaville illuminates an instance of negotiation and subversion by which foreign fashions are absorbed into preexisting fashion systems: "These various clothing traditions, whether homespun or foreign, converged in the new town where strangers jostled with each other in constructing social relations. In this environment, the importance of clothing was only enhanced, for goods expressed new cultural and social categories in a visible and intelligible manner."[21] Martin describes the long history of clothing's close association with power and status, from the eighteenth-century royal control over distribution and use of raphia cloth to the twentieth-century obsession with European haute couture. Her analysis of the role of clothing in the shifting power relations of the colonial and postcolonial periods indicates the subtle ways in which garments and the ways they are worn may be mobilized as tools for both domination and resistance. At the turn of the century, European employers and government officials strictly enforced prohibitions on the wearing of shoes by "natives." Although other garments might be acceptable, shoes brought locals too close to the prerogatives that separated Europeans from Africans.[22] Yet those same "natives" demonstrated their defiance by making Western clothing their own, as local men rejected the model of European comportment by wearing their Western-style shirts untucked, flouting convention.[23] Clothing was adjusted to suit new needs, worn in new combinations, imbued with new significance as garments passed from Europeans to Africans, both literally and figuratively, for clothing was both handed down from white employers to their employees and created by African tailors who reshaped and copied the cast-off clothing.

Karen Tranberg Hansen's analysis of the adaptation in contemporary urban Zambia of *salaula*, used clothing shipped in bales from New York and other Western centers to be sold in markets in Lukasa and other African cities, also points to the use of non-local clothing to assert local cultural identities.[24] Even as they purchase used American clothing—though, as Hansen reminds us, the U.S. origin of the clothing is complicated by its manufacture "in Third World locations by foreign firms and multinational companies"[25]—Zambian consumers transform the garments into local statements. Through retailoring and shifts in use patterns, such as the wearing of women's clothing by men, the clothes are "de-Westernized": "In the very act of appropriating them into 'the latest,' Zambians undercut their Western imprint."[26] For many of the Zambians who sell and buy salaula, the adaptation of non-local garments to suit local fashions communicates a pride in national identity, a means by which to "proudly and aggressively define their individual rights."[27]

The Congolese phenomenon of *sapeurs*—a self-assigned abbreviation for Société des Ambianceurs et Personnes Elégantes—thoroughly documented by Congolese sociologist Justin Gandoulou, provides another illustration of the ambiguity of clothing adaptations as a part of changing fashions in urban Africa.[28] Sapeurs stand outside "respectable" urban society, their clothing a form of protest against and rejection of mainstream Congolese society. The obsessive fascination with Western haute couture in contemporary Brazzaville and Kinshasa, a continuation of the long history of sartorial culture discussed by Martin, differs dramatically from the cultural politics that surround the wearing of such attire in Paris, New York, and other Western cities. Status is attained through the acquisition of clothing, specific designer names carrying varied amounts of status. Through travels to Paris to acquire the latest fashions and spending far beyond their means, sapeurs participate in an extreme version of consumer culture, transforming fashions into potent symbols of wealth, power, and status within a precisely ordered hierarchy. For sapeurs, Western-style clothing provides an arena for rebellion rather than compliance. Jonathon Friedman, in his discussion of the system of consumption by which sapeurs construct identities through fashion, describes the effectiveness of this rebellion: "The parody of elegance turns the sapeur into a delinquent, an intolerable sociopath, a danger to the very foundations of society. The amount of propaganda directed at destroying a group of youth who merely dress elegantly is indicative of the real threat that they pose to the state-class."[29]

Kobena Mercer's analysis of hairstyles of the African diaspora, primarily in North America, provides a similar example of strategic adaptations and subversions of the dominant cultural group's body adornment practices. Hair straightening, or "conking," a practice that attained great popularity in the 1940s, has been broadly accepted as evidence of the desire of black men and women to eliminate all signs of their difference from the white "ideal," to become as white as possible. Mercer posits that such practices are in fact a means of reinforcing differences:

> [T]he element of straightening suggests resemblance to white people's hair, but the nuances, inflections and accentuations introduced by artificial means of stylization emphasized difference. In this way the political economy of the conk rested on its ambiguity, the way it "played" with the given outline shapes of convention only to "disturb" the norm.[30]

Thus, like the high fashion clothing of the sapeurs, the mid-twentieth-century African American conk demonstrates the active role played by the peoples who are supposedly passive as goods and styles of a dominant culture are imposed upon them.

In an investigation of the immense popularity of Western goods, from food to clothing, in contemporary Belize, Richard Wilk refutes the conception of non-Western consumers as victims of foreign products. To attribute such passivity to consumers is to "ignore a century of market research in the United States that finds people's motivations for buying goods to be complex, deeply symbolic, social and personal and contextual."[31] Wilk's work addresses the complex nature of consumption, as foreign goods gain local significance, part of a history of adaptation: "Creoles have never lived in the kind of stable, traditionally bound regime of consumption beloved of anthropologists, so their present desires cannot be depicted as a disoriented response to the invitation of a new global mode of production."[32] Clearly, in Africa as in the African diaspora, clothing and personal adornment "speak" in many voices. Adaptation of Western-style garments may signal respect for and emulation of Western cultures or, with subtle alterations to those adaptations, they may indicate a rejection of Western cultures.

### Revivals of Tradition as Fashion

Within the field of fashion studies, a particular substudy may be discerned that focuses on the revival of fabrics and garments associated with the past, a period often viewed nostalgically as more culturally pure than the present. The world over, clothing revivals have been used as a form of protest against the economic, political, and religious policies of a ruling class. Specifically, in Africa and other former strongholds of colonial power, clothing and fashion have served as potent tools in struggles for independence. As such, cloth and clothing may come to serve as symbols of nationalistic sentiment.

Wilk's work in Belize offers one theoretical explanation for this return to traditional attire—as an expression of anticolonial sentiment. He writes of these renewals of tradition as struggles against the flow of "colonial time" and its implications for colonial "subjects": "In colonial time the colony is described using metaphors that blend the connotative meanings of time, distance and cultural development. *Primitive, backward,* and *underdeveloped* are such blending terms."[33] Wilk describes fashion's role as a highly visible symbol of the purported backwardness of the colony, for clothing styles in colonies, far from the metropole where contemporary fashion is "made," lag behind several years. Locals may seek the same contemporary moment as the colonizers, yet they reveal their underdeveloped state by failing to "keep up" with changing fashions. Revivals of indigenous textiles and garments imply a refusal to participate in this system: "Only when people obtain and consume objects outside the flow of colonial time, do they challenge and resist the social order of the colonial system."[34] In historical moments of resistance and of emerging national identity, indigenous clothing and fashion thus come to serve as symbols of the colonized population's rejection of the colonial culture.

Georg Simmel's 1904 analysis of fashion, though dated in many respects—his characterization of the fear of change among the "savage" races certainly reflects his era—does provide a cogent investigation of the mechanisms by which fashion operates, particularly illuminating the question of fashion as a marker of time. In a passage that seems to presage the bogolan clothing of the 1990s, Simmel describes the liminal temporal quality of much fashion:

> Fashion always occupies the dividing line between the past and the future, and consequently conveys a stronger feeling of the present, at least while it is at its height, than most other phenomena. What we call the present is usually nothing more than a combination of a fragment of the past with a fragment of the future.[35]

Bogolan clothing stands at this moment, between future and past, combining the two in varied proportions. As we have seen, bogolan in its many forms is deeply implicated in negotiations of tradition and modernity, both weighty cultural concepts in contemporary Mali, one associated with the past, the other with the future. For some designers, merchants, and consumers of bogolan clothing, the garments' appeal lies in their strong ties to the past, while others are drawn to their striking modernity. The same shirt, robe, or hat may be read as reaching back into the past or stretching forward into an innovative future.

Simmel's essay also addresses fashion revivals, which he describes as a natural outcome of the "element of feverish change"[36] that characterizes much fashion, as the fashion conscious strive to remain one step ahead of the broader society that follows their trends. Yet, as he notes, "like all phenomena it [fashion] tends to conserve energy":

> For this very reason, fashion repeatedly returns to old forms, as is illustrated particularly in wearing-apparel; and the course of fashion has been likened to a circle. As soon as an earlier fashion has partially been forgotten there is no reason why it should not be allowed to return to favor and why the charm of difference . . . should not be permitted to exercise an influence similar to that which it exerted conversely some time before.[37]

Thus, in the cycle of fashion certain forms and styles show a disposition to be fashionable and those forms, once they have gone the way of all fashion to become last year's model, may be later revived by those who seek always to distinguish themselves from their neighbors. Sometimes, in fact, the standard bearers of fashion deliberately champion styles that oppose the fashion of their day, for "extreme obedience to fashion . . . can also be won by opposition to it."[38] Hence, the appeal of revived fashions may lie precisely in their recent rejection as passé.

Simmel does not consider the possibility of fashion revivals as political statements that critique dominant fashions or celebrate indigenous forms, yet his analysis illuminates the workings of fashion by which politicized revivals may be transformed, moving from the realm of social statement into the world of fashion. Such is the motivation behind much bogolan clothing. Many of the painters highlighted in Chapter 6 described their use of bogolan in terms of its role as a symbol of Malian identity, contrasted with the dominance of Western-style media and iconography. Bogolan clothing often serves the same purpose. Although there is no evidence to suggest that bogolan's role as a national symbol dates to the era of Mali's movement toward independence from French rule in the 1940s and 1950s, bogolan clothing (like bogolan painting) did gain political significance during the struggle for democracy after decades of dictatorial rule. An examination of several past instances of clothing and fashion as tools for social mobilization helps provide context for bogolan's recent revival.

Ali Mazrui notes several instances of the mobilization of fashion in the service of African social movements, among them the paradoxical circumstances surrounding the Tanzanian government's 1968 condemnation of indigenous Maasai dress, viewed as a refusal to accept Western-style dress, the emblem of modernization and progress. The Maasai resistance to Western-style attire constituted, as Mazrui eloquently states, "rebellion by withdrawal, a cultural assertion by a quiet defiance."[39] Simultaneously, the Tanzanian parliament took up a measure to ban miniskirts, viewed as an emblem of corrupting Westernization.[40] Thus, clothing was held up as the exemplar of stubborn resistance to progress and, simultaneously, as a sign of unchecked progress. Mazrui also describes a more dramatic instance of clothing as political tool: Eliud Mathu, the first African member of the Kenyan Legislative Council, "once tore his jacket off at a public meeting in a dramatic gesture of rejecting Western civilization [saying,] 'Take back your civilisation—and give me back my land!'"[41]

Mazrui also discusses the complex role of the veil in the Algerian war for independence, whose violence lasted for nearly a decade (1954 to 1962) and whose tactics included the French attempt to "win over" Algerian women by coercing them, through propaganda or by force, to shed their veils. Citing Frantz Fanon's seminal 1967 essay, "Algeria Unveiled,"[42] Mazrui notes that in the complex culture of wartime Algeria, the veil became a weapon, used to conceal grenades and guns. At the same time, the absence of the veil became a disguise for women, who shed the garment in order to "pass" as French loyalists.[43] As Homi Bhabha describes, this relatively simple garment bore powerful resonance:

> The colonizer's attempt to unveil the Algerian woman does not simply turn the veil into a symbol of resistance; it becomes a technique of camouflage, a means of struggle—the veil conceals bombs. The veil that once secured the boundary of the home—the limits of woman—now masks the woman in her revolutionary activity.[44]

Betty Wass has documented the role of dress in Nigeria's independence movement, describing how non-European styles of dress became a sign of solidarity with the nationalist cause. Although European-style attire became increasingly popular during the early twentieth century, a sign of prosperity and sophistication, by mid-century "nationalistic feelings fueled by the independence movement prompted Nigerians to use dress as one means of severing themselves from the colonialists and identifying with the political cause."[45] Local Nigerian garment types, such as *agbada* or *riga* (long robes) and women's headties, were adopted by supporters of the nation's independence movement.

In their far-reaching analysis of the colonial encounter in South Africa, John and Jean Comaroff describe the complex negotiation of modernity and ethnic identity as the southern Tswana people adopted, transformed, and in some cases abandoned British dress over the course of the nineteenth century.[46] Clothing played a complex role in the interactions between British missionaries and their prospective converts. As the British sought to "civilize" the Tswana by bringing them dresses, shirts, and collars, the Tswana drew these and other garments into their existing systems of attire, transforming them into statements of their distinctly non-British identities. Elements of Western dress might be combined with preexisting garments, the foreignness and expense of European clothing often augmenting the status communicated by the local garment. In other instances, wholly new styles were created by blending garments, as in the case of the Tswana chief Sechele, who in 1860 had a European-style suit fashioned of leopard skin.[47] Like tailored bogolan clothing, leopard skin serves here as both a potent symbol of power and as a reference to distinctly local identities. Creative combinations of Western and local attire provided a new sartorial vocabulary with which to communicate in the changing social environment: "Western dress, in short, opened up a host of imaginative possibilities for the Africans. It made available an expansive, expressive, experimental language with which to conjure new social identities and sense of self, a language with which to speak back to the whites."[48]

The retention of local dress can become, in situations of dramatic cultural collision, a form of resistance or a means of negotiating change. Comaroff and Comaroff note that some Tswana leaders resisted "the missionary challenge by reverting, assertively, to *setswana* ["the Tswana way"] costume—and by insisting that their Christian subjects do likewise."[49] The return to precontact practices, one might argue, carries more weight as an act of political resistance than would the consistent retention of local attire; having adopted some aspects of "civilization," these Tswana leaders dramatically rejected those practices, flying in the face of missionary efforts.

Certainly the best-known and most thoroughly documented instance of clothing revival as political statement is Gandhi's revival of *khadi,* locally spun and woven cloth, as part of India's resistance to British colonial rule. By embracing the use of local cloth at a time when European cloth and clothing styles were increasingly prevalent, Gandhi struck a chord with millions of Indians, creating a symbol around which anti-British sentiment congealed.[50] It should be noted that the harnessing of clothing as a tool for resistance is far from an exclusively non-Western phenomenon. Ireland at the end of the nineteenth century experienced a growing nationalism that also found voice in the celebration of clothing styles associated with the rural, idyllic past and Celtic ethnicity. As in many parts of Africa, where colonial powers discouraged or forbade the wearing of local attire, clothing in Ireland held particularly powerful potential as a symbol of resistance.[51] In the developing Home Rule movement, the wearing of Irish linens and lace, though tailored into British-style garments, became a subtle form of protest, both fashionable and political.[52] Bogolan is used in an analogous manner.

Clothing and fashion may serve as tools for the negotiation of differences within societies as well as between them; ethnic groups, genders, and other social sectors use attire to define themselves as distinct from others. In their ongoing investigation of styles of dress among the Kalabari, a minority Nigerian ethnic group centered in the Niger Delta region, Joanne Eicher and Tonye Erekosima describe how attire may declare ethnic rather than national identity. The relatively small Kalabari population uses clothing to set itself apart from the majority Hausa, Ibo, and Yoruba populations and from the smaller, more closely related Bonny, Nemba, and Okrika peoples.[53] In Nigeria today, the espousal of distinctive, ethnic clothing serves new purposes, reflective of contemporary concerns:

> [M]embers of ethnic groups like the Kalabari and other Nigerian peoples wear their own ethnic garments as proven and familiar vehicles of attachment to the past. Perhaps by wearing ethnic outfits as a cushion of security, Nigerians feel better able to cope with the challenges of transition to industrial modernization.[54]

Misty Bastian's investigation of contemporary fashion in a predominantly Ibo region of Nigeria demonstrates how clothing styles may be used by women and young men as tools of resistance against the social dominance of older men.[55] Women in Onitsha and elsewhere in Nigeria adopted aspects of dress, including the flowing robe (agbada), in rich brocade, associated with wealthy Nigerian men or *al-hajjis*.[56] In so doing, they expressed the "transformations in gender, education, and economic status that they had already experienced or that they considered the obvious next step in 'development' for their country."[57] Not only were they stepping into the sartorial realm of men, they were also rejecting the predominance of Western-style attire, for the new al-hajji fashions were "partially a response to several decades of Nigerian women's (Westernized) dress practice that stipulated tight skirts, nipped-in waists, low-cut necklines."[58] Thus, female al-hajjis challenged the male prerogatives of access to wealth and power and also rejected the association of Western attire with female status.

Bastian also discusses a young male clothing designer in Onitsha whose reshaping of the agbada transformed it into a modern challenge to the garment's close association with an idealized Nigerian "tradition." He streamlined the voluminous robe, emphasizing the lean bodies of younger men, and used dark colors associated with mourning in Onitsha and with Western-style business suits everywhere. Through fashion, this designer and the young men who commissioned his work blended tailoring and color that references Western attire with the traditional agbada form, an elision that their elders found "profoundly disturbing."[59]

Fashion is, clearly, a subtle yet powerful means of declaring diverse identities, whether subsuming the non-local into local systems of value (sapeurs, salaula), associating past styles with new meanings (agbadas and khadi as symbols of anticolonialism), or combining two systems of fashion in an effort to harness the power of both (a leopard-skin suit). Bogolan clothing, in its varied forms, takes part in all of these varieties of fashion as social statements.

### Bogolan: Outside the Mainstream

A key prerequisite for the mobilization of clothing as political or cultural symbol is the predominance of non-local fabrics and garments. The creation of a "tradition" to be the object of nostalgia requires the existence of a definable non-traditional that puts into relief the practices once accepted as simply quotidian. The effectiveness of bogolan clothing as a statement of pride in cultural identity is partially dependent upon the predominance of Western-associated attire in Bamako, much as bogolan's effectiveness as a medium for painting is partially predicated upon the prevalence of oil painting and other Western media. The strength of the recent revival of bogolan is, in other words, a result of and a reaction to the T-shirts, jeans, business suits, miniskirts and other Western-associated attire that fill the streets of urban Bamako.[60]

Bogolan makes a powerful political statement in Bamako today, but Western-associated clothing as a category of fashion "speaks" little. Rather than making a statement, Western-style suits and dresses have become the norm, thus dulling their communicative power. Whereas Western-style fashion was, when rare, a declaration of the wearer's wealth and aspirations to Western-style education and professions, today "traditional" clothing is exceptional in urban contexts and therefore a more effective communicative device. Esther Pasztory asserts that "ethnic or polity styles emerge primarily as a way of dealing with others, and their purpose is the creation of difference."[61] In urban Mali, where Western-style clothing predominates, bogolan fashion can effectively "speak" its message.

In the early to mid-1990s, bogolan clothing was a recent and flourishing aspect of contemporary fashion in Mali. Mansour Ciss, the Senegalese sculptor resident in Bamako for several years, noted from 1988 until 1992 the increasing number of designers making use of bogolan and, in turn, the growing number of residents wearing the cloth.[62] Artisanat director Racine Keita, a keen observer of the shifting popularity of textiles and other products under his purview, said that in the mid-1980s bogolan clothing attracted more attention abroad than in Mali.[63] Mamadou Keita, owner of the Galerie Indigo, one of Bamako's most successful private art galleries, also noticed the interest in bogolan clothing abroad before it developed at home. In an effort to popularize the cloth, Keita wore shirts made of bogolan that met with great approval and interest in Canada and in Europe, but in Mali he found little interest until the late 1980s, when he began to see more and more bogolan garments on the city's streets.[64]

Although a great many Malians, particularly in urban areas, continue to wear clothing imported from Western producers—Tommy Hilfiger and Calvin Klein clothing are every bit as highly valued in Bamako as in New York City—a new and growing clientele seeks out clothing made of locally produced fabrics. In all of its forms, bogolan clothing meets a fashion demand that is not derived from Western precedents. Bogolan vests, baseball caps, and other garments often serve as accessories, worn to accent a denim skirt or a T-shirt (Figure 17), creating a bricolage of garments all considered to be equally chic by the young people who wear them. Few of the young bogolan consumers I spoke with in 1992–93 discussed the cloth in terms of national or ethnic identity. None felt that the blending of bogolan and Western-style garments in any way diminished the impact of the locally produced cloth and its characteristic patterns.[65] Bogolan's value as a signal of revived pride in and awareness of Mali's distinct cultural history is not dependent upon the explicit statement of nationalistic sentiments by those who wear it. Rather, the cloth has become chic, moving from national symbol to personal statement of one's fashion sensibility.

In the tourist art market the construction of Malian identity also owes much of its appeal to the immense popularity of non-local material culture. The Malian identity constructed in the tourist art market, however, is distinct from that created by participants in the bogolan clothing market. In the tourist market, bogolan is produced for the benefit of an external audience, the foreign consumer. As discussed in Chapters 3 and 4, tourist art offers non-Malians a condensed, readily legible version of Malian culture, created in response to the perceived expectations of the intended audience. Dean MacCannell, in his analysis of the cultural politics of modern tourism, labels such identity production for external consumption "reconstructed ethnicity," which he de-

Figure 17. Boy wearing bogolan shorts. Bamako, 1993.

*Bogolan tailored to create a wide range of garments is today worn by people of all ages and genders.*

scribes as "the kind of touristic and political/ethnic identities that have emerged in response to White culture and tourism."[66]

The consumption of bogolan fashion by Malians is no less a reconstruction, but it constitutes a very distinct type of ethnicity or nationality construction—one that is directed inward rather than outward. The fact that Malians are the primary consumers of bogolan clothing does not bring the identity they construct any closer to "authenticity," that mythic goal of revivals of tradition. Preservation or revival of tradition only takes place in opposition to something that is not traditional. As Mac-Cannell succinctly describes, "A tradition that is guarded as such, as in 'this is our sacred way,' always marks another way that is not sacred."[67] The revival of bogolan as fashion operates in this manner, signifying tradition by distinguishing itself from dominant cultural modes of dress. As in the tourist art market, bogolan's precise resemblance to the traditional cloth is relatively unimportant. In none of its sartorial manifestations does bogolan clothing reproduce the iconography and the labor-intensive manufacture of bogolanfini, yet it never strays far enough from its orgins to completely leave tradition behind.

# 8

# MAKING IT MODERN

## Bogolan Clothing's Dual Directions

As in the fine art and tourist art bogolan markets, the making and marketing of bogolan clothing is deeply implicated in diverse conceptions of cultural and personal identity. The wearing of bogolan might be associated with either Western or Malian identity, with tradition or with modernity; the producers of bogolan clothing may invoke either set of associations depending upon the combination of the tailoring of the garments, the materials of which they are made, and the motifs with which they are adorned. Discussions with artists and consumers of bogolan clothing reveal the range of motivations for wearing the cloth, from those who consider bogolan clothing to be a political statement to those who find it attractive without awareness of its broad context, treating the cloth as a fashion trend to be followed.

For these two sets of consumers, two types of bogolan apparel have developed, each of which draws from distinct precedents—one in the tourist art market and the other in art galleries and museums: "couture" bogolan clothing and "fine art" bogolan clothing. The two "schools" of bogolan fashion have distinct motivations, though as in other markets for bogolan the boundaries between these categories are permeable. One school, fine art, aims to update bogolan while preserving many of its distinctive traits, creating a uniquely Malian fashion trend, while the other, couture, seeks to adapt bogolan to Western fashion, making the cloth international rather than specifically Malian. Both schools transform bogolan from its rural, "traditional" forms into innovative types of garments, using new iconography, and new production techniques.

As noted earlier, when used in rural contexts bogolanfini is associated with hunters and with girls following initiatory rituals, serving in both instances as a tool for spiritual protection. Along with its spiritual functions, bogolanfini can communicate information about the identity of the wearer, including occupation, age, and region of origin.[1] Although few of the artists who created bogolan clothing in Bamako in the 1990s and none of the consumers who wore it spoke of the cloth's protective roles in its original contexts, all made note of its role as a marker of identity. For some the cloth marks Bamana identity, for others the cloth refers to Malian nationality, and for visitors to Mali the cloth may stand in for Africa as a whole. Through all of its changes at the hands of artists, designers, and consumers, bogolan clothing retains its function as a marker of identities.

To serve so broad a range of significatory functions, bogolan clothing is read-

Aujourd'hui moi je fais du bogolan léger, du bogolan lourd, je fais du bogolan de tout parce que techniquement moi je suis dans une autre dimension que même les auteurs du bogolan. Il y a que le graphisme qui m'intéresse et plus c'est une identité culturelle. (Today I make bogolan of light fabrics, bogolan of heavy fabrics, all kinds of bogolan because technically I am in a completely different realm from the originators of bogolan. I am interested only in the graphic quality of the designs, and it's also a matter of cultural identity.)
*Chris Seydou, Malian fashion designer*

African designers do not, like most artists, want to be African designers but simply designers, who do not disown their origins but who draw their modernity from the source of their countries. For Africa is not a reservoir of a living age-old tradition, it is also rooted in the now commonplace modernity of lycra and knitwear, anchored in the hazy identity of urban culture.
*Jean Loup Pivin, "Rebirth of an African Style"*

ily adjusted to suit different needs. A similar adaptability is evident in the tourist art and fine art versions of the cloth; in all of the markets for contemporary bogolan, the artist may adjust the style of his (or, less frequently, her) designs, the type of cloth used as a support, and the compositions of pigments. Only in the case of clothing, however, is the cloth fashioned into one of many distinct forms; the variety of boubous, pants, headwear, dresses, shirts, and other articles of clothing offers a vast range of possibilities and opportunities to transform bogolan still further.

The bogolan clothing worn by increasing numbers of young people in Bamako constitutes, in essence, a return to the cloth's original function as clothing, made to be worn rather than hung on the walls of a museum or displayed as a souvenir. Yet the stylistic distance between the bogolan clothing currently popular in Bamako and that worn by hunters and young girls in village contexts is vast. The distinction between the bogolan garments worn in these diverse environments is complicated by the fact that many of the artists in Bamako who create bogolan attire do so with the intention of re-creating Malian traditions, viewing their work as a revival of or an homage to past clothing styles. Conversely, another group of clothing designers have adapted bogolan in an effort to move away from the past, taking the cloth into modern, international arenas.

## "COUTURE" BOGOLAN: TAILORING TRADITION

The labeling of one category of clothing as "couture" bogolan is a reference to both tailoring[2] and to the culture of Western fashion. Rather than being made into distinctly Malian or West African garments—the flowing robes called boubous, loose-fitting pullover shirts, or wide, drawstring pants—this bogolan clothing typically takes the form of jackets, miniskirts, dresses, and other garments. In all of these forms, couture bogolan is extensively tailored, an important distinction that resonates with broader implications. Distinctly Malian garments, in contrast, require minimal cutting and sewing. Boubous, for example, require but three seams: the two sides are each partially sewn leaving wide openings that serve as sleeves, and the robe is stitched around the neck opening. The distinction between the two approaches to the creation of attire could hardly be more dramatic.

The degree of tailoring is much more than a stylistic distinction, for the effect of a garment and practical aspects of its production and marketing change dramatically with the emphasis on tailoring. Like most Malian-style clothing, boubous and drawstring pants reveal little of the shape of the wearer's body; the voluminous, billowing fabrics accentuate the body's movements rather than closely following its contours. A typical Western-style shirt or jacket, conversely, conforms closely to the outlines of the wearer's body. Whereas the same boubou might fit a large or a small person, Western clothing is sized quite precisely. The making of jackets and dresses and pants requires a great deal of cutting and sewing, so that the artists and entrepreneurs who make "couture" bogolan clothing must either work with a tailor or themselves have tailoring skills.

Although tailoring is essential to this style of attire, its producers need not possess any bogolan-making skills. Many make clothing of fabric purchased in the tourist art market or commissioned from bogolan makers in Bamako or elsewhere. The tailoring of the cloth, the design of the garments, is for them the most important creative act, putting their personal stamp on the clothing. Paradoxically, the use of bogolan made for the tourist market produces both the most expensive (haute couture) bogolan ensembles as well as the most inexpensive, quickly produced, clothing and accessories.

The growing market for bogolan clothing has, thus, created a new clientele for textile merchants in the tourist art market—consumers who purchase the already fabricated cloth in order to make vests, hats, and other garments for their own use or for sale. Although in some instances the purchase of cloth is a pragmatic response to a producer's lack of bogolan-making skills, more often it is a strategic decision. The tourist market cloth is practical economically, because it costs very little, approximately 2,000 CFA per pagne (in 1993, six dollars), when purchased from a large supplier in the Grand Marché. Financial practicalities alone do not fully account for this use of tourist market bogolan, for several of the designers in this market have the resources to purchase whatever cloth they desire; occasionally, they commission cloth from the same sources in order to maintain close control over the colors and patterns. The artists who create fine art bogolan garments create their own bogolan, painting or stenciling designs onto the cloth after it has been tailored into garments.

Most of the professional and amateur designers making tailored bogolan clothing know little of bogolanfini's symbols and the cloth's uses in small towns and villages. Those who do make their own cloth rarely learned bogolan techniques through rural apprenticeships, instead acquiring the basic rudiments from friends in Bamako or in classrooms at the Institut National des Arts. Many of the young producers and consumers of bogolan clothing remembered the cloth from their childhood, having encountered it during visits to relatives in their home villages, but few knew anything of its production before taking it up in Bamako.[3]

For the designers and tailors who produce bogolan clothing, adherence to labor-intensive techniques and symbolic patterns of bogolanfini is of less importance than the retention of key characteristics, for example, color and the use of strip-woven cloth, to maintain the cloth's association with bogolanfini. As noted earlier, the artists and entrepreneurs of the tourist art market are experts in the creation of strategic resemblance to bogolanfini. It comes as little surprise, then, to find that tourist market bogolan suits the needs of designers who wish to adapt the cloth to international markets, where bogolan loses its specificity as a Malian art form.

Although they express a lack of concern with the details of bogolanfini's symbolic, broadly "traditional" functions, producers of bogolan garments simultaneously express pride in the cloth's history and respect for its significance in rural, "traditional" settings. One major designer alluded to the difficulty he had in cutting, sewing, and reshaping a well-made piece of bogolanfini, made for a ritual purpose and created with its own compositional logic.[4] Although these artists may not have a rural hunter's respect for the cloth's power of protection or respect like that of the Groupe Bogolan Kasobane and others who work to preserve bogolanfini techniques, they generally view the cloth as more than simply a means to attract consumers. Some actively promote the cloth's value as a cultural treasure, while others experiment with techniques and pigments to expand the medium's versatility and its popularity.

In many instances, the tailored, Western-style garments reach audiences that the makers of fine art bogolan clothing do not. Couture bogolan garments are economically attainable for average Malians as well as for wealthy Malians and foreigners. For those who can afford the more expensive designer dresses and jackets, bogolan clothing may represent the height of fashion and, simultaneously, a recognition of national heritage (Figure 18). Those who cannot afford the high-end garments can easily find a tailor to fashion a bogolan vest, tie, or cap. In Bamako, as in many other West African cities and towns, tailors are widely available, and their work is generally affordable for the average Malian.[5] The clothes in this category thus range from the extremely exclusive to the broadly available, appealing to a variety of potential consumers.

One name is repeatedly cited by the artists, designers, and observers of the Malian arts scene in discussions of the revival of bogolan: Chris Seydou. He is credited with bogolan's revival through fashion in Mali, and with the cloth's popularity outside Mali. Because his story is a rich illustration of bogolan's biography in the international and local markets, and because he was particularly reflective about the implications of his use of bogolan in contemporary, tailored garments, an overview of Seydou's contributions to the revival of bogolan is in order.

Figure 18. Oumou Sangaré wearing a dress made of bogolan-patterned factory cloth, 1993. Photograph courtesy of Adama Coulibaly.

*One of Mali's most popular singers, Oumou Sangaré is increasingly prominent in the world music scene. Here she performs at a concert in Bamako.*

### Chris Seydou, the African Dior

Contemporary Mali's most talked about, most internationally successful, and at one time the most widely recognized visual artist in Bamako and abroad is not a painter or a sculptor but a clothing designer. Chris Seydou's work has been published in numerous French, German, Ivorian, Senegalese, as well as Malian fashion magazines. He worked and showed his designs with internationally renowned designers, most notably Paco Rabanne and Yves Saint-Laurent, and changed his name in homage to Christian Dior. He made a place for himself in the competitive Parisian fashion industry and was a pioneer in the continuing effort to promote African fashion designers in the international market.

Nearly all of the material on artists, merchants, designers, and entrepreneurs presented in this study is based on personal interviews and observations, because written sources of information are virtually nonexistent. Only Chris Seydou had the international profile that encouraged journalists, both abroad and in Mali, to devote attention to his work, providing a rich resource from which to now draw. Sadly, Seydou died on March 4, 1994, at the age of forty-five; the loss to Mali's—and Africa's—artistic community has been great. Obituaries appeared in French as well as Ivorian and Malian newspapers and magazines, and he was the subject of a French broadcasting company profile aired soon after his death.[6] The designer's importance as an ambassador of Malian culture was celebrated in these obituaries, as was his crucial role in bogolan's revival. According to one obituary by a Malian journalist, "Through his creations, Mali became better known throughout the world for its cultural treasures, all the way to America, where black Americans today make bogolan into a source of cultural identity."[7] Ivorian jewelry designer Michaël Kra notes Seydou's importance as a source of validation of local textiles and fashions: "He was the pioneer of African fashion, the man who made African women proud of African style, the first to . . . honor the celebrated bogolan textiles made by African weavers."[8]

Seydou was best known for his use of bogolan in contemporary, distinctly Western-style garments, tailoring the cloth into tight-fitting miniskirts, short jackets, and suit-coats (Plate 17). In a description of the "Chris Seydou phenomenon," journalist Macy Domingo catalogues several of his distinctive garments: "very sophisticated little camisole blouses which are very low-cut, shoulder-straps, strapless bras; sewn ensembles cut at the waist, very tight, with pompoms everywhere; short dresses."[9] Although he used other fabrics, such as damask, to create flowing boubous, Seydou never used bo-golan to create clothing in local, Malian styles. Unlike the Groupe Bogolan Kasobane, Seydou's interest in the cloth was piqued not by its potential popularity in Mali but by its potential in the international fashion market. His use of the cloth was radically dif-ferent from its previous incarnations as boubous, pagnes, and hunters' tunics: "He flouted every convention, showing *bogolan* made into mini-skirts or bustiers, as large berets or full-fitting coats and even as a fitted suit worn by the President's wife, Adam Bâ Konaré, for the opening of a film festival in Marseilles in 1993."[10]

Chris Seydou's role in the revitalization of bogolan in urban Mali has been dis-puted by other members of Bamako's artistic community, part of an ongoing debate concerning the innovators who first utilized bogolan in contemporary contexts. Some artists and entrepreneurs assert that Seydou was the first to recognize the cloth's po-tential,[11] while others insist that his role has been overemphasized.[12] In discussions, his name is mentioned immediately when the topic turns to bogolan; clearly his high profile has made him Mali's most visible proponent of contemporary bogolan. While the Groupe Bogolan Kasobane and other bogolan innovators were at work in Ba-mako, Seydou was living in Ouagadougou, the capitol of Burkina Faso, in Abidjan, the capital of the Côte d'Ivoire, and in Paris. It will be argued here that it was par-tially due to his separation from Mali that Seydou came to adapt bogolan, his dis-tance from its source, his homeland, permitting him to view it anew.

Chris Seydou was born Seydou Nourou Doumbia in 1949 in Kati, a small military town forty kilometers north of Bamako. In an extensive interview, Seydou described the early development of his interest in clothing design and construction.[13] Because Sey-dou's mother worked as an embroiderer, he was from an early age familiar with the tools of the clothing trade. As important, his mother had copies of European fashion magazines that impressed Seydou greatly; he recalled his fascination from the age of seven with the clothing and the beautiful women the magazines pictured. At fifteen, he left school to pursue his interest in fashion. His mother supported him in this decision and allowed him to apprentice himself to a local tailor in Kati named Cheickene Ca-mara.[14] In 1968 Seydou relocated to Ouagadougou, and the following year he moved to Abidjan. He changed his name from Seydou Nourou Doumbia when he embarked on his professional career, adopting the prénom "Chris" as a tribute to Christian Dior, whose work had a great influence on his early development, but keeping "Seydou" in order to preserve an aspect of the name his family gave him.[15]

In 1969, as now, Abidjan was known for its fashion industry. Merchants, artists, and the fashion conscious often repeated the West African fashion truism: "Bamako for cloth, Dakar for tailors, Abidjan for designers." Abidjan is home to the UNIWAX textile company, a major producer for the whole of Africa and sponsor of the Ciseaux d'Ivoire (Ivory Scissors) award for African designers.[16] Seydou moved back and forth between Abidjan and Paris several times and helped to bring international attention to Abidjan's role as a center for the African fashion trade. Seydou met with great success in the city, designing clothing for many of Abidjan's wealthy and influential women.[17]

Beginning in 1972, Seydou spent seven years in Paris, where he studied the traditions of European couture. He also continued to produce and, whenever possible, to show his work. His designs were worn by celebrities and luminaries, including Bianca Jagger,[18] Princess Beatrice of the Netherlands, and Madame Mobutu, wife of the infamous former president of Zaire.[19] Seydou met famous designers, acquaintances that increased his cachet on his return to Africa, where he himself attained celebrity status. Seydou found that his work appealed to African women who sought "la mode occidentale" (Western style) and that European women appreciated his "exoticism."[20] As Seydou explained, people did not buy his work because he was African, but because he "brought an African sensibility" to his designs.[21]

Seydou's decision to return to Bamako was more of a surprise to Malians than his success abroad. Having moved back and forth between France (where he feared losing touch with his African origins) and Abidjan (where he feared he would lose the connections and the prestige he had gained in France), Seydou decided in 1990 to return to his country of birth. After years abroad, few expected his return because, as one obituary described, "Mali was practically a punishment for Chris because he loved living the big city life under the sun of Abidjan, New York or Paris."[22] Seydou returned to Bamako in search of "the authors, the origins" of "the real African traditions."[23] Although Abidjan was, for Seydou, an important center for the fashion market, only in Mali did he feel he had access to the sources of his craft: Malian weavers and dyers. He also returned in order to promote Malian arts, which he felt suffered on the international market due to the lack of infrastructure for the production and export of artisanal products. He describes his intentions on his return to Mali: "In spite of the richness of Malian art, it lacks the structures that will insure its competitiveness on an international level. I am now devoting myself to providing structure for this art . . . that is just waiting to blossom."[24]

Much of Seydou's attention was focused on bogolan, which he had used for years and which he felt was at risk of deteriorating, ironically, due to the new popularity that he had helped to create. His efforts to support and protect bogolan took very different forms from the research and documentation-based projects of the Groupe Bogolan Kasobane. His work was as much entrepreneurial as it was altruistic; he hoped his own work might benefit from the amelioration and regulation of the bogolan industry, for he often bemoaned the low quality of the bogolan he found in Bamako's markets.[25]

Seydou began using bogolan in Paris, in 1975–76, though at first it did not attract much attention or approval from his fellow designers or his clients.[26] He described his first recognition of bogolan's potential: On returning to Paris in 1973 after a visit home, Seydou found in his suitcase several pieces of bogolan that he had received as gifts. He was already familiar with bogolan from his childhood in Kati, but there he associated it with hunters and ritual rather than with his own interest in fashion. In unfamiliar Paris the familiar cloth was transformed into a reminder of the place and the people of home.[27] Like the foreigners who purchase bogolan in the tourist art market, at a hotel, restaurant souvenir stand, or the airport shop at the end of a trip, Seydou's use of bogolan embodied his memories of Mali while he was resident in France.

Seydou's appreciation for and celebration of the culture of his country of origin once separated from that country might be considered part of the larger history of expatriate Africans embracing the cultures of "home." The Négritude movement, a broad cultural and political assertion of the value of indigenous African and Afro-Caribbean cultures, developed in the 1940s and 1950s among expatriates dwelling in Paris. According to Anya Peterson Royce, "Emigré intellectuals frequently develop nationalistic feelings before their counterparts at home do."[28] One factor in this transition can be glimpsed in the words of Skunder Boghossian, an Ethiopian painter in Paris in the 1950s, who describes the coming together of Africans and people of African descent outside their homelands: "I met Brazilian guys who looked as black as me. I thought they were Africans from some place like Kenya because of their curly hair. I had no concept of black people other than the Nigerians and Ghanaians in London."[29]

Like Senghor, Césaire, and the other poets and writers of the Négritude movement, Seydou met other African artists and designers in Paris, eventually organizing the Fédération Africaine de Prêt à Porter (African Federation of Ready-to-Wear Designers), an association for promoting African designers in the international market. Although the focus of these two groups of expatriate Africans in Paris—one setting the tone for decades of political and cultural policy in Africa, the other based in the promotion of African clothing and textiles—were on two completely different sights, a similar recognition of indigenous culture through separation from that culture appears to have been operative in both instances.

According to Seydou, the popularity of bogolan in Bamako and abroad in the early 1990s can be traced to his own use of the cloth. When asked why bogolan was so popular abroad, he replied drolly, "It's my fault."[30] When asked why the cloth was so popular in Bamako, he explained, "If a Malian designer like me goes to France . . . and I return to say that I am behind bogolan, what is everybody going to do? . . . I valorized the cloth."[31] Indeed, Seydou's high profile in Bamako gave his work extraordinary visibility, making his fashion shows major events and his designs immediate fashion trends.

Seydou carefully considered the implications of his use of bogolan, proving to be among the Malian artists who responded most fully and thoughtfully to queries regarding the tension between "tradition" and "modernity" in the contemporary bogolan market. During his years abroad, Seydou, like many African artists, found himself classified as an "African designer" rather than simply a "designer." Such experiences led him to consciously decide where he wanted to be viewed in the "Africa" of Western imagination. He determined to position himself within the same international arena as designers he worked with in Paris. Also at this time, he asserted his Malian identity through his choice of fabrics, creating a bricolage intended to please a wide variety of clients, African and European.

As he worked to attain a balance between Western garments and African fabrics, between Western expectations of "traditional" Africa and the modern cosmopolitan nature of his career, Seydou confronted many of the same challenges as Malian artists who sought to show their work in galleries and museums but were frequently marginalized as African artists. Seydou's resolution of these challenges differed from that of other artists, because he consciously dispensed with any "loyalty" to the cloth, focusing his attention on specific technical and stylistic features; he freely altered or abandoned aspects of the cloth that other artists preserved. That is, while many other artists and designers focused their attention on preserving bogolan's technique while adapting it to contemporary uses, Seydou seemed to disregard any doubt of bogolan's relevance to contemporary pursuits; no explanation for the cloth's adaptation to miniskirts and bustiers was necessary, and none was offered.

Seydou claimed that as a Malian, he was naturally interested in the cloth, but that he viewed it as a point of departure, a "cultural foundation" out of which his artistic work could emerge.[32] Ismaël Diabaté, Sidicki Traoré, the Atelier Jamana, the Groupe Bogolan Kasobane, and other artists, entrepreneurs, and designers adapting bogolan, whether for the fine art or the fashion markets, all present their work as part of a tradition—a claim that is central to their works' appeal. Preservation of tradition was not a part of Seydou's work. Recognizing the relevance of traditional arts to contemporary practice and refining them to suit contemporary tastes was his strength.

Seydou was firm in the separation of his work from the cultural and aesthetic roots of bogolanfini. Both technically and conceptually, he viewed the cloth as the raw material for contemporary fashion, changing its form in accordance with his needs. Editing, modifying, or discarding the format and the media that characterize bogolan were central to his design practice. In his words, "I am a contemporary designer who knows what I can do technically and how to do it. Bogolan can simply be a cultural base for my work."[33]

One of Seydou's primary modifications of the cloth concerned the density of its designs, altered to suit his use of bogolan as a medium for tailored garments. The number and variety of distinct motifs on a single pagne often makes cutting and assembling a garment extremely difficult, for no two portions of the cloth are identical. The variety of patterns is particularly evident in bogolanfini pagnes that combine symbols in a carefully ordered composition. According to Seydou, this cloth is "too full"; "there are ten designs in the same pagne, one can make ten patterns from a single one."[34] Describing his aversion to working with such densely adorned cloth, Seydou said, "Even to tailor this fabric with my French technique and everything, I was very afraid to cut it. . . . The graphic quality of the cloth was not made to be cut."[35]

Figure 19. Industrially produced bogolan cloth and garment designed by Chris Seydou, 1993.

*This cloth, commissioned by the ITEMA textile company, was used to create a variety of dresses and shirts that Chris Seydou sold at his shop in the Quartier du Fleuve, an upscale Bamako neighborhood, and at the San Toro cultural center.*

Though he spoke of it only in passing and without elaboration, Seydou's reluctance to utilize cloth adorned with symbolic motifs also reflected his respect for the cloth's protective significance in rural contexts. Although Seydou may not have held the same beliefs or understood the specific significations of the symbols, he was aware of those beliefs and, as a Malian of Bamana ethnicity himself, respectful and proud of their relevance to his cultural background. Seydou was sensitive to the shifts in the cloth's meaning as it changes locales, losing specific symbolic power but maintaining its powerful effect: "In the traditional society, this [a particular symbol] means one thing but when it moves outside it has no meaning. . . . [But] if it once had a meaning . . . it [the symbol] is still powerful."[36] Awareness of this power made him hesitant to cut the cloth when he first started using it: "For me it was symbolic. For me, I didn't want to cut bogolan early on; it was difficult to put my scissors to it."[37]

Seydou responded to the difficulties in utilizing the cloth available to him by creating his own versions of bogolan, isolating a single pattern in a process he referred to as "decoding" the cloth.[38] The resultant cloth facilitated the cutting and assembly his designs required. Because he did not have the skills to make bogolan, Seydou commissioned artists to produce the cloth according to his specifications. He quickly learned that bridging the gap between his conception of the cloth and the practices of rural women who continue to make the cloth for local use would be a great challenge. Seydou and some friends traveled to Kolokani, bogolanfini artist Nakunte Diarra's home and the village with a reputation for the production of quality bogolanfini, planning to commission cloth that they might use in tailored garments. He found that the village women simply "don't operate that way"; they would not copy his designs, which to them likely appeared preposterous.[39] His specifications, which required that the cloth be made with only one motif, essentially stifled the cloth's communicative capabilities.[40] Seydou also found that the women made the cloth too slowly for his purposes, as they were accustomed to making it only for local use.

Unable to secure the cloth he sought in Kolokani, Seydou turned to bogolan producers in Bamako. He found the Groupe Bogolan Kasobane, Ismaël Diabaté, and others of their circle "too artistic to serve in an artisanal context,"[41] a comment that accurately reflects the stance of the artists. Instead he hired a young man who had studied bogolan techniques at the Institut National des Arts to produce cloth according to his specifications. Seydou also continued to utilize cloth from the tourist art market, which was cheap and abundant.

Seydou additionally adjusted bogolan to suit his designs by applying bogolan patterns to a variety of supports, moving beyond the strip-woven cotton cloth to poplin and other factory-produced fabrics. The cut of his garments determined the weight of the cloth he used; for his 1992 designs, Seydou used a stretch spandex-like material to create tight, full-body suits with bogolan designs printed on them. He worked to realize whatever permutations of bogolan he could imagine, taking the cloth far from the strip-woven, locally dyed fabric that inspired him during his early Parisian sojourn in 1973. As Seydou explained, referring to the locally woven and dyed cloth, "It's beautiful like this, full of imperfections; people like it because it's ethnic, because it's this or that, but one can go beyond this."[42]

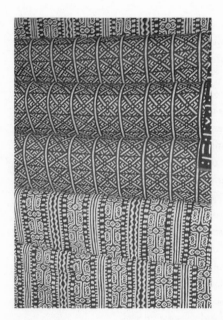

Figure 20. Industrially produced fabrics with bogolan motifs made by the Texicodi textile factory, Côte d'Ivoire. Textile stall, Grand Marché. Bamako, 1997.

*Textiles that replicate bogolan's patterns and colors are made in factories throughout West Africa and beyond.*

Among Seydou's most popular and influential bogolan-related projects was his 1990 collaboration with the Industrie Textile du Mali (ITEMA), a textile manufacturer in Bamako for which he designed a bogolan-inspired fabric that was printed and sold in 1990–91. Seydou had designed factory cloth previously; in the mid-1980s he had designs printed by the UNIWAX company in Abidjan. Unfortunately, the ITEMA factory was among some of the government-owned companies damaged during the 1991 coup d'état, which caused enough destruction to close the factory temporarily and stop the supply of Seydou's cloth; as a result, only a small amount actually reached the market. Other projects were derailed by the change in government, as described in one of the obituaries that recounted Seydou's career: "[T]he wind of democracy carries away with it all the meticulously prepared dreams for success: good-bye artisanal center, distribution firm from Mali to Europe."[43]

In 1993, Seydou was using his stock of ITEMA cloth to create layered dresses, vests, and jackets (Figure 19). Produced with brown and indigo blue patterns, the cloth featured designs based in bogolanfini but printed in subtly modulated tones that hinted at the handmade imperfections of the cloth. Because it was not available in the local textile markets, consumers who desired the cloth would have had to purchase Seydou's expensive clothes, which few could afford. In the meantime, other textile companies, such as Gonfreville, Texicodi, and UNIWAX (all in Côte d'Ivoire), had begun printing their own versions of bogolan, finding a receptive market (Figure 20). Factory-cloth versions of bogolan continued to proliferate through the 1990s, creating an entire subcategory of factory-printed textiles that have found a strong market in Mali and abroad.

In all of his designs with bogolan, Seydou preserved a single aspect of the cloth's original appearance: the bold, linear designs. This is the same quality that, in his view, puts the cloth at risk as the designs are copied, transferred, and recycled in every conceivable form, from bedsheets to dinnerware. The internationalization of bogolan was a matter of concern for Seydou and for other Malians seeking to support the production of bogolan as a source of income and recognition for Malians. Seydou's design for the ITEMA factory cloth may initially appear to contradict his stated concern for bogolan producers, for certainly industrially produced cloth does not provide employment for rural bogolan producers. In fact, Seydou's intention was to secure the patterns for a Malian textile company so that, at the least, the cloth would bear a "Made in Mali" label. Seydou spoke of his consternation at seeing bogolan-patterned industrial cloth in the window of the Parisian furniture and housewares store Roche-Bobois that was labeled "tissu Mexico" (Mexico fabric).[44] He also expressed dismay at the adaptation of the patterns by U.S. fabric and clothing designers, beginning with Norma Kamali in the early 1980s, who used a bogolan fabric that reproduced even the smudged edges of the hand-painted designs.[45] Though his method and his philosophy of promoting and preserving the cloth differed from those of the Groupe

Bogolan Kasobane, Ismaël Diabaté, and the many other artists who used the technique to create paintings and garments, Seydou was working toward the same objective. Chris Seydou's work inspired others to transform bogolan into a medium for the creation of garments in contemporary styles. None have achieved Seydou's great success, but each has developed his own style.[46]

### Youssouf "Nialë" Sidibe

In 1993 Youssouf Sidibe, who is known by his nickname, Nialë (after a popular soccer star), was a twenty-six-year-old lead guitarist and singer for a rock band called Tombouctou, which was popular at several of Bamako's bars. He also had a second career as a creator of bogolan clothing, which he initially made specifically for his stage performances. When I first saw the band perform at Le Bar Bozo, a Bamako nightclub, Sidibe wore a sharply tailored coat in the style of a short motorcycle jacket and elaborately adorned with motifs painted in bogolan pigments. The designs included a musical staff with notes and on the reverse the name of the band (Figure 21). At other public performances, he wore bogolan-dyed shirts and vests, each adorned with bold designs.

Sidibe, whose family is from Segou, northeast of Bamako, had learned bogolan-making techniques around 1992. He is essentially self-taught, having acquired his skills by observing a friend's brother, who was one of the many young men trained in bogolan techniques at the Institut National des Arts.[47] Sidibe did not take up bogolan as a means of earning money but instead viewed it as a complement to his musical career, raising his band's profile through the use of bogolan costumes. As he honed his skills, making shirts of cotton poplin, which he found easier to work with than strip-woven cloth (because it has a smoother surface), and jackets of strip-woven cloth, Sidibe's friends and acquaintances began commissioning clothing, often paying through barter. Whenever he wore his bogolan garments, people inquired about commissioning clothing for themselves.[48]

In the early 1990s Sidibe made a limited number of garments, though he spoke of his intention to devote more time to the potentially lucrative activity. He also expressed interest in bogolan paintings, an activity he considered taking up after he learned of Ismaël Diabaté's work. The young musician was impressed by Diabaté's willingness to move beyond the "traditional" limits of bogolan, painting on factory-woven cotton, using an aerosol applicator, radically altering the cloth's style. Sidibe, who had never previously studied art, found himself fascinated by the potential of this long-familiar art form.

Sidibe's technique and his style are distinctive, likely the result of his distance from the major bogolan producers, most notably the Groupe Bogolan Kasobane, who have had a powerful influence on the work of their students and apprentices. Sidibe does not use stencils or depict prototypically Malian subjects or ideograms. Instead, he paints shapes using distinctively thick, soft-edged lines. The resultant bold, sweeping designs are quite unlike the hard-edged stencils and the intricately drawn compositions of the Atelier Jamana, the Groupe Bogolan Kasobane, or other former students at the Insititut National des Arts.

Figure 21. Youssouf "Nialë" Sidibe wearing a bogolan jacket. Bamako, 1993.

*Made in collaboration with a tailor, this jacket by Youssouf Sidibe is a particularly successful example of the "home-made" designs created by young people in Bamako. Tombouctou is the name of Sidibe's band.*

Sidibe has also experimented with bogolan pigments. For example, he adds n'gallama leaves directly to the fermenting mud rather than using them solely in the dye bath that prepares the cloth for the application of mud. He has found that this use of n'gallama deepens the mud's color. He has also experimented with using the leaves and bark other bogolan artists employ without pre-dyeing the cloth in the n'gallama dye that fixes the colors, though at the time he had not yet found an alternative means of making the colors fast.[49] Sidibe prides himself on the immediacy of his technique, which enables him to move directly from conception to finished product. Unlike other producers of bogolan clothing, Sidibe applies pigment directly onto the cloth or garment without sketching or measuring first. He reports that he is able to create a shirt in three days and jackets in one week, working only in his spare time.

Sidibe's ethnic background makes him a particularly interesting example of the broadening of bogolan's appeal across all of Mali's ethnic groups. He explained that the Peul, or Fulani,[50] traditionally nomadic herdspeople, have customary prohibitions against the wearing of bogolan, which is associated with the settled, agricultural Bamana.[51] Because his mother is Peul, Sidibe was strongly discouraged from involvement with the cloth. His persistence reflects a belief that "one shouldn't be imprisoned by tradition."[52] Like the other young men adapting this traditionally feminine art form, altering its style and its techniques, Sidibe steps outside of the past restrictions associated with the cloth's production, demonstrating the power of bogolanfini to inspire contemporary, urban Malian artists.

### Mamadou Diarra

Mamadou Diarra is another young man who created and marketed bogolan clothing in the early 1990s, though by 1997 he had abandoned bogolan to work in film and television. In 1992, he was selling his work at the Centre Culturel Français from one of several stalls located on the veranda at the back of the building.[53] Most of Diarra's wares consisted of dresses, vests, scarves, and other garments, all adorned in bogolan pigments (and occasionally indigo dyes) applied using a wide range of techniques. Diarra's work belongs in the couture category, for he worked with a tailor to create garments that he then decorated with colors and patterns using bogolan techniques. He occasionally applied the pigments directly to several meters of cotton cloth, which he then had made into garments by a tailor.

Diarra, like many young men in Bamako, struggled to earn a living and had attempted several pursuits before turning, for a time, to bogolan clothing. He had worked briefly as an electrician before taking up his real passion: the creation of art. He sculpted in clay, meeting with little success. During a visit to the Centre Culturel Français, he saw Ismaël Diabaté's paintings and was inspired by bogolan's artistic potential and its uniquely Malian character.[54] He worked briefly in the Groupe Bogolan Kasobane's workshop, though his own work seemed to owe little to their influence. He spoke of his frustration at the group members' insistence that he work with sketches, carefully designing garments before working with the bogolan pigments. According to Diarra, "I don't need sketches. I can make five outfits in a single day."[55] Much of Diarra's work is closer to Diabaté's gestural painting than to the Groupe Bogolan Kasobane's carefully worked compositions. Diarra is like the group members, however, in his desire to focus his efforts on bogolan paintings rather than clothing. He was not yet prepared to show his paintings in 1993, and relied on his rapidly produced bogolan clothing to provide an income in the meantime.

Diarra's garments incorporated a number of innovative techniques and iconographic elements. He experimented with a combination of batik and bogolan, painting designs in wax then dyeing the fabrics in bogolan pigments so that the areas covered by the wax remained undyed. He sometimes splattered pigments onto strip-woven cloth or factory-woven cotton poplin. He also applied bogolan pigments to gauzy cotton cloth, used by Tuareg men as turbans and veils, creating chic scarves and wraps that he said had sold well among Malian and non-Malian women.[56] Diarra also experimented with the iconography of bogolan, most notably in his incorporation of words into the motifs that adorn his cloth. In addition to using abstract patterns as well as Komo ideograms, Diarra also designed several shirts and dresses that incorporate the Bamana names of several types of leaves, roots, and bark used in bogolan pigments. The words were written in pigments made from those materials—an acknowledgment of the technique in a very literal form. Diarra explained that this innovation was a response to bogolan's popularity and a celebration of its distinctly Bamana character.[57] Though the shirts and dresses bear no stylistic resemblance to the bogolanfini of Bamana villages, they constitute an urban designer's tribute to a rural art form.

## THE "FINE ART" SCHOOL: TRADITIONAL CLOTH FOR NEW MARKETS

Much like the bogolan paintings created for display and sale in museums and expensive galleries, "fine art" bogolan clothing is characterized by labor-intensive production, elaborately worked surfaces, and vast expanses of cloth. The artists who create fine art bogolan garments almost without exception consider themselves to be artists rather than designers or tailors, unlike the makers of couture bogolan clothing. Most, in fact, are professional artists who also use bogolan to produce paintings for the gallery trade. The prices of their garments also reflect their connections to the exclusive fine art trade; their intricately worked robes and pants are sold at prices far beyond the reach of the vast majority of Malians.

Despite the limited local market for fine art bogolan clothing, the ornately adorned garments have wide visibility in Bamako and abroad, because bogolan clothing in contemporary styles is popular among musicians and other entertainers, worn on stage and in music videos. Performers who wear bogolan clothing include musicians Habib Koita, Toumani Diabaté, and Oumou Sangaré (see Figure 18). Mali's most prominent film directors also make use of fine art bogolan attire in costume and set designs. Artists have also begun applying bogolan techniques to less expensive articles of clothing, such as scarves and hats, broadening their customer base.

### The Groupe Bogolan Kasobane

Just as the analysis of the fine art trade in bogolan in Chapter 6 began with the Groupe Bogolan Kasobane, so too does the following discussion of fine art bogolan clothing. The group, which has had great success in the fine art realm, has been equally successful in the production of clothing made for sale at boutiques and bazaars, on commission from customers, and for theatrical and film costumes. Other artists who began their careers as students or assistants of the Groupe Bogolan Kasobane have themselves also gone on to become important producers of both clothing and paintings. Like numerous other artists producing bogolan clothing, the members of the Groupe Bogolan Kasobane view clothing as a means to an end, for the money they earn enables them to finance their paintings.

The group's earliest efforts toward the revitalization of bogolan were in the realm of clothing design. Soon after meeting as students at the Institut National des Arts in 1974, before bogolan gained sufficient popularity to enable them to charge high prices for their work, they began earning money through the production of matching sets of bogolan clothing for members of youth groups and other organizations.[58] As described in Chapter 6, the members of the group have long emphasized the importance of their work to preserve and promote bogolan techniques. In the realm of clothing, as in their paintings, the group members seek to create amalgamations of traditional and contemporary styles aimed at both local and international markets.

Through the films of two renowned Malian film directors, Cheik Oumar Sissoko and Souleyman Cissé, the Groupe Bogolan Kasobane's garments have reached international audiences. Group member Kandiora Coulibaly is employed by the National Ministry of Cinema, where he works as a costume and set designer. Through his work, the Groupe Bogolan Kasobane's robes have appeared in numerous films, including Cissé's *Yeelen* (Brightness), which won the 1987 Special Jury Prize at the Cannes Film Festival. The group members were more extensively involved with Cheik Oumar Sissoko's 1995 film, *Guimba: Un Tyran, Une Epoque* (released in the United States as *Guimba the Tyrant*), which also received international acclaim. Groupe Bogolan Kasobane members Baba Fallo Keita and Boubacar Doumbia, the film's production designers, won the Grand Prix for set design at the Festival Pan-Africain du Cinéma de Ouagadougou,[59] the prestigious biannual film festival held in Burkina Faso (Plate 18). Coulibaly designed the film's costumes, which were singled out for praise in the 1995 *Toronto Film Festival Catalogue*'s description of the film: "The architecture is remarkable, the colours vibrant, the clothes to die for."[60]

In a discussion of the Groupe Bogolan Kasobane's costume and set designs for film, Coulibaly described how they worked to create a universally appealing form of bogolan that would communicate to viewers wherever the films might be shown:

We tried to simplify the signs [bogolan's motifs] by transposing the patterns of the interior decoration of homes onto the fabrics of the costumes, so that these patterns updated to today's tastes made them easier to read. In addition, we highlighted the signs that are easier to read and that had a special meaning which could be understood by everybody. . . . We designed a catalogue for filmmakers who wanted our collaboration so that they could understand the meanings of the signs. This has always aroused their interest.[61]

Film set and costume designs, thus, are another resource in the group's efforts to broaden bogolan's appeal, teaching filmmakers and viewers about bogolan's symbolism, just as they teach their students at the Institut National des Arts. Their clothing designs for films are based on extensive research, documenting and adapting existing garments to artfully evoke the films' fictional settings. According to Boubacar Doumbia, the group members conducted research for three years in preparation for *La Genèse* (Genesis), a 1999 film directed by Cheik Oumar Sissoko.[62]

The Groupe Bogolan Kasobane's clothing is, in some respects, remarkably similar to their large, ornately worked paintings. The garments they most frequently produce, men's and women's robes, or boubous, involve large expanses of cloth much like the vast canvases of their paintings. Along with boubous the Groupe Bogolan Kasobane's clothing production includes the drawstring pants typical of local Malian garment traditions and diaphanous lengths of fabric for use as scarves and headties, similar to those created by Mamadou Diarra. Occasionally other garments may be produced to temporarily expand the group's inventory for bazaars and exhibitions or on commission, including vests, hats, and bags. The group does not, however, create bogolan-dyed miniskirts, baseball caps, or other clearly Western-associated garments, thus distinguishing themselves from the "couture" bogolan clothing producers.

That the group focuses on characteristically Malian (or, more broadly, West African) garments further articulates their interest in maintaining bogolan's traditional character. In the streets of Bamako, boubous are very much in evidence despite the prevalence of Western-style garments such as T-shirts, suits, and tailored dresses. The large, flowing robes, made of factory-produced cottons and synthetic fabrics, are worn by both men and women in marketplaces, offices, and nightclubs. At special events, such as weddings and baptisms, boubous are virtually required dress (Plate 19). An elaborately embroidered boubou made of the finest locally dyed bazin—for women worn along with an elaborately wrapped head tie—remains today the most potent marker of high status and wealth, far more impressive than a dress or a tailored suit.

The Groupe Bogolan Kasobane retain the size, shape, and decorative organization of traditional boubou types in their bogolan versions of the garment. Most factory-cloth boubous are adorned with embroidery at the neck, often extending around the yoke and across the front of the garment in intricate patterns (Figure 22). These patterns have long been applied by hand, stitched by specialists who in some parts of West Africa were also calligraphers and Muslim scholars.[63] Today, most embroidery is applied using sewing machines and paper patterns, a shift analogous to the adaptation of stencils in the creation of bogolan in the tourist market and in the clothing market as well.

Stencils and paper patterns enable artists and tailors to work more quickly, increas-

Figure 22. Bogolan boubou, Groupe Bogolan Kasobane. Bamako, 1993.

*The patterns that encircle the yoke and extend down the front of this garment have been stenciled onto the strip-woven cotton cloth, a process illustrated in Figure 7.*

ing their production, and both have encouraged the use of increasingly standardized forms. Stenciling facilitates the use and re-use of bogolan motifs in a variety of combinations, much as the tailors who adorn boubous on commission for clients offer a selection of designs from which to create various arrangement of motifs. Stencils and paper patterns enable clothing producers, like tailors, to operate workshops employing numerous young men who apply stencils or stitch embroidery onto garments.

There are further parallels between embroidery and the Groupe Bogolan Kasobane's adaptation of bogolan to "traditional" garments such as boubous. Consider, for example, the placement of decorative motifs on bogolan and boubous. The group's boubous maintain the customary focus on yokes and chests as locations for design elements. In addition, the bold arabesques and repetitive patterns created with bogolan pigments reflect prevalent styles of garment embroidery. Thus, although the Groupe Bogolan Kasobane's use of bogolan to adorn garments such as boubous is innovative, their innovation is founded in a familiar, "traditional" precedent. Recognition of this precedent does not diminish the group's status as a major creative force, for the artful fusion of bogolan techniques and an important form of indigenous formal attire is itself a creative achievement.

Like their paintings, the Groupe Bogolan Kasobane's garments are adorned with abstract symbols reminiscent of but not identical to the symbolic designs of bogolan-fini. Bamana and Dogon ideograms are incorporated into clothing designs as they are into paintings. The motifs operate as abstract patterns and, when sold along with information on their symbolic significance, as elements of cultural context that enhance the garments' appeal for many non-Malian consumers. Figurative designs are few; stenciled images of ci waras, ideograms, and masks are occasionally used, as are abstract or symbolic motifs, integrated into the overall abstraction of garment designs.

### Housewares: Dressing the Home

The success of their bogolan clothing led the Groupe Bogolan Kasobane to apply the medium to other products, such as housewares, beginning in the early 1990s. Using elaborate stenciling and dyeing techniques, the group members and their apprentices create pillows, curtains, tablecloths, and other bogolan-based items. Many of the pillows and curtains designed by the group are adorned with ideograms, usually stenciled but occasionally painted by hand. The same stencils may in fact be applied to both clothing and housewares, creating matching ensembles of pillows, scarves, and boubous.

Although the production and marketing of the Groupe Bogolan Kasobane's home decor and clothing overlap in many respects, their housewares have for the past three years incorporated one innovation that has not been applied to clothing: the use of indigo dyes. Curtains, wall hangings, bags, pillows, and other items are available in indigo blue as well as in the browns and tans of bogolan. In response to inquiries concerning their use of indigo only for select products, group members explained that although bogolan clothing finds a ready market, indigo-dyed garments would likely have less appeal.[64] Indigo dyeing is widespread in West Africa, as in other parts of the world, so the technique does not have bogolan's appeal as a uniquely Malian textile. The point is explicitly made in an article on the Groupe Bogolan Kasobane's work in a Malian periodical: "If indigo dyeing is found throughout West Africa, it appears to be undeniable that 'bógólan' is an ancestral technique unique to the Malian region."[65]

The group's housewares are sold in the same boutiques and bazaars as their clothing, filling a similar market niche among Bamako's cultural and economic elite. Musée National director Samuel Sidibe has found that most Malians are resistant to the use of bogolan in their homes, preferring the European- or Middle Eastern–style decors that have long served as markers of status.[66] Just as expensive bogolan clothing indicates the wearer's identification as Malian, the adornment of a home with bogolan announces the owner's conscious identification with Malian traditions, rejecting the overwhelming popularity of brightly decorated factory cloths and shiny plastic fixtures.[67]

Like the group's paintings, their other products' prices place them beyond the reach of most Malian consumers. At a 1993 opening for an exhibition and sale of the group's garments and housewares at the Galerie Indigo, prices for large boubous were as high as 80,000 CFA (one hundred thirty dollars), as expensive as the highest priced boubous in bazin with elaborate embroidery; curtains cost as much as 40,000 CFA. Clearly, the group's efforts to create elegant, uniquely Malian garments are aimed at the wealthy Malians and expatriates who also buy their paintings. The group has begun, in recent years, to create increasing numbers of inexpensive items, such as scarves, though these too are more expensive than most Malians would likely spend for such garments. The work of the Groupe Bogolan Kasobane is, certainly, the most expensive of Bamako's fine art bogolan clothing.

### The Atelier Jamana

The members of the Atelier Jamana are likely Mali's most prolific producers of bogolan clothing. They work in a broad range of styles and techniques, constantly experimenting to create new products and new designs. Like their former professors, the members of the Groupe Bogolan Kasobane, the artists of the Atelier Jamana create clothing as a means of financing their primary effort—large, elaborately worked paintings.[68] Also like the Groupe Bogolan Kasobane, the Atelier Jamana's repertoire includes a variety of housewares, such as pillows, tablecloths, and bags.

Much of the Atelier Jamana's clothing is similar in style to that of the Groupe Bogolan Kasobane. They too produce large and small boubous adorned with ornate patterns at the neck and yoke. Their early boubous (ca. 1990) were exceptionally ornate, combining stenciled and painted patterns to lacelike effect (Plate 20). The amount of labor these garments required made them impractical, for to make a profit the group members had to price them far higher than the market would bear. Their more recent clothing is less labor intensive, with simplified designs. They also produce a great many matching shirt and pants sets in a style associated with traditional attire, most notably drawstring pants and a short shirt with a pocket in front. Both shirt and pants are adorned with a combination of stenciled and hand-painted designs.

The Atelier Jamana's work is clearly distinguishable from that of their former mentors in the Groupe Bogolan Kasobane despite their stylistic and technical similarities. The Atelier Jamana artists make extensive use of the splattered application of bogolan pigments, creating mottled, translucent colors similar to the camouflage-style bogolan of hunters' tunics. Varied stencils are applied over these patterned backgrounds, creating distinctive combinations of dark, deeply saturated motifs on a light ground (Plate 21). Using stencils in an innovative manner, the Atelier Jamana artists create what might be described as "negative" motifs—placing the solid stencils on cloth and painting or splattering bogolan pigments so that, on removing the stencil, the image remains, outlined in the energetic drips and puddles of pigment.

The members of the Atelier Jamana, unlike the Groupe Bogolan Kasobane, create a number of garment types clearly associated with Western-style attire, using bogolan dyes to adorn neckties, fanny packs, and hats. According to group member Rokiatou Sow, these garments are important sources of income, purchased in great numbers by expatriates and tourists at Christmas bazaars and boutiques.[69] In 1997 the Atelier Jamana artists were directing much of their efforts toward the production of these items, having found a growing local Malian audience to supplement their sales at bazaars and other events.

Stenciled pagnes made using intricately designed plastic or cardboard stencils provide another source of steady income for the group. The patterns that adorn these cloths are not based in bogolanfini's symbolic motifs but are abstract designs inspired by a wide range of sources, from elements of the natural world to patterns borrowed from factory-printed textiles. Using coordinated sets of stencils, the Atelier Jamana artists create multicolored pagnes, layering mud and n'beku bark pigments in varied intensities onto the surface so that the cloth beneath each element of the interlocking stencils receives pigment of a different color. The step-by-step development of the patterns, each color applied using a different stencil, is a technique used by other artists as well. Stenciled pagnes can be made quickly—ten or more concurrently—with each layer of stencils applied to all and the cloths then dried and washed simultaneously.

The Atelier Jamana's pagnes exemplify simultaneously contemporary urban bogolan's references to and distance from "traditional" clothing. Bogolanfini is commonly made in pagne form to be worn as wraps by girls and women. The composition of the cloth, the placement and selection of the motifs, reflects the pagne's characteristic shape and size, which is in turn reflective of the cloth's function as a wrap. The Atelier Jamana's pagnes are identical in size and shape to bogolanfini pagnes, yet they are never worn as wraps. The wearing of pagnes as wraps is associated with rural life or with informal wear; women in Bamako might wear pagnes as wraps in their homes but in any formal social setting they would likely be worn only under long robes if at all. Instead, bogolan pagnes are used as tablecloths, as wall hangings (primarily by non-Malians), and tailored into other garments, such as vests. The reference to a form widely considered to be traditional—the pagne—is clearly deliberate, yet the shift in use transforms the cloth into a contemporary urban product.

The Groupe Bogolan Kasobane and the Atelier Jamana are by far the most successful and best-known producers of fine art bogolan clothing. Few other artists use bogolan to create garments in specifically Malian styles. Those who do include former students of the Groupe Bogolan Kasobane as well as self-taught artists who make clothing for friends and relatives, selling their work only occasionally.

### Sekou Traoré

In the late 1980s, Sekou Traoré's family lived next door to Kandiora Coulibaly of the Groupe Bogolan Kasobane, a fortuitous circumstance that exposed Traoré to bogolan dyes and their many applications to art and garment production.[70] From Coulibaly, Traoré learned to mix and apply bogolan pigments, and he observed the Groupe Bogolan Kasobane at work on paintings as well as garments. Traoré was in 1993 a recent graduate of the Ecole Normale Supérieur, Bamako's most prestigious high school. Like many recent graduates, he was unable to find employment and so turned to bogolan as a means of earning money. He also learned tailoring skills from friends, enabling him to cut basic garments. Depending upon the shape and complexity of the garment, Traoré applied bogolan dyes either before or after the pieces were assembled. Like the Groupe Bogolan Kasobane, Traoré works with Malian-style garments such as boubous and short, wide shirts.

Stylistically, Traoré's work resembles the Groupe Bogolan Kasobane's paintings

rather than their clothing. Without using stencils, Traoré fills every available surface of his garments, melding ornate linear abstractions with depictions of masks, dancers, and other typically "Malian" subjects (Figure 23). Unlike the Groupe Bogolan Kasobane, the Atelier Jamana, and other artists discussed in previous chapters, Traoré's clothing is not a secondary aspect of his oeuvre. Because his aim is not to finance the "real work" of gallery and museum-oriented paintings, as is the case for the Groupe Bogolan Kasobane and the Atelier Jamana, Traoré devotes all of his artistic energy to the production of clothing.

Traoré's garments, however, function much as canvases, adorned with ornate compositions that incorporate elaborate figurative and abstract elements carefully delineated in lines of varied widths and intensities. He often combines letters, numbers, and other emblematic elements. When asked to explicate these designs and characters, Traoré did not offer any specific interpretations, asserting that his aim was to paint beautiful patterns rather than to communicate specific ideas.[71] Indeed, the abstract forms, letters, and figures appear to be organized with visual composition in mind rather than "syntax."

Traoré had not, in the mid-1990s, moved beyond friends and family as clients for his clothing. His prices varied according to the amount of time devoted to a particular garment's production, ranging between 10,000 and 25,000 CFA (thirty to seventy dollars). He often decreased his rates in exchange for goods and services, enabling more of his peers to purchase garments. As a means of earning a small income, bogolan clothing served Traoré well.

**Figure 23.** Sekou Traoré (*kneeling*), Victoria Rovine, and a friend of Traoré wearing bogolan garments made by Traoré. Bamako, 1993. Photograph by Morna Foy.

*Using garments much like canvases, Sekou Traoré covers all available surface with intricate designs, some of which are based in bogolanfini's symbolic motifs.*

### Alou Traoré

Alou Traoré is another young man who began making bogolan garments in the early 1990s.[72] He is from San, the city famous as a source of inexpensive, quickly produced bogolan aimed primarily at the tourist art market in Bamako. Traoré is a schoolteacher by training, and he worked briefly as an instructor in Bamako before losing his job in 1991 during the disengagement de l'état, the government effort to reduce the country's bloated bureaucracy. Traoré learned basic bogolan-making skills as a child in San, where many of his friends and acquaintances made bogolan to be sold in Bamako: "I am not an artist by training but since I was born in a city where people make bogolan, when I found myself unemployed I began to make bogolan."[73]

Traoré works exclusively with stencils, elaborating the technique to create layers of richly hued designs (Figure 24). His garments, like those of the Groupe Bogolan Kasobane and the Atelier Jamana, are distinctively Malian in style, primarily boubous, drawstring pants, and shirts, but he also occasionally makes scarves and vests.[74] His work differs dramatically from much of the bogolan clothing sold in Bamako. Not having studied or apprenticed with other urban artists, he developed his techniques and his style independently. Instead of concentrating his stenciling around the yokes of his boubous, Traoré covers the entire surface of his garments with carefully composed, often precisely symmetrical patterns (Plate 22). Because he approaches the entire garment as a surface to be ornamented, Traoré's clothing appears to be closer to boubous made of patterned factory cloth than to hand-embroidered gowns. Factory-cloth boubous, though they may be embroidered over the patterned surface, create an impression of overall patterning, rather than emphasizing particular portions of the body. Traoré's garments function similarly, each portion of the robes receiving equal attention, adorned with equally dense designs.

Traoré's stencil designs include a wide range of abstract forms, none of which are based in bogolanfini's patterns. As noted earlier, some resemble European-style textile designs, many of which appear on factory-printed cloth. On inquiry, Traoré did not indicate that he had been directly influenced by factory cloth, but he did explain that he absorbs influences from every aspect of his visual environment.[75] Traoré's work also incorporates many of the motifs that typify contemporary Malian art, including ci waras, cowrie shells, and dancers. In his use of identifiably Malian motifs, Traoré reflects the broad Malian celebration of local cultures evident in the fine art as well as in the fashion markets.

The prices of Traoré's garments separate him from other artists using bogolan to create traditional-style garments. While in 1997 the Groupe Bogolan Kasobane or the Atelier Jamana might easily have priced an elaborately worked boubou at 50,000 CFA (one hundred fifty dollars) or more, Traoré had fixed the price of his large boubous at 15,000 CFA (about forty dollars). His intended market is not expatriate and tourist-based, but rather local Malians who purchase the garments for special occasions, as gifts, or to be tailored into vests and other garments. His pagnes, many of which are adorned with multicolored stencils, are sold for 4,000 CFA (twelve dollars); this is a significant amount of money for most Malians, yet not completely out of range for the average salaried worker.

Traoré's government service background and his lack of pretensions to artistic status may have predisposed him to approach the production of bogolan clothing in a more efficient, businesslike manner than many of his fellow artists. Much of Traoré's work is created on commission; his clients select garments and patterns from his catalogue of carefully photographed and organized samples, either commissioning the garments exactly as pictured or customizing them with selected stencil patterns and colors.[76] Business among Malian artists and craftspeople is generally conducted in an informal atmosphere, but Traoré schedules his delivery dates with great specificity and generally adheres closely to his schedule.

Because he did not embark upon this second career with the connections of a graduate of the Institut National des Arts or a former apprentice of the Groupe Bogolan Kasobane, and because his work is difficult to classify, Traoré initially met with some dif-

Figure 24. Alou Traoré stenciling a boubou. Bamako, 1993. Photograph courtesy Alou Traoré.

*Alou Traoré works with stencils cut from plastic, using a paint brush to apply pigments.*

ficulty in finding outlets for his work. I first encountered it in an unlikely location: a stall in the Marché Medine (see Plate 6). Here, trucks arriving from the countryside bring mountains of mangos, coconuts, and plantains to be divided for dispersal to the city's many other markets and to the many women who sell fruits and vegetables from stalls and on the streets. The market is also the center of production for trunks, hoes, coolers, and myriad other items fashioned of recycled cans, tires, barrels, and the like. The Marché Medine is not, in short, a likely stop for visiting tourists or art merchants, but rather a center for wholesalers and distributors.

Here, Alou Traoré had made an arrangement with a stall owner to display and sell his boubous and pagnes to passersby. The rest of the stall was devoted to medicinal products, including animal parts, bark, leaves, and other items used in the production of charms and medicines. The cloths hanging from the shelves and plastic roof of the stall provided a shelter for the merchant while drawing attention to his wares, and Traoré hoped that the occasional non-Malians who visited the market would stop to view these "exotic" items. Traoré sold few garments from this location, yet the chance encounter with a textile aficionado or an entrepreneur in search of new products made his presence there valuable. Between 1992–93 and 1997, Traoré's business increased significantly. He hired assistants and made contacts with sponsors and merchants, including the painter Sidicki Traoré, whose shop on a busy street corner provides high visibility for the artists whose work he sells (see Figure 12).[77]

### Yaya Sylla

In 1992, Yaya Sylla was thirty-five years old and had been working with bogolan for more than ten years. Sylla, who was born and raised in Bamako, first encountered bogolan in tourist market shops, including the stall owned by his father. As an antiquities dealer, his father sold primarily masks and other sculpture, though occasionally he sold cloth as well.[78] When Sylla decided that bogolan might find a ready market in Bamako, he traveled to a village near San to study the technique, a location he selected after learning that several bogolan stalls in the tourist market were stocked with cloth from there. He lived in the village for six months, a month at a time, over the course of several years. In his effort to "get to the roots of bogolan,"[79] Sylla learned all he could of the varied leaves and roots used in the area and of the meanings of the symbols that adorn the cloth. He said that although most artists in Bamako use only two or three colors in varied intensities to dye bogolan, he planned to create cloth made of more than two hundred different vegetal and mineral colors.[80]

Sylla's goal is to establish a training center for the study of bogolan in Sebenikoro, a small town on the bank of the Niger River that has now become essentially a suburb among Bamako's urban sprawl. There he had found mud suitable for bogolan production and a number of residents who were supportive of his efforts.[81] Like the Groupe Bogolan Kasobane, Sylla's aim is to preserve and perpetuate the making of bogolan among young people. Also like the group members, his ambitions extend beyond Mali's borders. He works with an assistant, a young man from Guinea. Sylla's intention is to train the young man and eventually send him back to Guinea to promote the making of bogolan there.

Sylla, like so many bogolan artists, divides his bogolan production among several markets. He makes small paintings, bags, and decorative hangings for sale at the Centre Culturel Français and other tourist-oriented locations, such as holiday bazaars. His clothing, primarily the short, wide shirts typical of local manufacture—essentially, two rectangular pieces of fabric sewn together, open at the neck and sides—is aimed at a Malian market. In the early 1990s Sylla had found few clients beyond his immediate friends and family, but he did not wish to expand his merchandise into baseball caps, neckties, and other inexpensive items that might have attracted different audiences. Instead, he wished to expand Malian audiences for the medium.

### Aminata Dramane Traoré and San Toro

Aminata Dramane Traoré—a sociologist, politician, entrepreneur, restauranteur, and patron of the arts—is a highly visible supporter of bogolan's revival in Mali and abroad. Although she is not an artist, she has done much to encourage the production of bogolan for contemporary urban markets through commissions, exhibitions, and public events. Her most visible public role as a supporter of the arts came at the end of the 1990s, when she served for two years as minister of arts and tourism. Whatever her official role, however, Traoré has long been at the forefront of Mali's rediscovery of its indigenous arts.

Beginning in 1983 at her restaurant, Le Djenne, and later at the cultural center she founded in 1992, San Toro (which also incorporates a restaurant and a boutique [see Map 2]), Traoré has provided venues for the exhibition and sale of work by bogolan artists.[82] At Le Djenne, dining areas are hung with paintings by numerous artists, including Ismaël Diabaté and the Atelier Jamana. Traoré herself has claimed that Le Djenne represents the first use of bogolan as interior decoration.[83] San Toro provides additional space for the display of paintings, though the focus of the business is clearly garments and housewares, all made using local media and techniques. Artists work with Traoré to adapt indigenous arts such as pottery, basketry, leatherwork, weaving, and dyeing to products aimed at urban, often non-Malian, audiences. Bogolan curtains, duffle bags, pillows, and bedspreads are sold alongside basketry lampshades, clay planters, and leather placemats (Figure 25). All are recognizably Malian, yet all bear the imprint of Traoré's contemporary style; these are not the textiles, baskets, and pots one finds in the tourist art market, where the aim is to create an often abbreviated form of a "traditional" art. San Toro's wares are part of Traoré's effort to take Malian arts in new directions, to retain the character of Mali's rich traditions while looking at them in a new way, or, as she put it, "to remain ourselves without rejecting other [influences]."[84] Her success as a patron and entrepreneur, and her status as a powerful and influential woman, make Traoré an exceptional participant in bogolan's revival.

Figure 25. Products for sale at the San Toro cultural center. Bamako, 1993.

*Duffle bags in various sizes, a knapsack, curtains, and scarves are all made by bogolan artists according to San Toro owner Aminata Dramane Traoré's specifications.*

Clearly, the two schools of bogolan fashion—couture and fine art—take distinctly different approaches to the challenge of adapting bogolan to contemporary clothing. Some designers transform the cloth into designs one might expect to find on the runway in Paris or on the rack in Bloomingdale's while others create garments that seem more at home in a museum or on a stage than in the streets. The cloth itself encourages these dual directions, for bogolan is simultaneously a versatile technique and a distinctive corpus of patterns, both of which may be adapted to a variety of contexts. The cloth's possibilities in the realm of fashion are limited only by the imagination of the artists and designers who find in bogolan a source of virtually endless creative inspiration.

# 9

# BOGOLAN ABROAD

## Reverberations in the United States

Much as this book opened with a set of epigraphs embodying diverse and, at times, contradictory readings of a single textile, this discussion of bogolan's North American marketing and consumption begins with a set of quotations that reveal the cloth's similarly multivalent character as it travels abroad. Even as bogolan is transformed in the United States, the cloth still retains its Malian roots, adding new layers of complexity to its biography. This coda extends the discussions that have come before, underscoring bogolan's adaptability to new circumstances and changing markets. Bogolan's appearance in the U.S. market represents a continuation of the textile's capacity as a cultural barometer, reflecting in its myriad forms a wide range of identities, attitudes, and conceptions of the "traditional," the "authentic," and the "African." As Thomas McEvilley notes, the meaning of objects necessarily shift as they move:

> When an object produced by one culture is received in another, there is bound to be cognitive slippage, an unintended misperception on the part of the receivers. But it is precisely this "off" quality that offers a window of rich openness, through which new options may arise on both sides.[1]

Although bogolan's travels in the U.S. market may indeed create new opportunities for understandings as well as misperceptions, its presence in the United States has also fulfilled the fears of Chris Seydou and other supporters of the cloth's revival—the bogolan-inspired products that are sold in the United States rarely benefit Malian producers of bogolan. In fact, the Malian origins of the cloth are often blurred or erased as the products are sold. Instead, the cloth is associated with ideas and identities unrelated to its history.

This study has investigated the ways in which bogolan's many Malian manifestations reverberate through a wide range of markets, styles, media, and symbolic overtones. The connotations the cloth carries with it, "tradition" and its attendant concept of "authenticity," shift with the location and identity of the viewer. The U.S. marketing of bogolan exemplifies the elastic nature of tradition, for the concept is transformed with the cloth, shifting to suit the changing desires and expectations of its consumers and expanding to encompass a vast diversity of forms and media.

A brief examination of bogolan's changing forms and fortunes in its U.S. manifestations reveals the potency of its associative powers, for even though the

Figure 26. "Mudcloth"
paper gift bag, The
Ashanti Collection,
1993. Photograph by
Ecco Wang Hart.

Bogolan patterns are re-
produced on paper as
well as a variety of other
media. Here, the style of
the cloth is imitated
closely, reproducing the
fuzzy edges of the hand-
painted cloth.

technique by which it is made, the products into which it is fashioned, and the contexts in which it appears bear little resemblance to its traditional incarnations in rural
Mali, bogolan continues to connote tradition. In the United States, the cloth's abstract designs and its black and white hues are often its sole defining features. As in
Mali's tourist art markets, designs are extremely simplified, most bearing little resemblance to bogolanfini's symbolic motifs. What marks their U.S. adaptations most dramatically are the media on which they appear; bogolan-style designs have been transferred onto a variety of materials, from cotton, rayon, and other fabrics to ceramics
and paper (Figure 26). Although these products may not be identified as Malian, they
are consistently associated with Africa, with the designs assigned names such as
"Totem Elephant," "Zanzibar," and "Zimbabwe."[2]

A fundamental distinction separates bogolan's adaptations to Malian markets from
the cloth's appearance in the United States: Rather than evoking a local culture or identity, bogolan in the United States becomes a signifier for the non-local, the foreign, and
the exotic, concepts that carry diverse associations. Just as bo-
golan in its Malian manifestations appears in several markets,
transformed into myriad forms, so too does the cloth appear in
many markets and many forms in the United States. The
epigraphs that open this chapter suggest the range of meanings
that accompany the cloth in the U.S. market, from signal of ethnic pride to artifact of the exoticized "other." All of these quotations derive from the U.S. marketing of bogolan or, as the fabric
is more commonly called in the United States, "mudcloth."

In some U.S. contexts, mudcloth denotes Africa as an
idealized place and is marketed as a source of cultural identity
and heritage directed to African American audiences. For the
wider consuming public, the cloth may carry reverberations of
Africa as the "Dark Continent," dangerous and tribal, a conception based in the long history of Western dominance over and classification of
non-Western peoples. Still other evocations of mudcloth's distinctive appearance are
primarily aesthetic in nature, as, for example, when the cloth is adapted to fashion
and home decor without any overt reference to its African origins. Bogolan's varied
"personalities" in its U.S. incarnations represent a continuation of the cloth's biography, confirming on an international stage the extraordinary adaptability that has
made bogolan a prominent symbol of contemporary Malian culture.

In her investigation of the formation and articulation of ethnic identity, Anya Peterson Royce provides a useful framework within which to view bogolan's transformations, particularly as the cloth moves abroad. As previous chapters have elucidated,
bogolan's varied forms all revolve around the creation and re-creation of "traditional"
arts and cultural practices, whether for local or for foreign consumption. Recognizing
the limitations of "tradition" as a conceptual category, with its connotations of stasis
and conformity, Royce adopts the term *style* to encompass the change that is always a
part of tradition. As she notes, "Style assumes choice and allows for change. It is not
burdened with the cultural connotations that we unconsciously attach to the term

'tradition.'"[3] Bogolan's many manifestations in Mali and in the United States strategically maintain elements of the prototypically traditional bogolanfini of rural Mali. As one might expect, U.S. adaptations of bogolan are the aspects of the cloth's biography most distant from its origins. Entrepreneurs and designers who market their products in the United States incorporate aspects of the cloth's form and function to create "bogolan style," making reference to bogolan's role as an embodiment of "tradition" by creating new histories and new styles.

"Style" also encompasses the idea of "stylization," a variation on a form, embellishing or distilling a form to create something new. As Z. S. Strother notes, the term *style* has in the past been used in a pejorative sense with reference to African art, bearing connotations of "convention and simplification" that result from a "*lack of creative thought.*"[4] In combating this characterization, Strother illustrates the many ways in which the Pende masks that are her subject of study are in fact creative, sophisticated abstractions from reality. Though the goal here is not to draw a direct parallel between Pende masks and contemporary bogolan, the two subjects share a tendency to interpret stylization as simplification. Both tourist market bogolan in Mali and the United States might be readily dismissed as "simplifications," unworthy of attention in the same contexts as traditional bogolan. The cloth's U.S. incarnations, however, like tourist market bogolan, are often creative and strategic responses to the desires and expectations of new markets, while at the same time artists, designers, and merchants work to preserve crucial ties to the idea of tradition through stylization.

Tradition becomes, in Royce's formulation, a range of possibilities ("styles") rather than a single, definable construction. The importance, indeed the inevitability, of choice and of change is generally taken for granted in studies of modern Western art, fashion, and other forms of expressive culture. In Western cultures, "tradition" is primarily a starting point from which to measure distance from the past, a foil for stylistic, iconographical, and technical innovation, a model in which successive artistic styles mark the passage of time, from classicism to romanticism to impressionism, fauvism, surrealism, and so on. Popular conceptions of non-Western cultures and their arts have too often focused primarily on the "traditional," constructing an image of Africa as frozen in an eternal "tradition."

In one example of this all too prevalent attitude, in January 2000 *New York Times* reporter Norimitsu Onishi wrote about the effect of drought in several towns near Djenne. Here, the reporter asserts, the lack of written history indicates that the townspeople have little concept of the passage of time: "There are no written records in Gomitogo, or in its neighboring villages, Soa and Kossouma, so questions about the history of the villages merely draw stares. . . . For the chief of Kossouma, Djanguino Karankou, a cheerfully ebullient man . . . such questions about history are unimportant."[5] The town, "seemingly unchanged in centuries," apparently stands outside of time: "Even by the standards of Africa, arguably the continent least concerned with dates and time, the people in Koussouma showed little regard for such details."[6] Gomitogo, an ancient town a mere nine miles from Djenne, a city whose rich history as a trade entrepot and a center for Islamic learning is well known, may not have a written history, but if asked about his village's founding, Karankou likely would have provided detailed information. Far from frozen in time, the village has seen many changes.

Interestingly, as Onishi implies that these changes are less significant than those that occur in developed, "high-tech" countries, he goes on to state that the slow pace of life in Mali is exemplified by changes in cloth production: "Far from lands where changes are measured in faster Pentium chips, people here note that at some point in the 20th century the production and weaving of cotton was largely abandoned in favor of ready-made cloth bought in Djenne."[7] Cloth, as we have seen in the Bamana regions of Mali, south of Djenne, is deeply embedded in cultural practices; that the residents mark time by dramatic changes in their local industries and styles of attire should come as little surprise. In this example, an image of Mali as static, bound to its past, is produced for U.S. consumption. Many such conceptions are at work in the marketing of bogolan, or mudcloth, in the United States.

As designers, manufacturers, merchants, and consumers adopt, adjust, and transform bogolan to suit new markets in the United States, the cloth is stretched to the limits of its identity, the few traits that remain recognizable becoming the fixed core at the center of a whirlwind of stylistic change. The word *style* is particularly apt as bogolan moves into the U.S. market, for here the connection to specific aspects of "traditional" cultures, such as the use of the cloth by Bamana hunters, becomes increasingly vague. Unlike the vast stylistic variations on bogolan's form and medium created by Malian artists for Malian markets, the U.S. adaptations of the cloth often leave behind specific references to tradition in favor of vague "traditional styles." With the broadening of bogolan's referenciality from specific cultural practices to a generalized sense of the traditional or the African, the cloth's formal characteristics are broadened as well to include a wide range of styles, media, and techniques, each of which recounts a different aspect of bogolan's biography.

One style of bogolan that has not made the transition to the U.S. market is, not surprisingly, the fine art version of the cloth, the paintings made for the museum and gallery trade. In the United States, bogolan is marketed to suit Americans' taste for the "exotic" and "authentic" and to suit the desires of those African Americans who find in the cloth an expression of their heritage. Among these audiences, bogolan paintings do not meet consumer demands as readily as bogolan clothing and other products. As noted in earlier chapters, the artists working in the fine art realm strain against an international art market that seeks to place African artists in the realm of the "traditional," not recognizing their work in modern, global idioms. They face the same struggle in the U.S. art market, where consumers are generally not attracted to work that does not sufficiently resemble the bold, abstract patterns and handmade quality associated with "traditional" bogolan. In addition, as in Mali, the relatively high cost of paintings also limits their potential market in the United States.

Among all of the artists whose work is described under the rubric "fine art" bogolan, only the Groupe Bogolan Kasobane has shown their work in a solo exhibit in the United States. Although the venue was in New York, a city in which artists receive valuable exposure, the exhibition was somewhat outside the art world mainstream—in a gallery at Lincoln Center.[8] Nakunte Diarra's work, which more closely conforms to U.S. expectations of "traditional" African art, was exhibited at the Fashion Institute of Technology's museum in New York as well as other venues.[9] A more recent exhibition of bogolan, at the Fowler Museum of Cultural History in Los Angeles, also focused on the rural versions of the cloth.[10] The work of the Groupe Bogolan Kasobane and other artists making use of bogolan to create paintings has not yet found a niche in U.S. markets and museums.[11] Instead, bogolan in the United States generally appears in the form of T-shirts, home furnishings, wrapping paper, towels, paper cups, and luggage.

## CREATING AFRICAN STYLE

One incarnation of the bogolan sold in U.S. shops, catalogues, and other outlets caters to Western expectations and preconceptions of the African continent as tribal, preindustrial, primitive, and timeless. The advertisement for the "Jungle Fever" line of fabric from S. Harris & Company exemplifies this construction of bogolan as "primitive." Other advertisements extol the cloth's handmade, labor-intensive production, focusing on the uniqueness of each item and on the exotic locales from which the cloth originates. So singular is the technique that consumers receive reassurance from the knowledge that not even the clothing sizes of bogolan garments are uniform, a notion that would likely cause consumers chagrin if applied to other articles of clothing: "All items are handmade and no two are exactly alike. Slight variations in color, design, and size from the items pictured in this catalogue [including bogolan vests] are guaranteed and should be considered a part of the unique crafts of Africa."[12]

The emphasis on handmade production and singularity is vividly emphasized in another catalogue description, which asserts that the bogolan dress offered for sale is so distinctive, so local, that its production is limited not only to Mali but to a single village there. The erroneous reference to tree sap as one of the materials used to make mudcloth only adds to the aura of this "exotic" technique:

> The Malian edge of the Sahara. This village is its own planet with its own art and its own quiet. . . . They cut up empty flour sacks and paint them with a mixture of mud and tree sap, painting and washing and painting again. The mud in Mali has its own chestnut pigment; the sap fixes the color to the cloth. No other village has their technique.[13]

Another catalogue, for Turtlewear, features clothing designed for travel in rugged places and made of "authentic durable African cotton." The clothes are, in fact, made of factory-printed cloth designed to resemble bogolan's patterns (and which may or may not have been made in Africa). The names of the garments, which include "Sienna Baobab," "Timbuktu Skyline," and "Marabout,"[14] vaguely evoke West Africa without specifically associating the patterns with their Malian source. Similarly, Bloomingdale's line of bogolan-style bedding, "Sahara," is described with more than a tinge of exoticism: "A beguiling study in black and tan recalls the tribal beauty of Africa. Our Sahara duvet cover . . . creates a smooth, soft covering; add accents of midnight black and tan motifs, reminiscent of ancient drawings and symbols."[15]

An interior decoration magazine, *Southern Accents,* encourages readers to make use

Figure 27. Bogolan, Brooklyn, street banner. Brooklyn, New York, 2000. Photograph by Liz Brown.

*This street banner, one of many hung along this Brooklyn neighborhood's main thoroughfare, declares Bogolan "The Soul of the Brooklyn Renaissance."*

of African textiles, spelling out their appeal in an alliterative list: "Alluring, alien, and ancient, the complex nature of Africa's tribal textiles has long provided the art world with creative and artistic reference points."[16] Alien, ancient, and tribal, African textiles like bogolan may readily serve as the bearers of tradition for U.S. consumers eager for "authentic" and "traditional" items.

Even a company assembling bogolan products in the United States identifies itself with tradition by providing (erroneous) information on the cloth's production and by assuring consumers that even garments assembled domestically are pieced by "native" workers. Here, an essentialist tone is evident: "Authentic mud cloth vests. Very special natural hand-dyed cloth from Mali, Africa. The color that is painted onto the cloth comes from ground rock in the local area. Sewn in the U.S. by a native African woman, each is unique."[17] Allusions to bogolan's symbolic patterns abound as well, often in reference to cloth adorned with motifs unrelated to bogolanfini: "Women in Mali's Dogon tribe have long used the earthy symbols printed on our richly textured kola cloth vest as a form of communication."[18]

Occasionally, borrowed adaptations of bogolan that are aimed at mass markets provide essentially accurate information on the cloth and its production: "Designer Claude Montana borrowed from Mali the art of mudcloth to create Traces bedding. Naive, yet ultimately modern in spirit, the abstract pattern was originally made by decorating cloth with a special type of mud with bamboo and dried in the sun."[19] Peet's Coffee and Tea, a Berkeley-based company, uses bogolan patterns on its cups and bags, identifying the pattern on its bags as "bogolanfini," and noting that its source is Mali (Plate 23). The cloth's adaptation to a variety of products may, thus, broaden awareness of African and, more specifically, Malian arts and products sold in the United States.

Clearly, as is the case in its Malian markets, the information that accompanies bogolan—often the domain of the middleman or cultural broker—is as crucial as the cloth itself in determining what exactly consumers are buying. The same vest or towel may be purchased as a token of an "exotic" culture, as an example of the influence of a Malian art form, or as a statement about the consumer's personal identity and ethnic heritage.

### Bogolan as Ethnic Pride

Other outlets for the sale of bogolan emphasize African American cultural identity, making the wearing of the cloth a personal statement, identifying oneself with the cloth rather than consuming it as an aspect of "exotic" cultures. The power of the cloth's associative powers is perhaps most evident in this category of U.S. bogolan, for here the cloth is heralded as a positive symbol of contemporary identity rather than incorporated into a category of objects that betoken remote "traditional" cultures.

Perhaps the most dramatic example of bogolan's role as an expression of African American culture is not, however, to be found as a garment or a set of sheets but something much larger: a neighborhood. In an act of community self-affirmation, a Brooklyn neighborhood formerly called Fort Greene renamed itself in the late 1990s. The largely African American neighborhood is now called Bogolan.[20] On Fulton Street, banners adorned with bogolan patterns hang from lampposts, declaring the neighborhood's ethnic identity (Figure 27). "Bogolan" likely would not have been selected as the emblem of the neighborhood's identity were it not for the plethora of bogolan-based products marketed to African Americans equating the cloth with African heritage. Bogolan's vivid patterns are immediately recognizable and readily reproduced in a range of media, making bogolan both practical and effective as a cultural symbol.

In the mid-1990s, *Ebony* magazine, in cooperation with the Spiegel clothing company, created "E-Style," a mail-order catalogue aimed at African American audiences. An early catalogue features a bogolan and *kente* cloth jacket and encourages readers, "Show your pride in this patchwork cardigan made of authentic African mud cloth, Kente cloth and printed silk" (Figure 28).[21] The second textile featured in this garment, kente cloth, has entered American markets in a manner much like bogolan. Both are frequently presented as markers of African and African American identity.[22] In their varied forms, the two textiles often appear in the same contexts, communicating the same pride in African heritage. Both also serve in their places of origin as symbols of local identity; like bogolan in Mali, kente cloth in Ghana has come to serve as a symbol of Ghanaian and Ashanti identity.[23] Only bogolan, however, has been adapted to the fine art market in its place of origin. Because it is, unlike kente cloth, a dyeing rather than a weaving technique, bogolan is more readily adapted to an immense range of iconographic and stylistic expressions. In the United States, however, the two are often conflated into a single African symbol, as in the "E-Style" jacket.

McCall's, a major producer of clothing patterns, used bogolan and kente as sample fabrics for its 1995 "Afrocentric Extras" line of hats, shawls, belts, and headties (Figure 29). J. C. Penney collaborated with Harlem Textile Works, a community-based company in New York City that trains teenagers in textile design and production, to create its "African Origins" series of products. These included a 1994 bed linen called "Mud Cloth," part of the African American–oriented catalogue's effort to give consumers opportunities to purchase products "inspired by your proud heritage."[24] Kerris Wolsky, one of the founders of Harlem Textile Works, revealed that bogolan was the most popular

Figure 28. "E-Style" catalogue advertisement for its Africa Jacket, 1994.

*Combining the two most popular African textiles in the U.S. market, this garment of bogolan and kente cloth is sold as an emblem of African American identity.*

motif in the group's design repertoire that year, favored for its adaptability to a variety of products and for the graphic strength of its patterns.[25] The Ashanti company, named for the Ashanti kingdom and ethnic group of West Africa, used a bogolan design that could have been taken directly from the pagne in Plate 1 to create a paper gift bag, reproducing even the slightly fuzzy edges of the cloth's patterns (Figure 26). The bag's pattern is, like the J. C. Penney sheets, called "Mudcloth."

Clothing companies also declare their African-centered identities by offering bogolan-based products from catalogues with names that imply their identification with Africa as a source of cultural identity, such as "Homeland Authentics" and "NU NUBIAN." Here, bogolan vests, hats, bags, ties, jogging suits, children's clothing, pillows, tissue box covers, and myriad other products are offered to Americans seeking to give their homes and their wardrobes a sense of cultural identity. Identified variously as African, West African, and Malian (and even Ivorian), bogolan patterns are used to create connections with African heritage.

The generalization of bogolan's identity—from Bamana to Malian, and from Malian to African—produces a blurred view of the African continent. Though glorified as an aspect of personal heritage, this generalized version of bogolan is often little closer to "authentic" bogolan than the "tribal" adaptations discussed above. Nii Quarcoopome notes this lack of specificity in his discussion of kente cloth's popularity in the United States, though his statement is equally applicable to bogolan:

> Kente's popularity as a symbol bespeaks a monolithic view of African culture, not unlike the idea of Black communal identity. Kente and other cultural tokens have come to broadly symbolize Africa, the Motherland. When coupled with buzz words like *rich, cultural, heritage, roots,* and *pride,* kente becomes a potent expression of Afrocentrism. Such a presentation does little to demonstrate the diversity in ethnic groups, colors, languages, and cultures that exist on the continent today.[26]

Figure 29.
"Afrocentric Extras," McCall's Fashion Accessories, pattern no. 218.

Using bogolan to model their Afrocentric line of hats, wraps, and scarves, McCall's clearly draws a connection between the cloth and African American heritage.

The broadening and generalization of bogolan's cultural referents may well be an inevitable part of its long journey; its ties to villages in Mali are increasingly blurred when those villages are viewed from a greater and greater distance. Such generalization occurs, of course, as objects and ideas travel, becoming less specific in their referents as they move. Bogolan's particular fascination, however, is in its adoption by new audiences as an emblem of their own personal identity.

### Bogolan as International Style

Many adaptations of bogolan's style are not accompanied by any information about its roots, Malian, African, or otherwise. In these instances, it is not the cloth itself but rather its characteristic patterns and colors that are adapted to new products, a continuation of bogolan's diverse biography. In these adaptations, bogolan becomes pure style, unattached to specific referents. A bogolan-style shirt from Banana Republic, for example, clearly

reproduces the kalaka sen bogolanfini motif without acknowledging its source (Figure 30). The cloth in this context becomes a part of the palette of designers seeking new inspiration, not unlike Chris Seydou's interest in the "graphic quality" of bogolan. Seydou, however, was committed to retaining the patterns' association with bogolan's Malian contexts. When bogolan's patterns appear on garments and other products made for sale in the United States without any acknowledgment (whether accurate or inaccurate) of their origins, they become part of a "generic vocabulary of chic," a phrase coined in a globally oriented issue of the *New York Times' Fashions of the Times*. Style editor Amy M. Spindler describes the motivation for the international focus:

> [T]his issue is dedicated to the epic odyssey that is every person's life today. Our odyssey in creating the issue lay in finding stories that still rang with the exoticism of the new. . . . Much of what designers are showing [today] is a generic vocabulary of chic, the fashion equivalent of architecture's International Style.[27]

"International Style" has, one might assert, long been a tenet of U.S. culture, making every part of the world a part of the global marketplace, making the non-local into the generically chic—from bogolan to "tribal" tattoos. In the same issue of *Fashions of the Times,* a spread on the home of artists Helen and Brice Marden sums up the celebration of the global reach of American chic: "When worlds collide: A chair by Jean Prouvé stands next to an African monkey figure [a Baule *gbekre* figure]. A four-panel painting by Helen Marden hangs above a mid-ninth-century temple frieze from Java. A painting by Richard Tuttle hangs under a Tantric painting."[28] Borrowing and adapting, drawing on the entire world, the aesthetic of global or international style does not require that cultural context travel with objects. In an issue of *Metropolitan Home,* for example, the Scandinavian-style home of a San Francisco couple who admire Mediterranean decor features a sparely furnished bedroom whose primary visual interest is a bogolan bedspread, identified as "African bark-cloth."[29] This blending of influences—Scandinavian style, Mediterranean style, and African style—requires little specificity. The styles may evoke tradition, which is part of their appeal, without being accompanied by any specific cultural context.

Figure 30. Banana Republic shirt with the kalaka sen motif, ca. 1992. Photograph by Ecco Wang Hart. Courtesy of Barbara Frank.

Bogolan's varied forms and its presence in the U.S. market point to the cloth's versatility and the strength of its formal properties to retain their distinctive appearance even when stretched into diverse media and forms. These characteristics lend bogolan the ability to serve, just as it does in Bamako, as a signifier of diverse identities. Although in some contexts bogolan is sold as an icon of African American cultural heritage, in others the cloth is presented as broadly "ethnic." The generalization of bogolan's connotations as the cloth progresses from specific Bamana ethnic identity to Malian nationality to African American cultural identity to vaguely "ethnic" is all part of its distinctive biography. Though its identity grows blurred at its outermost extremes, bogolan still remains recognizable.

# I O

## CONCLUSION

## Making the Traditional Modern

B ogolan's widely varied biography demonstrates that locally based, handwo-ven and dyed cloth can coexist and even prosper alongside textiles produced by factories and cloth and garments imported from abroad. Not only have Malians sustained old demands and developed new markets for bogolan, as Dale Idiens prescribes, but demand outside Mali has also created new audiences for artists and merchants. In a 1991 United Nations report on the economic poten-tial of West African textile industries, Felicia Johansen focuses her attention on bogolan, specifically noting the cloth's promise both as an export product and as a luxury good.

The recent explosion of interest in and production of bogolan reveals the ways in which a multilayered artistic movement may reflect and take part in po-litical, economic, educational, and broadly cultural shifts in a major urban cen-ter. Indeed, bogolan's changing styles, media, production patterns, techniques, and markets have led this investigation through the complexities of contempo-rary Bamako, a city in which "tradition" and "modernity" coexist, meld, and produce new forms. Implicit in the analysis of bogolan's multiple forms and sig-nifications is an acknowledgment of the active role of African artists, merchants, and consumers in the creation and manipulation of traditions. The Malians who make and market bogolan in all of its forms are skilled in the selection and the modification of specific stylistic and contextual features of the cloth to appeal to preexisting notions of traditional Malian culture. The distinctive colors of bo-golan's mineral and vegetal pigments, the strip-woven cotton cloth, and the in-corporation of geometric designs (whether alone or in combination with figura-tive elements) are retained in nearly all of bogolan's incarnations. Even when one element is discarded, as in the case of factory-printed bogolan cloth, links to the cloth's "traditional" forms may be retained through accompanying contextual in-formation provided by merchants, designers, and artists.

Occasionally, the transformation of bogolan becomes evident in striking en-counters between diverse aspects of the cloth's revival. At the festivities surround-ing a 1993 opening at the Musée National du Mali, for example, bogolan ap-peared in two very distinct and, for the purposes of this study, revelatory forms. On a platform at the center of the museum's outdoor courtyard, a folkloric dance ensemble provided entertainment for those attending the opening (Figure 31). The troupe, which performed routines based on Bamana and Dogon dances,

Traditional African textiles reveal the remarkable quality and versatility that can be achieved by a simple craft technology, but unfortunately it appears that this tra-dition is soon destined to become a part of Africa's past....Today there are cotton mills and weaving factories in Africa built with the help of European technology, and as their production develops hand weaving will dwindle further, unless Africans themselves can maintain a demand.
*Dale Idiens, "An Introduction to Traditional African Weaving and Textiles"*

Mud cloth, unique to Mali, is successfully exported as pagnes to the United States and France. Courtiers and interior designers transform the cloth into exclusive finished products, and the pagnes are very popular in stores featuring high quality international crafts.
*Felicia Johansen, Opportunity Study for the Development of the African Textile Industry*

Figure 31. Malian
dancers performing at
the Musée National du
Mali. Bamako, 1993.

*This folkloric troupe
wears bogolan costumes
as they perform tradi-
tional Malian dances.*

wore costumes made of bogolan; the female dancers wore bogolan pagnes wrapped around their waists, while male dancers wore loose, knee-length drawstring pants made of the cloth. Meanwhile, a European woman, likely a visitor to Mali, stood in the audience wearing a tailored jacket also made of bogolan.

In this moment, a public spectacle celebrating local Malian culture, bo-golan's rich biography is vividly illus-trated: On stage, bogolan appears as one element in the creation of a "tra-ditional" performance, underscoring the folkloric character of the dances. The cloth and the clothing styles have been self-consciously selected by the troupe's organizers, for such garments would not be worn in any ordinary, quotidian context, indicating the organizers' recognition of bogolan's effectiveness as an evocation of Malian traditions. Simultaneously, bogolan appears in the audience as fashionable at-tire rather than as costume, cut and tailored to be worn along with jeans, shorts, skirts, and the like. Wearing a bogolan jacket would be equally appropriate in a non-Malian setting, in Europe or the United States, for example, where the cloth likely would not be identified as specifically Malian or African. At the museum opening, bogolan served a distinctly modern function, part of the construction of traditional culture in an urban, international setting where it contributes to the "authentic" ex-perience of audience members, and where non-Malian spectators may themselves partake of the "authenticity" created around them.[1]

During a visit to the bustling Marché Medine, I observed another encounter be-tween various aspects of bogolan's "biography." I was visiting the stall of bogolan pro-ducer Alou Traoré while accompanied by a French friend and a long-time Bamako res-ident, who wore a boubou created by Traoré; the boubou was adorned with a silhouette of a masked dancer. We stood in front of the hanging boubous and pagnes, all stenciled in bogolan pigments with a variety of patterns and motifs (see Plate 6). Nearby, looking at Traoré's display, and at the Frenchman wearing a bogolan boubou, stood a Malian man clad in a bogolan-dyed hunter's shirt, clearly a hunter visiting Ba-mako (Plate 24). The juxtaposition of the two forms of bogolan created in an instant a dramatic illustration of bogolan's wide-ranging significance in Bamako. The cloth ex-ists simultaneously as Alou Traoré's intricate, decorative stenciled pagnes and boubous and as the hunter's camouflage-style bogolan tunic. The former is a recent adaptation of the technique by a young, urban artist offered for sale to Malians and foreigners alike, while the latter is a distinctly rural garment believed to possess protective powers and made for use by members of an exclusive Bamana occupational group.[2]

Bogolan's malleability and the strength of its associative powers was vividly demonstrated at the museum opening and in the Marché Medine. In its many forms, bogolan reverberates through a wide range of markets, styles, media, and symbolic connotations as it is adapted to Bamako's urban environments. This study has explicated bogolan's changing forms, use patterns, markets, and production techniques, which together create an environment in which distinct forms of the cloth coexist and occasionally interact.

As bogolan has been adapted to non-Malian markets, the same juxtapositions between distinct phases of the cloth's biography may occur. An exhibition I curated, *Renewing Tradition: The Revitalization of Bogolan in Mali and Abroad,* was presented at the University of Iowa Museum of Art from March through June 2000.[3] I had arranged for four bogolan artists to appear at the museum, where they would present bogolan demonstrations and offer goods for sale at the museum's shop. The visit by these artists, who included Klétigui Dembélé of the Groupe Bogolan Kasobane and Lalla Tangara Touré, the bogolan entrepreneur,[4] occasioned numerous revealing cross-cultural encounters. More than one visitor to their demonstrations at the museum and at area high schools expressed surprise that the artists wore jeans and, in the case of two younger artists, T-shirts and sneakers, clearly expecting that they would dress in distinctly "African" attire. The artists, in turn, were amazed by the Americans' expectations. Some visitors to the museum's shop expressed surprise at the "modern" style of the bogolan scarves sold there that were made by members of Touré's bogolan-making cooperative, Segui-So. The artists, through presentations and discussions with the public, directly addressed these and other preconceptions about Africa and African art, using bogolan to illustrate the vitality of Mali's contemporary cultures.

For their part, the artists were bemused by the section of my exhibition devoted to the varieties of bogolan sold in the U.S. market, including pieces of luggage, coffee cups, towels, and garments adorned with bogolan-style patterns. They commented on the meaning of the patterns that they could decipher, interested to note which motifs seemed to "speak" to U.S. audiences. The fact that these artists traveled with their work, giving them the all-too-rare opportunity to experience their medium's, or, in the case of Dembélé, their work's reception in the United States, provided the artists with insight into the appeal of an indigenous Malian art form for distant audiences. For me, the experience was equally revelatory, bringing full-circle my investigation of bogolan's multiple constructions of tradition and modernity in Mali and in the United States.

The subjects addressed here have included the production and marketing of tourist art, classifications of contemporary arts in Africa, the economic shifts that accompany political change, art education, and changing gender roles in artistic production. Underlying all of these topics is a single conceptual issue—the negotiation and renegotiation of a society's conception of its own traditions, both for internal and external audiences. All of bogolan's many manifestations operate simultaneously as signifiers of Malian tradition—from inexpensive souvenirs to highbrow fine art, from garments worn as costumes to those worn as fashionable attire—no single manifestation compromising the efficacy of the others.

Bogolan is particularly well suited to a wide range of formal adaptations, because the cloth may be defined by both its medium and by its iconography. Any textile that is adorned with patterns that reproduce or resemble bogolanfini motifs, whether locally woven cotton or factory-printed rayon, carries bogolan's many connotations. Similarly, any surface adorned with bogolan's characteristic pigments, whether depicting ci wara figures, Dogon dancers, or elaborate abstractions applied with an aerosol applicator, is a part of the traditions with which bogolan is associated. Further still, bogolan possesses the malleability, literally as well as metaphorically, that characterizes textiles. It can be folded, stacked, stretched to create a canvas, cut and tailored to create traditional garments or haute couture fashions, and adorned with patterns and figurative depictions as wide ranging as an artist's imagination. One can scarcely imagine another medium so ideally suited to the circumstances of urban Mali, where local traditions are celebrated even as modernity and international cultural influences are adapted and adjusted to suit local tastes and desires.

This study offers but one indication of the rich potential of art historical research to elucidate broad social themes in the complex environment of contemporary Africa and its diaspora, in which global cultural influences are as much a part of daily life as local, indigenous practices. Adaptability and variation have characterized African arts for centuries, and studies of contemporary movements offer an opportunity to document political, economic, and broadly cultural changes as they occur alongside stylistic changes. In Bamako today, bogolan has inspired an astounding number of artists and designers while offering valuable insight into the complexity of contemporary Mali's relationship with its "traditional" past, reworking symbols of that past to serve as tourist market commodities, as fine art, and as fashion.

Figure 32. *Iowa,* by Klétigui Dembélé, 2000. 36.5″ × 23.5″ (93 × 60 cm). Collection of the University of Iowa Museum of Art.

I close with a recent work of art by a leading bogolan artist that embodies the versatility, creativity, and receptivity of the artists who have adapted bogolan to a wide array of markets and meanings in contemporary Mali. After his sojourn in Iowa City for the opening of *Renewing Tradition,* Klétigui Dembélé sent the University of Iowa Museum of Art a bogolan painting inspired by his visit (Figure 32). The painting condenses many of his impressions of the place, weaving together rolling farm fields with the major agricultural icons of the region, pigs and corn. Through Dembélé's artistic vision, Iowa becomes a symbol for fertility and plenty, succinctly communicated in bogolan's rich browns and tans, made of the very earth that sustains fields of millet in Mali and rows of corn in Iowa. Once again, the medium proves itself to be, in the hands of talented artists and designers, a rich amalgamation of the "traditional" and the "modern," providing a tool for the expression of the relevance each holds for the other.

# NOTES ▨

## I. INTRODUCTION: BOGOLAN'S BIOGRAPHY

*All interviews were conducted in Bamako unless otherwise noted.*

1. The word *bogolan* has numerous alternate spellings, including *bógólan* and *bOgOlan,* the former borrowing accents from French, the latter based in an alphabet created by the Malian members of the Club Amadou Hampate Bâ (named after a renowned Malian author). Because all of the variants are approximations of a word in the Bamanakan, or Bamana, language, I have used the spelling closest to English standards for stylistic reasons. My thanks to Ibrahim Iba N'Diaye for information on the Club Amadou Hampate Bâ alphabet.

2. Alternatively, this group may be identified as Bambara. Following most current usage, I have here adopted the spelling "Bamana."

3. Pascal James Imperato and Marli Shamir, "Bokolanfini: Mud Cloth of the Bamana of Mali," *African Arts* 3, no. 4 (Summer 1970): 41.

4. Here the term *traditional*'s common associations are called into question, signaling that the word's meanings will be reshaped in response to the realities of twenty-first-century urban life in Africa and elsewhere.

5. Henry Drewal, "Contested Realities: Inventions of Art and Authenticity," *African Arts* 25, no. 4 (October 1992): 24.

6. Igor Kopytoff, "The Cultural Biography of Things: Commodification as Process," in *The Social Life of Things: Commodities in Cultural Perspective,* ed. Arjun Appadurai (New York: Cambridge University Press, 1986), 68.

7. Ibid., 68.

8. Ibid., 64.

9. June Spector of Spector Travel in Barbara Murray, "Tumultuous Past Lives: Black and White Americans Visit Places with Ties to Slavery," *National Geographic Traveler,* January–February 2000, 22.

10. Franz de Zeltner, "Tissus Africains à Dessins Réservés ou Décolorés," *Bulletin et Mémoires: Société Anthropologie de Paris,* ser. 16, 1 (1910). See page 8.

11. James Clifford, "The Others: Beyond the Salvage Paradigm," *Third Text,* no. 6 (Spring 1989): 74.

12. These include, along with Clifford, Sally Price, *Primitive Art in Civilized Places* (Chicago: University of Chicago Press, 1989); Christopher B. Steiner, *African Art in Transit* (New York: Cambridge University Press, 1994); Kwame Anthony Appiah, "The Postcolonial and the Postmodern," in *In My Father's House: Africa in the Philosophy of Culture* (New York: Oxford University Press, 1992); and several essays in George E. Marcus and Fred R. Myers, eds., *The Traffic in Culture: Refiguring Art and Anthropology* (Berkeley: University of California Press, 1995), and Ruth B. Phillips and Christopher B. Steiner, eds., *Unpacking Culture: Art and Commodity in Colonial and Postcolonial Worlds* (Berkeley: University of California Press, 1999).

13. John Picton, "In Vogue or the Flavour of the Month: The New Way to Wear Black," *Third Text,* no. 23 (Summer 1993): 92.

14. David Koloane, "The Identity Question: Focus on Black South African Expression," *Third Text,* no. 23 (Summer 1993): 102.

15. Janet Wolff, *The Social Production of Art* (New York: New York University Press, 1984), 94.

16. Marvin Cohodas, "Elizabeth Hickox and Karuk Basketry: A Case Study in Debates on Innovation and Paradigms of Authenticity," in *Unpacking Culture: Art and Commodity in*

*Colonial and Postcolonial Worlds,* ed. Ruth B. Phillips and Christopher B. Steiner (Berkeley: University of California Press, 1999), 146.

17. Ibid., 149.

18. Estimates of the dead range from one hundred to several hundred.

19. Years into its new national experiment, Mali received attention from unexpected quarters, including a 1996 *New York Times* editorial that pointedly notes, "Mali has moved without fanfare from 35 years of single-party rule and 23 years of military dictatorship to a multi-party democracy. This feat might be better known if a single high-level American official had troubled in recent years to visit Bamako, Mali's capital." "Democracy in Mali," *New York Times,* April 29, 1996, A26.

20. The archives include those of the Institut des Sciences Humaines, the Bibliothèque Nationale, and the Institut National des Arts, all located in Bamako.

21. There are references to bogolanfini that predate de Zeltner's article, but they are merely mentions of the cloth amid lists of other aspects of Bamana material culture.

22. De Zeltner, "Tissus Africains," 225.

23. Introduction in Henri Clouzot, *Tissus Nègres* (Paris: A. Calavas, [1920–25?]).

24. "Participation du Soudan au Salon de la France d'Outre Mer, 1940," doc. IQ-1329, Archives Nationales, Bamako.

25. "Exposition Coloniale Internationale de Paris, 1937–1940," dossier 1, doc. IQ-1750, Archives Nationales, Bamako.

26. For these earlier, published descriptions of bogolan's production and use based on original research, see Imperato and Shamir, "Bokolanfini"; John B. Donne, "Bogolanfini: A Mud-Painted Cloth from Mali," *Man* 8, no. 1 (March 1973): 104–7; Patrick R. McNaughton, "The Shirts That Mande Hunters Wear," *African Arts* 15, no. 3 (May 1982): 54–58, 91; Sarah Brett-Smith, "Speech Made Visible: The Irregular as a System of Meaning," *Empirical Studies of the Arts* 2, no. 2 (1984): 127; eadem, "Symbolic Blood: Cloths for Excised Women," *RES* 3 (1982): 15–31. More recently, see Tavy Aherne, *Nakunte Diarra: A Bógólanfini Artist of the Beledougou* (Bloomington: Indiana University Art Museum, 1992); Pauline Duponchel, "Formes, Fonctions et Significations des Textiles Traditionnels de Coton Tissés et Teints du Mali" (mémoire de DEA, Université de Paris I–Pantheon-Sorbonne, 1990); eadem, *Du Bogolan Traditionnel au Bogolan Contemporain*

(Bamako: Centre Culturel Français, 1995); eadem, *Textile de Coton—Bogolan du Mali* (Paris: Ecole Practique des Hautes Etudes, Section des Sciences Religieuse, 1997); and Toma Muteba Luntumbue, *Bogolan: Un Art Textile du Mali* (Brussels: Editions les Alizés, 1998).

27. Like many other large cities without extensive infrastructure, Bamako's city limits sprawl into settlements that resemble conglomerates of villages, mud brick structures often built by their owners without electricity or a water supply. The municipal government is increasingly working to document these new, ever-growing areas where residents are reluctant to declare their presence for fear of unwelcome visits by tax collectors.

28. *Post Report: Mali* (Washington, D.C.: U.S. Department of State, 1992), 1.

29. *Country Profile: Côte d'Ivoire and Mali* (London: Economist Intelligence Unit, 1994), 38.

30. Pascal James Imperato, *Mali: A Search for Direction* (Boulder: Westview Press, 1989), 8.

31. Claude Meillassoux, *Urbanization of an African Community: Voluntary Associations in Bamako* (Seattle: University of Washington Press, 1968), 8.

32. Arjun Appadurai, *Modernity at Large: Cultural Dimensions of Globalization* (Minneapolis: University of Minnesota Press, 1996); Kwame Anthony Appiah and Henry Louis Gates Jr., *Dictionary of Global Culture* (New York: Knopf, 1997); Homi K. Bhaba, *The Location of Culture* (London: Routledge, 1994); Jon Bird et al., eds., *Mapping the Future: Local Cultures, Global Change* (New York: Routledge, 1993); Frederick Buell, *National Cultures and the New Global System* (Baltimore: Johns Hopkins University Press, 1994); David Morley and Kevin Robins, *Spaces of Identity: Global Media, Electronic Landscapes and Cultural Landscapes* (New York: Routledge, 1995); Saskia Sassen, *Globalization and Its Discontents* (New York: New Press, 1998).

33. All of these identities are subject to much negotiation.

34. B. Marie Perinbam, *Family Identity and the State in the Bamako Kafu, c. 1800–c. 1900* (Boulder: Westview Press, 1997), 110–12.

35. Esther Pasztory, "Identity and Difference: The Uses and Meanings of Ethnic Styles," *Studies in the History of Art* 27 (1989): 35.

36. John Tomlinson, *Cultural Imperialism* (Baltimore: Johns Hopkins University Press, 1991), 69.

37. Eric Hobsbawm and Terence Ranger, eds., *The Invention of Tradition* (New York: Cambridge University Press, 1983).

38. Aherne, *Nakunte Diarra*, 15.

39. Djenne-Jenno ("Old Djenne") is one of West Africa's most important archaeological sites, located near Djenne, or Jenne, a city on the Niger River north of Bamako. The terra-cotta sculptures from Djenne-Jenno and surrounding sites date from the twelfth to the fifteenth century and are among the most coveted types of African sculpture in the West. The Malian government's efforts to safeguard the sculptures, which have been pillaged from their sites and illegally exported, led to groundbreaking U.S. emergency import restrictions in 1993.

## 2. THE RURAL ROOTS OF BOGOLAN

1. Kandiora Coulibaly, interview, February 6, 2000.

2. Sarah Brett-Smith, personal communication, September 9, 2000. Brett-Smith notes that the cloth was displayed in the 1900 Exposition Universelle.

3. Pauline Duponchel, *Textile de Coton—Bogolan du Mali* (Paris: Ecole Practique des Hautes Etudes, Section des Sciences Religieuse, 1997), 94.

4. Sarah Brett-Smith, "Symbolic Blood: Cloths for Excised Women," *RES* 3 (1982): 16.

5. Brett-Smith, personal communication, September 9, 2000. The cloths are in the collections of the Museum für Völkerkunde in Basel and the Museum für Völkerkunde in Berlin.

6. According to Pascal James Imperato and Marli Shamir, who recorded bogolanfini production over the course of 1966 to 1970, "While the technique for making this cloth is known throughout the Bamana country, it is popularly recognized that the center for its production is the Beledougou area which lies to the north and northeast of Mali's capital, Bamako." Pascal James Imperato and Marli Shamir, "Bokolanfini: Mud Cloth of the Bamana of Mali," *African Arts* 3, no. 4 (Summer 1970): 32.

7. The Beledougou region is particularly known for its history of animism and resistance to Islam, but today many of the region's residents would likely identify themselves as Muslims even as they retain many beliefs and practices rooted in pre-Islamic religions.

8. Sarah Brett-Smith, *Bamana Mudcloths: A Female Language of Power* (forthcoming). In "Symbolic Blood," 15, Brett-Smith illustrates cloths that are classified as red—basaie and *n'gale*—adorned with stripes that differentiate them from white bogolan.

9. Tavy Aherne, *Nakunte Diarra: A Bógólanfini Artist of the Beledougou* (Bloomington: Indiana University Art Museum, 1992), 4.

10. Strip weaving is typical of many West African regions, its design potential epitomized by *kente* and related styles of cloth made by Akan and Ewe weavers in Ghana and Côte d'Ivoire. Here, too, the looms on which strip cloth is woven, horizontal in orientation, are used almost exclusively by men.

11. Both tafé/taafé and pagnes refer to a rectangular, wrap-sized piece of fabric, approximately 40 in. × 60 in. (1 × 1.5 m). *Pagne,* used in many parts of Francophone West Africa, is the term more commonly used in Bamako.

12. Julianne Freeman, "Muso Korobaya: Practice, Embodiment, Transition, and Agency in the Lives of Senior Bamana Women of Mali" (Ph.D. diss., Indiana University, 1996), 205.

13. Brett-Smith, personal communication, September 9, 2000.

14. Claire Polakoff, *Into Indigo: African Textiles and Dyeing Techniques* (Garden City, N.Y.: Anchor Books, 1980), 130.

15. Adire is a Yoruba indigo-dyed textile made using cassava paste as a resist.

16. I first met Diarra during a trip to Kolokani in February 1993. I next saw her a year later in a very different setting—Cleveland, Ohio. She was visiting the United States during an exhibition of her work (curated by Tavy Aherne) at Cleveland State University. These dramatically divergent locales encapsulate the breadth of Diarra's career—from Kolokani to Cleveland, essentially bypassing the markets of Bamako with the help of her European and American clientele. For the exhibition catalogue, see Aherne, *Nakunte Diarra*.

17. Significantly, Aherne's exhibition and catalogue sparked an exchange in the pages of *African Arts* that centered on the important role of innovation among bogolanfini artists in the ostensibly traditional—in the eyes of both residents and observers—region of Beledougou. In her discussion of large *tapis* (literally, "rug") bogolanfini made by Nakunte Diarra and other women in Kolokani, Aherne cites Diarra's explanation that in the early 1980s, a Western researcher, Sarah Brett-Smith, began commissioning women to make these big cloths; they were as large as 75 in. × 70 in.

(187 × 162 cm) (Aherne, *Nakunte Diarra,* 15).
In his review of the exhibition and catalogue,
Pascal James Imperato notes that, in fact, he
and Marli Shamir had illustrated a tapis in
their 1970 *African Arts* article on the cloth,
asserting that artists in the region had been
making tapis since the 1960s (Imperato and
Shamir, "Bokolanfini," and Pascal James
Imperato, review of *Nakunte Diarra: A
Bógólanfini Artist of the Beledougou,* by Tavy
Aherne, *African Arts* 27, no. 2 [April 1994]:
79). Innovation, clearly, is not a recent
phenomenon in the Beledougou. In a
subsequent letter to the editor, Brett-Smith
contributed another story of innovation,
concerning the distinctive composition of
some tapis in which the surface of the cloth is
divided into four quadrants, each adorned
with a different motif. This she traces to a
specific event in 1984, when Fatmata Traoré, a
bogolanfini artist in Kolokani, was inspired by
a providential gift of food in the midst of a
famine to create a particularly innovative
cloth. Traoré presented the cloth to Brett-
Smith's supervisor, who accompanied Brett-
Smith on a relief mission by the U.S. Agency
for International Development during which
they brought the Traoré family much-needed
rice (Sarah Brett-Smith, "On the Origin of a
New *Tapis* Mud-Cloth Design," *African Arts*
27, no. 4 [Autumn 1994]: 16–17, 90). Brett-
Smith speculates that other artists in Kolokani
(including Diarra) admired Traoré's work and
later adapted the style. Although the
dynamism of tradition is epitomized by
bogolan's urban transformations, artists in
Kolokani and other rural towns innovate with
more subtlety than in Bamako but with no less
creativity.

18. Aherne identifies these leaves as *cengura* in
*Nakunte Diarra.* "Cengura" is likely an
alternate spelling for "n'tjankara." Brett-Smith,
personal communication, September 9, 2000.
Aherne notes that Diarra uses a variety of
leaves, separately or in combination, including
n'gallama and, more frequently, cengura.
Eadem, personal communication, September
5, 2000.

19. Alou Traoré, interview, February 1, 2000.

20. The five sections are detailed in *Bogolan et Arts
Graphiques du Mali* (Paris: ADEIAO and Musée
des Arts Africains et Océaniens, 1990) and
Duponchel, *Textile de Coton.* ADEIAO is the
Association Pour le Développement des
Echanges Interculturel au Musée des Arts
Africains et Océaniens.

21. Aherne, *Nakunte Diarra,* 12.

22. Imperato and Shamir, "Bokolanfini," 38.

23. Freeman, "Muso Korobaya," 168.

24. John B. Donne, "Bogolanfini: A Mud-Painted
Cloth from Mali," *Man* 8, no. 1 (March 1973):
105.

25. Aherne, *Nakunte Diarra,* 9.

26. Imperato and Shamir, "Bokolanfini," 39.

27. Brett-Smith, personal communication,
September 9, 2000.

28. Imperato and Shamir, "Bokolanfini," 39–40.

29. Brett-Smith, "Speech Made Visible: The
Irregular as a System of Meaning," *Empirical
Studies of the Arts* 2, no. 2 (1984).

30. Imperato and Shamir, "Bokolanfini," 37.

31. Brett-Smith, "Speech Made Visible," 128.

32. See Chapters 5 and 6.

33. Brett-Smith, "Speech Made Visible," 142.

34. Ibid. Brett-Smith further notes that sajume
kama is often paired with *dabi kams,* its
negative counterpart pattern. The latter
pattern also refers to a bird, the standard
nightjar, which is associated with sorcery.
Personal communication, September 9, 2000.

35. I am grateful to Klétigui Dembélé for his
exegesis of the motifs. In my description of the
motifs' meanings, I have also made use of
Duponchel, *Textile de Coton;* Aherne, *Nakunte
Diarra;* and Imperato and Shamir,
"Bokolanfini."

36. Lalla Tangara Touré, personal communication,
February 9, 2000.

37. *Bogolan et Arts Graphiques,* 34–35.

38. This function's urban, international manifestations are discussed in Chapters 7 and 8.

39. Brett-Smith, "Symbolic Blood."

40. Heidi Jones et al., "Female Genital Cutting
Practices in Burkina Faso and Mali and Their
Negative Health Outcomes," *Studies in Family
Planning* 30, no. 3 (September 1999): 219–30.
The authors note that "Mali has declared the
elimination of FGC [female genital cutting] a
priority as part of a strategy for increasing
women's empowerment" (p. 220). In another
contribution to the study of excision in Mali,
Claudie Gosselin found that 96 percent of the
223 Malian women she interviewed were
excised. Claudie Gosselin, "Handing Over the
Knife: *Numu* Women and the Campaign
against Excision in Mali," in *Female
"Circumcision" in Africa: Culture, Controversy,
and Change,* ed. Bettina Shell-Duncan and
Ylva Hernlund (Boulder: Lynne Rienner
Publishers, 2000), 193–214.

41. Brett-Smith, "Symbolic Blood," 25.

42. McNaughton defines *nyama* as "the world's
basic energy, the energy that animates the
universe." Patrick R. McNaughton, *The*

*Mande Blacksmiths: Knowledge, Power, and Art in West Africa* (Bloomington: Indiana University Press, 1988), 15.

43. Brett-Smith, "Symbolic Blood," 27.

44. Patrick R. McNaughton, "The Shirts That Mande Hunters Wear," *African Arts* 15, no. 3 (May 1982): 54.

45. Ibid., 56.

46. Freeman, "Muso Korobaya," 170.

47. Ibid.

48. Ibid., 170–71.

## 3.THE TOURIST ART MARKET: COMMERCE IN AUTHENTICITY

1. The Grand Marché is also known as the Marché Rose ("Pink Market"), a reference to the color of its main building.

2. See Chapter 6.

3. Susan Vogel, *Africa Explores: Twentieth Century African Art* (New York: Center for African Art; Munich: Prestel-Verlag, 1991), 238.

4. Ruth B. Phillips and Christopher B. Steiner, "Art, Authenticity and the Baggage of Cultural Encounter," in *Unpacking Culture: Art and Commodity in Colonial and Postcolonial Worlds,* ed. Ruth B. Phillips and Christopher B. Steiner (Berkeley: University of California Press, 1999), 9.

5. Although the structure had been rebuilt by August 1997, when I visited Bamako in February 2000 merchants had yet to return to the new market. Thanks to textile merchant Brehima Konaté, I got a bird's-eye view of the new building from a second-story balcony. The pristine new market is, like the old market, based in Sudanese-style architecture, with rounded turrets and softly curving walls. Konaté and many other merchants expressed great frustration at the continuing delays that keep them crowded in the overflowing side streets while the spacious market stands empty. The most recent delay was reportedly caused by infighting among the merchants' representatives over the sizes of the stalls.

6. The cliff villages of the Dogon, among the most thoroughly studied groups in Africa (largely due to the many French researchers who worked with ethnologist Marcel Griaule), are a major tourist attraction in Mali. Dogon figurative sculpture and masks are represented in most Western collections of African art, having attained nearly iconic status.

7. The supermarkets, for example, are the only places in Bamako where one can purchase brie and other cheeses, a variety of European and American candies, and several brands of rum, brandy, and the like, all at exorbitant prices.

8. Paul Guillaume and Thomas Munro, *Primitive Negro Sculpture* (New York: Hacker Art Books, 1968), 2.

9. Harry R. Silver, "Beauty and the 'I' of the Beholder: Identity, Aesthetics, and Social Change among the Ashanti," *Journal of Anthropological Research* 35, no. 2 (1979): 204.

10. Brian Spooner, "Weavers and Dealers: The Authenticity of an Oriental Carpet," in *The Social Life of Things: Commodities in Cultural Perspective,* ed. Arjun Appadurai (New York: Cambridge University Press, 1986), 226.

11. Sidney Kasfir, "African Art and Authenticity: A Text with a Shadow," *African Arts* 25, no. 2 (April 1992): 53.

12. Nancy Nooter, in Susan Vogel, *The Art of Collecting African Art* (New York: Center for African Art, 1988), 9.

13. The Indianapolis Museum of Art's 1996 exhibition *Art and Technology: Africa and Beyond* offers a dramatic example of the scientific approach to authenticity, incorporating techniques such as atomic absorption spectroscopy and CAT scans.

14. Spooner, "Weavers and Dealers," 222.

15. Sharne Algotsson and Denys Davis, *The Spirit of African Design* (New York: Clarkson Potter Publishers, 1996), 10.

16. Christopher B. Steiner, *African Art in Transit* (New York: Cambridge University Press, 1994), 136.

17. Arjun Appadurai, "Introduction: Commodities and the Politics of Value," in Appadurai, *Social Life of Things,* 47.

18. Susan Stewart, *On Longing: Narratives of the Miniature, the Gigantic, the Souvenir, the Collection* (Baltimore: Johns Hopkins University Press, 1984), 136.

19. This is Steiner's term, which effectively summarizes the important role of merchants in Africa's tourist art markets. Steiner, *African Art in Transit,* 155.

20. *Ci waraw* are wooden headdresses that represent antelope and are worn by young Bamana farmers at festivals that celebrate agricultural prowess.

21. I am grateful to Mansour Ciss and Aziz Diop, two Senegalese artists then resident in Bamako, for introducing me to Madi Sissoko in October 1992.

22. Madi Sissoko, interview, October 22, 1992.

23. Discussion of these art forms in the context of "fine art," rather than as ethnographic objects, can be found in several publications, including John Picton, *The Art of African Textiles: Technology, Tradition, and Lurex* (London:

Barbican Art Gallery, 1995); Philip Ravenhill, *Dreams and Reverie: Images of Otherworld Mates among the Baule, West Africa* (Washington, D.C.: Smithsonian Institution Press, 1996); and Tom Phillips, *Africa: The Art of a Continent* (Munich: Prestel, 1996).

24. This development is discussed in Chapter 5.

25. I had such an experience in 1992, when Racine Keita, who was then director of the Artisanat, took me to meet a local sculptor. In the sculptor's family compound, located in a neighborhood on the outskirts of Bamako, I saw rows of identical Bamana, Dogon, and Senufo figures in varied states of completion. The artist proudly showed me the well-worn pages of a French catalogue on African art from which he had copied the sculptures that filled his yard. Here, clearly, was an artist well aware of the expectations of his patrons.

26. Arnold Rubin, "Artists and Workshops in Northeastern Zaire," in *Iowa Studies in African Art,* vol. 2 (Iowa City: School of Art and Art History, University of Iowa, 1987), 8.

27. Christopher B. Steiner, "Authenticity, Repetition, and the Aesthetics of Seriality: The World of Tourist Art in the Age of Mechanical Reproduction," in Phillips and Steiner, *Unpacking Culture,* 97.

28. Larry Shiner, "'Primitive Fakes,' 'Tourist Art,' and the Ideology of Authenticity," *Journal of Aesthetics and Art Criticism* 52, no. 2 (Spring 1994): 226.

29. Bennetta Jules-Rosette, *The Messages of Tourist Art: An African Semiotic System in Comparative Perspective* (New York: Plenum Press, 1984), 17.

30. Nelson H. H. Graburn, *Ethnic and Tourist Arts: Cultural Expressions from the Fourth World* (Berkeley: University of California Press, 1976), 17–19.

31. Ruth B. Phillips, *Trading Identities: The Souvenir in Native North American Art from the Northeast, 1700–1900* (Seattle: University of Washington Press; Montreal: McGill-Queen's University Press, 1998), 104.

32. These bracelets are equally popular with Malians and tourists.

## 4. TOURIST MARKET BOGOLAN: CHANGING DEMANDS, CHANGING FORMS

1. Instead of bleaching out the yellow n'gallama pigment as in bogolan from San, color for the Bandiagara region is enhanced through the application of several dye baths.

2. Youssouf "Nialë" Sidibe, interview, March 1, 1993.

3. Susan Stewart, *On Longing: Narratives of the Miniature, the Gigantic, the Souvenir, the Collection* (Baltimore: Johns Hopkins University Press, 1984), 148.

4. Paula Ben-Amos, "Pidgin Languages and Tourist Arts," *Studies in the Anthropology of Visual Communication* 4, no. 2 (Winter 1977): 129.

5. Tavy Aherne, *Nakunte Diarra: A Bógólanfini Artist of the Beledougou* (Bloomington: Indiana University Art Museum, 1992), 10; and eadem, personal communication, September 5, 2000.

6. They remark, "The artists from Beledougou consider all of these cloths to be of inferior quality." Pascal James Imperato and Marli Shamir, "Bokolanfini: Mud Cloth of the Bamana of Mali," *African Arts* 3, no. 4 (Summer 1970): 39.

7. See Chapters 5 and 6 for discussion of bogolan created for display in galleries and museums.

8. Patrick McNaughton and Barbara Frank, personal communications, 1994.

9. Interviews: Brehima Konaté, January 11, 1993; Hama Guro, December 22, 1992; Klétigui Dembélé, July 30, 1997; and Sidicki Traoré, December 11, 1992.

10. Hama Guro, interview, December 12, 1992.

11. Assistants may also be used in the creation of more traditional bogolanfini. They sometimes prepare dyes and mud, or they may fill in areas already outlined by the artist. The sure hand of the experienced artist, however, is required for the bulk of the work.

12. See the inventory in Chapter 1.

13. During a visit to Mali in January 2000, I saw cloth in many sizes depicting women wearing Fulani-style earrings, sporting intricately braided hair, and wearing only waist wraps with "Bonne Année" (Happy New Year) prominently placed at the top or bottom of the cloth.

14. See the discussion of the work of the Atelier Jamana below and in Chapter 6.

15. Ruth B. Phillips, *Trading Identities: The Souvenir in Native North American Art from the Northeast, 1700–1900* (Seattle: University of Washington Press; Montreal: McGill-Queen's University Press, 1998), 137.

16. In visits to the Grand Marché in 1997 and 2000, I saw no ci wara stenciled cloth, though the antelope figures do appear in the stenciled robes made by Alou Traoré, whose work is discussed below. Masked dancers, on the other hand, have remained popular motifs.

17. Guro, interview, December 22, 1992. All the members were in their mid-twenties when I first met them in 1992. The group's formation is discussed in Chapter 6 as part of an

investigation of the paintings that are at the core of their bogolan production. The group added a new member in 1997, though I did not have the opportunity to conduct interviews with him.

18. Ibid.

19. Boureima Diakité, interview, January 20, 1993.

20. Hama Guro, interview, January 20, 1993.

21. Diakité, interview, January 20, 1993.

22. Several group members, interview, February 4, 1993.

23. See the discussion of the Atelier Jamana's paintings in Chapter 6.

24. The distinction between fine art and decorative art or craft is evident at the most basic levels of Malian art education. See Chapter 5.

25. Guro, interview, December 22, 1992.

26. Members of the Atelier Jamana, interview, December 1992 and January 1993.

27. Oumar Almani, interview, January 21, 1993. The Groupe Bogolan Kasobane's work is discussed in Chapters 5 and 7.

28. In recognition of contemporary bogolan's complex biography, impossible to neatly classify, Traoré appears again in Chapter 8, where his innovative contributions to the field of fine art bogolan fashion are discussed.

29. Traoré is among the most common Malian last names. None of these artists and entrepreneurs are directly related, and their common involvement with bogolan is coincidental.

30. Alou Traoré, interview, March 8, 1993.

31. Alou Traoré, interview, January 30, 2000.

32. Yet, Diarra, in her involvement with the teaching of young men from Bamako, plays an active role in the adaptation of bogolan to new markets.

33. Hama Barry, personal communication, July 1997.

34. Pascal James Imperato, *Mali: A Search for Direction* (Boulder: Westview Press, 1989), 74.

35. A transition government led by Amadou Toumani Traoré and a council of ministers guided the country through a reshaping of the constitution and elections and then passed power on to President Alpha Oumar Konaré.

36. For example, Alou Traoré, the maker of stenciled bogolan, was a schoolteacher before losing his job to government cutbacks.

37. Among the thirty students in the bogolan class I attended at the institute, only one woman was enrolled. Unlike many of the young men in the class, Sira Traoré, the sole female student, did not intend to earn a living making the cloth. Most of the men in the class spoke of their desire to sell clothing or

paintings made using their bogolan skills. Sira Traoré, interview, February 6, 1993.

38. Imperato and Shamir, "Bokolanfini," 41.

39. Lalla Tangara Touré, personal communications, January and February 2000.

40. Nakunte Diarra, interview, Kolokani, February 1, 1993.

41. Aherne, *Nakunte Diarra,* 14.

42. Richard Roberts, "Women's Work and Women's Property: Household Social Relations in the Maraka Textile Industry of the Nineteenth Century," *Comparative Studies in Society and History* 26, no. 2 (April 1984): 229–50.

43. Peter Wollen, "Tourism, Language and Art," *New Formations,* no. 12 (Winter 1990): 50.

44. Jane Schneider and Annette B. Weiner, "Cloth and the Organization of Human Experience," *Current Anthropology* 27, no. 2 (April 1986): 183.

45. Klétigui Dembélé, professor of bogolan at the Institut National des Arts, personal communication, November 10, 1992.

46. See Imperato and Shamir, "Bokolanfini," 34.

47. Oumar Almani, the creator of stenciled labels for bogolan discussed earlier, is her son.

48. Bennetta Jules-Rosette, *The Messages of Tourist Art: An African Semiotic System in Comparative Perspective* (New York: Plenum Press, 1984), 41.

49. All of the merchants with whom I spoke (in 1992–93 and 1997) mentioned having done so. Artisanat director Racine Keita mentioned such exports as well, noting that the government maintains essentially no control over exporters, many of whom do not declare the hundreds of cloths they ship in their luggage, therefore avoiding taxes. Racine Keita, interview, December 6, 1992.

50. Brehima Konaté, interview, January 11, 1993.

51. More than one weaver I spoke with worked for a female entrepreneur, a natural extension of the extensive female involvement in the retail marketing of factory-printed textiles. The numerous women in the market sold only in limited quantities, directly to consumers rather than wholesale. I could not find any women among the owners of large-scale textile outlets; none of the textile shops or stalls in the Grand Marché employed women.

52. I was unable to ascertain Konaté's labor costs, because none of the merchants and cloth producers who work with him wished to reveal that information. Clearly, the weavers and dyers receive only a small fraction of the cloth's selling price. Awareness of the negative response such information might receive among Western researchers is widespread, discouraging merchants from sharing such details.

53. This situation has parallels all over the continent, where middlemen pay minimal prices for products that they resell at triple the price (or more). In Mali, several entrepreneurs, often with assistance from international aid organizations, have attempted to rectify this imbalance. They have established artisan cooperatives, producing bogolan as well as other textiles.

54. Ronald Waterbury, "Embroidery for Tourists: A Contemporary Putting-Out System in Oaxaca, Mexico," in *Cloth and Human Experience,* ed. Annette B. Weiner and Jane Schneider (Washington, D.C.: Smithsonian Institution Press, 1989), 244.

55. Ibid.

56. Youssouf Kalilou Berthe and Abdoulaye Konaté, *Un Mode de Teinture: "Le Bogolan"* (Bamako: Musée National du Mali, 1985), 10: "A San, où le bogolan est devenu un art populaire, toutes les générations présentes s'adonnent avec joie à cet art qui ici, risque d'être purement commercial."

57. Imperato and Shamir, "Bokolanfini," 37.

58. Aherne, *Nakunte Diarra,* 10.

59. Wali Mariko, interview, February 3, 1993.

## 5. FINE ART BOGOLAN: BETWEEN CATEGORIES

1. Chapter 6 discusses the practical effects of these issues on the careers of artists currently at work in Bamako.

2. Christopher B. Steiner, *African Art in Transit* (New York: Cambridge University Press, 1994), 129.

3. Both artists are discussed in Chapter 6.

4. Alpha Oumar Konaré, interview, in Jean-Loup Pivin, "Le Mémoire en Marche," *Revue Noire,* September 1991, 1.

5. During a 1997 visit to Bamako, for example, the recent appearance of telephone booths in many neighborhoods was a matter of great pride for residents, part of the modernization of their city.

6. Such figurative use is not unique to the fine art versions of bogolanfini. As noted in Chapter 4, much of the bogolan produced for the tourist market is representational, often depicting characteristically "Malian" scenes, such as masked Dogon dancers and the famous Djenne mosque. The goal of such tourist-oriented cloth is efficiency; figures and scenes are schematic and standardized. Figurative paintings made for display in museums and galleries are more carefully nuanced, whether the artist's goal is naturalism or stylization.

7. Since the devaluation of the West African CFA in 1995, prices have dramatically increased. In 1997, artists in Bamako told me that paintings in some exhibitions were priced as high as 700,000 CFA.

8. Anthony Appiah, *In My Father's House: Africa in the Philosophy of Culture* (New York: Oxford University Press, 1992), 59.

9. Ibid., 6.

10. Mamadou Diarra, interview, October 20, 1992.

11. Paula Ben-Amos, "African Visual Arts from a Social Perspective," *African Studies Review* 32, no. 2 (1989): 4.

12. See Chapter 3.

13. Identifying the paintings as objects of visual contemplation is not to imply that they are purely decorative. Many bogolan paintings have significant secondary functions, such as statements on contemporary social issues or historical events. The importance of these secondary functions in the work of artists such as the Groupe Bogolan Kasobane and Ismaël Diabaté is discussed below.

14. My discussion of art education in Mali that follows indicates the pervasiveness of these classificatory systems, which shape the training of young artists.

15. Anne-Marie Willis and Tony Fry, "Art as Ethnocide: The Case of Australia," *Third Text,* no. 5 (1988–89): 10.

16. Enwonwu's work was celebrated in the 1950s in London, where renowned sculptor Jacob Epstein purchased one of his pieces, and he received prominent public sculpture commissions. Marshall W. Mount, *African Art: The Years since 1920* (Bloomington: Indiana University Press, 1989), 176.

17. Ben Enwonwu, "Le Point de Vue de l'Afrique sur l'Art et les Problèmes Qui Sont Posents Aujourd'hui aux Artistes Africains," in *Colloque: Fonction et Signification de l'Art Nègre dans la Vie du Peuple et pour le Peuple* (Paris: Editions Présence Africaine, 1966), 430.

18. These include the Groupe Bogolan Kasobane, Atelier Jamana, Sidicki Traoré, and others discussed in Chapters 6 and 8.

19. Kofi Awoonor, *Breast of the Earth: A Survey of the History, Culture, and Literature of Africa South of the Sahara* (New York: Nok Publishers International, 1975), 342.

20. Mount, *African Art,* 75.

21. Ibid., 75.

22. V. Y. Mudimbe, "'Reprendre': Enunciations and Strategies in Contemporary African Arts," in *Africa Explores: Twentieth Century African Art,* ed. Susan Vogel (New York: Center for African Art; Munich: Prestel-Verlag, 1991), 278.

23. Frank McEwen, "Return to Origins: New Directions for African Art," *African Arts* 1, no. 2 (Winter 1968): 23.

24. Frank McEwen, "La Peinture et la Sculpture Africaines Modernes," in *Fonction et Signification,* 443.

25. Clémentine Deliss, "7 + 7 = 1: Seven Stories, Seven Stages, One Exhibition," in *Seven Stories about Modern Art in Africa,* ed. Clémentine Deliss (New York: Flammerion, 1995), 16.

26. Mount, *African Art,* 147.

27. Everlyn Nicodemus, "Inside. Outside," in Deliss, *Seven Stories about Modern Art in Africa,* 35.

28. Yacouba Koné, interview, March 9, 1993. The bogolan paintings of Yacouba Koné and Brehima Koné, another member of the Samé group, are discussed in Chapter 6.

29. Sidicki Traoré, interviews, December 10, 1992, and February 9, 1993.

30. Vogel, *Africa Explores,* 282.

31. Kofi Antubam, "From Ghana Folk Art to Kofi Antubam Art," in *Catalog of an Exhibition Held at Accra Central Library* (December–January 1962), as cited in Mount, *African Art,* 5.

32. Simon Njami, "An African in New York," *Revue Noire,* June–July–August 1992, 47.

33. Thomas McEvilley, *Fusion: West African Artists at the Venice Biennale* (New York: Museum for African Art, 1993), 71.

34. Ly Dumas, interview, Paris, April 10, 1993.

35. Nicholas Serota and Gavin Jantjes, in *From Two Worlds,* ed. Rachel Kirby and Nicholas Serota (London: Trustees of the Whitechapel Gallery, 1986), 6.

36. James Clifford, *The Predicament of Culture: Twentieth Century Ethnography, Literature, and Art* (Cambridge, Mass.: Harvard University Press, 1988), 225.

37. In one prominent example, in the 1987 exhibition and catalogue *Perspectives: Angles on African Art* by Susan Vogel (New York: Center for African Art, 1987), the ten co-curators were asked to select their favorite African art objects from a group of photographs. All but the sole "traditional" African artist (a Baule sculptor) were invited to choose among objects from many different regions and ethnic groups. The Baule sculptor was shown only Baule art for, according to Vogel, "Showing him the same assortment of photos the others saw would have been interesting, but confusing in terms of the reactions sought here" (p. 17 n. 2).

38. *Magiciens de la Terre* (Paris: Editions du Centre George Pompidou, 1989).

39. Deliss, "7 + 7 = 1," 15.

40. dele jegede, "African Art Today: An Historical Overview," in *Contemporary African Artists: Changing Tradition* (New York: Studio Museum in Harlem, 1990), 39.

41. Emma Ejiogu, "African Art in Transition," *African Commentary: A Journal of People of African Descent* 2, nos. 4–5 (May 1990): 67.

42. E. J. de Jager, "African Art and Artist: A New Identity?" *African Insight* 18, no. 4 (1988): 202–3.

43. Sidney Kasfir, "One Tribe, One Style: Paradigms in the Historiography of African Art," *History in Africa* 11 (1984): 183.

44. Research into individual artists and artistic creativity includes a groundbreaking edited volume on African sculptors, potters, and musicians (*The Traditional Artist in African Societies,* ed. Warren D'Azevedo [Bloomington: Indiana University Press, 1973]), which includes essays by Roy Sieber, Robert Farris Thompson, and others. See also work by Roslyn Walker on Olówè of Isè (*Olówè of Isè: A Yoruba Sculptor to Kings* [Washington, D.C.: National Museum of African Art, 1998]), Ruth B. Phillips on Mende carvers (*Representing Woman: Sande Masquerades of the Mende of Sierra Leone* [Los Angeles: Fowler Museum of Cultural History, 1995]), Patrick R. McNaughton on blacksmiths (*The Mande Blacksmiths: Knowledge, Power, and Art in West Africa* [Bloomington: Indiana University Press, 1987]), Sarah Brett-Smith on Bamana carvers (*The Making of Bamana Sculpture: Creativity and Gender* [New York: Cambridge University Press, 1994]), and an increasing number of other publications.

45. Magnin is the French curator and collector who co-curated the famous and infamous *Magiciens de la Terre* exhibition.

46. Ismaël Diabaté, interview, October 13, 1992.

47. William Rubin, ed., *"Primitivism" in Twentieth Century Art: Affinity of the Tribal and the Modern* (New York: Museum of Modern Art, 1984).

48. Michelle Wallace, in Lucy Lippard, *Mixed Blessings: New Art in a Multicultural America* (New York: Pantheon Books, 1990), 26.

49. Ola Oloidi, "Abstraction in Modern African Art," *New Culture* (Ibadan) 1, no. 9 (August 1979): 12.

50. Demas Nwoko, "Contemporary Nigerian Artists and Their Traditions," *Black Art* 4, no. 2 (1980): 48.

51. Miss. Mosunmola Omibiyi, "The Artist in Contemporary Africa," *Pan-African Journal* 8, no. 1 (1975): 111.

52. It is important to note that the original

(African) audience for African abstraction likely would not have viewed that art as abstract, for abstraction is a category that only exists in contrast to Western notions of naturalism. The labeling of much African sculpture as "abstract" is, thus, a Western construct.

53. Rasheed Araeen, "From Primitivism to Ethnic Arts," in *The Myth of Primitivism: Perspectives on Art,* ed. Susan Hiller (New York: Routledge, 1991), 175.

54. "L'objectif final étant . . . la formation . . . de producteurs aptes à promouvoir un artisan modern, à concevoir et à mettre en oeuvre de petits projets utiles . . . et gérés de façon rationnelle" (p. 2).

55. "L'introduction de la perspective est la principale nouveauté dans cette section" (p. 2).

56. Frederick Hartt, *Art: A History of Painting, Sculpture, Architecture,* 2d ed. (Englewood Cliffs, N.J.: Prentice-Hall; New York: Harry N. Abrams, 1985), 516. Taking Hartt's extrapolation a step further, one might assert that the colonial era in Africa is directly linked to the development of three-point perspective, for how else could early British, French, and Portuguese explorers have sailed around the continent's coasts?

57. The first Malian professors were Moussa Dambilé, who taught decorative arts, and Mamadou Somé and Salif Kanté, both of whom taught painting. Professors Oumar Coulibaly and Modibo Diallo, interviews, October 18, 1991.

58. The marble Thera uses is quarried in the Kayes region in western Mali. He combines his Dogon heritage with European influences such as Michelangelo and Rodin. Demy Thera, interview, October 30, 1992.

59. Examples of stone carving in sub-Saharan Africa include Nomoli and Pomdo figures (Kissi, Sapi, and related groups, Guinea and Sierra Leone), steatite memorial markers (Yombe and Kongo peoples, Democratic Republic of Congo), and monoliths, or *atal* (Ekoi and related peoples, Cross River region, Nigeria).

60. The *Programmes Officielles* calls for "étude des masques chez les authentistes (sculpteurs traditionnels)" (p. 102).

61. Marie-Françoise Becchetti-Laure, "Aperçu de la Jeune Peintre à Bamako, République du Mali, 1960–1990: Formation-Création-Diffusion" (mémoire de maîtrise, Université de Provence, Aix-Marseille, 1990), 54.

62. Baba Moussulu Touré, "Arts et Peuples du Mali: Tradition et Tendances Modernes" (thèse de doctorat d'art, Ecole Supérieur des Arts Industriels du Moscou, 1991): "Dans les années

1975–1985 on a fait les premières démarches réelles pour révaloriser, diffuser et emprunter les formes traditionnelles et les motifs. . . . On voit se développer d'une façon productive l'art décoratif et graphique (bocolan), y compris les motifs traditionnels et les symboles ('ideogrammes')."

## 6. THE FINE ART MARKET: FROM BOGOLAN TO LE BOGOLAN

1. The revival of bogolan in the realm of fashion and clothing is discussed in Chapter 8.

2. John Povey, "First Word," *African Arts* 23, no. 4 (October 1990): 6.

3. The fact that most of the artists I spoke with relied on one person—Frank Pythais, a Libero-American painter—to frame their work for exhibition is illustrative of this lack of artistic materials. Frank Pythais, interviews, November 18, 1992, and December 15, 1992.

4. Although Sidibe died in 1987, I was fortunately able to see several of his paintings in the Musée National du Mali, where they are being stored until his survivors determine where they are to be permanently housed. Because the paintings have not been accessioned into the collection, I was unable to photograph them.

5. Djelemakan Sacko, interview, November 10, 1992, and Yacouba Koné, interview, March 9, 1993. Marie-Françoise Becchetti-Laure, "Aperçu de la Jeune Peintre à Bamako, République du Mali, 1960–1990: Formation-Création-Diffusion" (mémoire de maîtrise, Université de Provence, Aix-Marseille, 1990), 286.

6. I was unable to ascertain the origins of Berthé's nickname. He had left Bamako many years before I arrived there in 1991.

7. Maryam Thiam, interview, February 11, 1993. Thiam's work exemplifies the importance of U.S., French, and other foreign assistance agencies in supporting the involvement of women in urban entrepreneurial activities. Many nongovernmental organizations target women's development issues with the aim of providing women with access to markets currently dominated by men.

8. Seydou's career is discussed in detail in Chapter 8.

9. Néné Thiam, interview, November 19, 1992.

10. Néné Thiam and Souleyman Guro, interview, November 9, 1992.

11. Coulibaly's thesis has since been lost.

12. Kandiora Coulibaly, interview, May 18, 1993.

13. Ibid.

14. Grin are groups of teenagers and young adults, often centered around the organization of

dances, parties, and other festivities where young people may gather. The wearing of matching outfits is a common indicator of social solidarity in Mali (as elsewhere in West Africa); friends might wear clothing tailored of the same cloth, families at weddings might wear matching ensembles, and members of the same grin often have some form of unified attire for special events.

15. Coulibaly, interview, May 18, 1993.

16. This event is a week-long celebration of Malian arts and culture, formerly held biannually in Bamako.

17. *La Voix des Artistes,* no. 7 (1989): 4: "La surprise attendait les visiteurs dans la première sale. Une statue de femme grandeur nature, habillée de deux pagnes bogolan et tenant dans ses bras un bébé qu'elle allaite, souhaitait la bienvenue à ceux qui entraient. Une manière originale d'annoncer les couleurs, car cette salle était reservée à l'exposition du bogolan. . . . C'etait là l'oeuvre du Groupe Bogolan, une association de jeunes artistes . . . chacun a maîtrisé les techniques du bogolan propres à sa région."

18. Baba Fallo Keita, interview, August 3, 1997. See Plate 9 for an example of these large paintings.

19. *Bogolan et Arts Graphiques du Mali* (Paris: ADEIAO and Musée des Arts Africains and Océaniens, 1990), 8.

20. Ibid., 27.

21. Keita, interview, August 3, 1997. *Nyama* is a deeply significant Bamana word whose most basic definition is "trash" or "refuse," reflecting the tendency to conceal the deepest signification beneath the least likely facade. As Chris Bird and Martha Kendall eloquently describe it, *nyama* is the "energy of action," the force that is released by actions of all kinds and that is required to animate the universe ("The Mande Hero," in *Explorations in African Systems of Thought,* ed. Ivan Karp and Charles S. Bird [Bloomington: Indiana University Press, 1980], vii–ix). Patrick McNaughton describes its crucial role in the work of blacksmiths, whose profession demands a high level of involvement with a dangerous force (*The Mande Blacksmiths: Knowledge, Power, and Art in West Africa* [Bloomington: Indiana University Press, 1988], 15–16).

22. "Fiche Technique" (Technical Form), providing basic information on each painting sold by the Groupe Bogolan Kasobane: "Nyama parle de la relation entre l'homme et les animaux, l'homme et la nature, entre les hommes eux mêmes . . . qu'on appelle 'Nyama' en Bambara et Carma chez les Hindou."

23. "Fiche Technique": "L'homme est en train de courir et pour aller plus vite il utilise les moyens scientifiques. Mais en réalité c'est l'homme lui même qui s'utilise et s'use mais apparemment il pense qu'il est satisfait. C'est comme en Afrique un enfant qui utilise la tige de mil comme cheval, il galoppe, il court avec, fait boire, manger la tige mais en réalité c'est lui même qui court et fini par se fatigué."

24. I did not have an opportunity to photograph these works. As plans were underway to display the paintings, group members did not wish to decrease their impact by permitting them to appear in reproductive form prior to their unveiling at an exhibition.

25. BIAO is the acronym for Banc International de l'Afrique de l'Ouest, a major West African banking conglomerate.

26. *Bogolan et Arts Graphiques.* In 1995, the Centre Culturel Français produced a catalogue (by Pauline Duponchel) to accompany the exhibition *Du Bogolan Traditionnel au Bogolan Contemporain,* which prominently included a work by the Groupe Bogolan Kasobane.

27. Susan Vogel, ed., *Africa Explores: Twentieth Century African Art* (New York: Center for African Art; Munich: Prestel-Verlag, 1991). Two paintings by the Groupe Bogolan Kasobane appear on page 183: *Ba Ka Kulushi* (Polygamy) and *Le Secourisme (Cameroun)* (Rescue [Cameroon]).

28. "Un Entretien avec le 'Groupe Bógólan': La Technique du Bógólan," *Jamana,* January–February 1987, 20.

29. Néné Thiam, interview, November 19, 1992.

30. Clément Tapsoba, "Les Signes du Bogolan Comme Base de Créativité," *Ecrans d'Afrique* 24, no. 2 (1998): 99.

31. Arouna Mouniratou, "Rapport de Stage: Bogolan et Batik," submitted to the Institut National des Arts, Bamako, May 1993.

32. Coulibaly, interview, May 18, 1993.

33. I am here adopting James Clifford's model for the Western desire to "rescue" disappearing traditions. James Clifford, "The Others: Beyond the Salvage Paradigm," *Third Text,* no. 6 (Spring 1989): 73–79.

34. Klétigui Dembélé, interview, November 10, 1992.

35. Kandiora Coulibaly, personal communication, February 6, 2000.

36. Clifford, "Others," 75.

37. "Un Entretien avec le 'Groupe Bógólan,'" 20.

38. Thiam and Guro, interview, November 9, 1992.

39. Other ethnic groups, including the Dogon and Minianka, also have long histories as bogolan producers. The Bamana are, however, by far the ethnic group best known for bogolan production.

40. See Chapter 8 for discussion of Youssouf "Nialë" Sidibe, a young clothing designer whose family attempted to discourage him from working with bogolan.

41. Catherine and Bernard Desjeux, "Bogolan Kasobane: Le Pluriel de l'Art," *Balafon* (Air Afrique magazine), July 1996, 31: "Chacun prend possession d'un coin de l'immense toile écrue et dessine avec une plume de canard en fonction de son inspiration nourrie des réflections des uns et des autres."

42. "Un Entretien avec le 'Groupe Bógólan,'" 21: "Les artistes mettent en commun leur sources d'inspiration, élaborent ensemble une composition, mais laissent le soin de la réalisation totale ou partielle à celui du groupe qui ressent le mieux le thème traité."

43. *Bogolan et Arts Graphiques,* 50: "Par leur création en commun les artistes du groupe dépassent l'individualisme, le subjectivisme et le 'moi' occidental."

44. Francesco Pellizzi, review of *Africa Explores: Twentieth Century African Art,* edited by Susan Vogel, *African Arts* 26, no. 1 (January 1993): 24.

45. Thiam, interview, November 19, 1992; Dembele, interview, November 10, 1992.

46. They have also begun to use indigo for their clothing, pillows, and curtains. They apply it in techniques similar to those used with bogolan. Indigo is not, however, used to create fine art.

47. This is discussed in Chapter 8.

48. Keita, interview, August 3, 1997.

49. Mansour Ciss, interview, October 15, 1992.

50. Interview, July 10, 1997.

51. Diabaté's shows include more than fifteen exhibitions in Mali (beginning in 1970) as well as group and solo exhibitions in China (Maison des Expositions, Beijing, 1983), Côte d'Ivoire (Hôtel Ivoire, Abidjan, 1993), Cuba (Deuxième Biennale de la Havane, 1986), France (Centre Jean Vilar, Angers, 1990; Salle André Malraux, Yerre, 1994), Senegal (Galerie 39, Dakar, 1991), and Switzerland (Ethnografiska Museum, Stockholm, 1988), among other international exhibitions.

52. Vogel, *Africa Explores,* 193.

53. Ismaël Diabaté, interview, October 13, 1992.

54. Ibid.

55. Ibid., and interview, July 31, 1997.

56. Diabaté, interview, October 13, 1992.

57. Amadou Chab Touré, ed., *Signes et Alphabets au Mali: Synthèse des Semaines de la Calligraphie* (Bamako: Club Ahmed Baba with the support of the Embassy of France to Mali, 1999).

58. Ibid., 26.

59. That Diabaté, already a well-established artist, chose to work with the Groupe Bogolan Kasobane indicates the degree to which the group members had become the designated experts in the use of bogolan.

60. Pauline Duponchel, *Du Bogolan Traditionnel au Bogolan Contemporain* (Bamako: Centre Culturel Français, 1995), 14: "il va évoluer vers un travail plus libre . . . qui n'est pas sans rappeler les 'dripping' de J. Pollock."

61. Ismaël Diabaté, interview, February 2, 2000.

62. Ibid. Yacouba Koné, interview, March 8, 1993; Mamadou Diarra, interview, March 12, 1993; Brehima Koné, interview, December 2, 1992. In the interest of preserving the artists' signature techniques I have refrained from providing specific information on these aspects of their work. I learned a great deal about the premium artists place on technical and stylistic innovation on those occasions when I introduced one bogolan artist to another. Upon meeting, Yacouba Koné and Youssouf Sidibe traded references to their varied innovations without revealing the essential information that would allow the other to duplicate the techniques, thus preserving the niche each had created, much as merchants in the tourist art market conceal the details of their commerce to prevent competitors from gaining access to their suppliers and clients.

63. Mary H. Nooter, "The Aesthetics and Politics of Things Unseen," in *Secrecy: African Art That Conceals and Reveals* (New York: Museum for African Art, 1993), 24.

64. His preference for Malian subjects was evident before he began to make use of bogolan. His titles of drawings and paintings from the early 1980s include *Bozo Dwelling, Young Peul Girl from Mopti,* and *Dogon Sun.* All of these titles refer to Malian ethnic groups. In French these translate as *Habitation Bozo, Jeune Fille Peul de Mopti,* and *Soleil Dogon.* Beccetti-Laure, "Aperçu de la Jeune Peintre à Bamako," 286.

65. Germaine Dieterlen and Youssouf Cissé, *Les Fondements de la Société d'Initiation du Komo* (Paris: Mouton, 1972).

66. Patrick R. McNaughton, *Secret Sculptures of Komo: Art and Power in Bamana (Bambara) Initiation Associations,* Working Papers in the Traditional Arts 4 (Philadelphia: Institute for the Study of Human Issues, 1979), 21.

67. McNaughton, *Mande Blacksmiths,* 130.

68. Dieterlen and Cissé, *Fondements.*

69. Diabaté, interview, October 13, 1992, and Becchetti-Laure, "Aperçu de la Jeune Peintre à Bamako," 287.

70. Diabaté, interview, July 31, 1997.

71. The exhibition was held at the Hôtel des Ventes Chave Jean Martin, June 1992.

72. Diabaté, interview, October 13, 1992.

73. Notably, one of *Fondements'* co-authors, Cissé, is a Malian scholar, adding yet another layer of ambiguity to the separation of Western from Malian influences. Only with great difficulty can an artist like Diabaté disentangle the two to create distinctively Malian art.

74. Diabaté, interview, October 13, 1992.

75. Dieterlen and Cissé, *Fondements*, 95.

76. For Traoré, as for many Africans who travel to France to seek their fortunes, life in Paris was physically and psychologically trying. Many Malians who had themselves tried their luck in France, or had friends and family members who had lived there, told me of the prejudice, menial labor, and lack of social interaction that made life in France exceedingly difficult.

77. Sidicki Traoré, interview, December 10, 1992.

78. Ibid.

79. Ibid.

80. Modibo Diallo, for example, exhibited a bogolan painting on interlaced cotton strips in the 1995 exhibition *Du Bogolan Traditionnel au Bogolan Contemporain* at the Centre Culturel Français, Bamako.

81. Sidicki Traoré, interview, February 9, 1993.

82. Sidicki Traoré, interview, July 23, 1997.

83. Duponchel, *Bogolan Traditionnel,* 26: "il lie avec harmonie ces deux techniques."

84. Traoré, interview, December 10, 1992.

85. Traoré, interview, February 9, 1993.

86. Becchetti-Laure, "Aperçu de la Jeune Peintre à Bamako," 133: "Le marché de l'art contemporain n'existe pas."

87. Diabaté, interview, October 13, 1992.

88. Djelemakan Sacko, interview, November 11, 1992.

89. Moussa Koné, interview, October 28, 1992.

90. Habib Ballo, interview, October 12, 1992.

91. In the realm of conceptual art, Abdoulaye Konaté has received international attention for his installation works.

92. Discussions with Malians and with the staff of the Musée National indicate that most residents of Bamako visit the museum once during their primary school years, or not at all.

93. Samuel Sidibe, interview, October 30, 1992.

94. In September 1986 the museum featured an exhibition on textile dyeing in urban Mali and in August 1987 a display on weaving in urban Mali.

95. Sidibe, interview, October 30, 1992.

96. These included one exhibition by the Chiffons de Samé group, two exhibitions of Ismaël Diabaté's work, one of Yacouba Koné's paintings, one of Brehima Koné's work, two Groupe Bogolan Kasobane displays, and one featuring paintings by Sénou Fofana. Soon after I left Mali in July 1993, another young bogolan artist, Alhousseney Kelly, was featured there in a solo exhibition. During a visit in 1997, I was told by several artists that the director who succeeded Decraene focused more on music than on visual art and had reduced opportunities for exhibitions.

97. The lack of Malian attention to galleries was dramatically evident by my difficulties in locating the Galerie Tatou; even the residents of a building next door were not aware of its existence.

98. Yacouba Koné, interview, March 9, 1993.

99. Roland de Livry's father owned Le Lido, a popular nightclub and restaurant that had closed by the time of my research. See Chapter 5 for more on de Livry.

100. The exhibition was held October–November 1989.

101. Yacouba Koné's exhibition took place October–November 1990.

102. Koné, interview, March 9, 1993.

103. Ibid.

104. Brehima Koné, interview, December 12, 1992.

105. The exhibition was held in December 1992. The paintings were tragically destroyed in the fire that razed the club on New Year's Eve.

106. Brehima Koné, interview, December 12, 1992.

107. I worked primarily with Sow, Guro, and Diakité. Aly Dolo did not live in Bamako but traveled there frequently to participate in group activities.

108. The Atelier Jamana's clothing and related products are discussed in Chapter 7.

109. Editorial, *Jamana,* October–December 1984, 1.

110. Boureima Diakité, interview, January 20, 1993.

111. Venues for Atelier Jamana exhibitions have included the Centre Culturel Français, Le Yanga, and the Galerie Tatou in Bamako. Atelier Jamana artists, interview, December 2, 1992.

112. Both events, which included workshops on the export of handcrafted products to the United States, were sponsored by the International Enterprise Development Program, a non-governmental organization.

113. One of the Atelier Jamana members, Hama Guro, is the younger brother of Souleyman Guro of the Groupe Bogolan Kasobane.

114. At the institute they were taught by members of the Groupe Bogolan Kasobane.

115. Hama Guro, interview, January 20, 1993.

116. Diakité, interview, January 20, 1993.

117. Rokiatou Sow, Boureima Diakité, and Hama Guro, interview, August 8, 1997.

118. Diakité, interview, January 20, 1993.

119. Sénou Fofana, interview, December 21, 1992.

120. Duponchel, *Bogolan Traditionnel*, 18.

## 7. CULTURE THROUGH CLOTHING: BOGOLAN AS FASHION

1. My use of the terms *fashion* and *clothing* should be addressed at the outset of this chapter. *Fashion* is narrowest in its signification, referring to the ephemeral, transitory nature of some forms of clothing. *High fashion*, or haute couture, is a specific subset of fashion, created by professionals, often deliberately exclusive in its marketing. *Clothing* is that which covers the body, whether for protection or for aesthetic enhancement, a category that includes "fashion."

2. This incarnation of the cloth that suggests bogolan's adaptability to markets quite distinct from those in operation on the streets of Bamako is addressed in Chapter 9.

3. Introduction in *Chic Thrills: A Fashion Reader*, ed. Juliet Ash and Elizabeth Wilson (Berkeley: University of California Press, 1992), xi.

4. I should note the intriguing coincidence that as I write this the *New York Times Magazine Fashions of the Times* features a "global" view of fashion with a simple premise: "We sent the planet's best-traveled photographers on assignment: shoot an iconic person in an iconic location" (p. 168). The sole African location is Bamako, with a local young woman modeling distinctly non-local clothes—a silk and wool dress worn with a wool turtleneck. The photograph is by Malick Sidibé, a portrait photographer who, like Seydou Keita, has successfully exhibited his work in U.S. galleries and museums. Here we see Bamako as iconic African locale, this fashion spread an all too rare indication of the city's presence in the orbit of international fashion. John Hyland, "Clothes Meet World," *New York Times Magazine Fashions of the Times*, Fall 2000, 168–83. I am grateful to Florence Babb for bringing this image to my attention.

5. Investigations of African fashion include Joanne B. Eicher, ed., *Dress and Ethnicity: Change across Space and Time* (Washington, D.C.: Berg, 1995); M. J. Hay, *Western Clothing and African Identity: Changing Consumption Patterns among the Luo*, Discussion Papers in the African Humanities 2 (Boston: African Studies Center, Boston University, 1989); Hildi Hendrickson, ed., *Clothing and Difference: Embodied Identities in Colonial and Post-Colonial Africa* (Durham, N.C.: Duke University Press, 1996); Judith Perani and Norma H. Wolff, *Cloth, Dress and Art Patronage in Africa* (New York: Berg, 1999). John Picton, ed., *African Textiles: Technology, Tradition, and Lurex* (London: Barbican Art Gallery, 1995); Elisha P. Renne, *Cloth That Does Not Die: The Meaning of Cloth in Bùnú Social Life* (Seattle: University of Washington Press, 1995); Doran H. Ross, *Wrapped in Pride: Ghanaian Kente and African American Identity* (Los Angeles: UCLA Fowler Museum of Cultural History, 1998); Els van der Plas and Marlous Willemsen, eds., *The Art of African Fashion* (Trenton, N.J.: Africa World Press; The Hague: Prince Claus Fund, 1998).

6. Important research on textiles and garments includes but is not limited to Lisa Aronson, "Akwete Weaving: Tradition and Change," in *Man Does Not Go Naked: Textilien und Handwerk aus afrikanischen und andern Ländern*, ed. Beate Engelbrecht and Bernhard Gardi (Basel: Ethnologisches Seminar der Universität and Museum für Völkerkunde, 1989), 35–64; Renée Boser-Sarivaxénvanis, *Recherche sur l'Histoire des Textiles Traditionnels Tissés et Teints de l'Afrique Occidentale* (Basel: Verhandlungen der Naturforschenden Gesellschaft, 1975); Justine M. Cordwell and Ronald Schwarz, eds., *The Fabrics of Culture: The Anthropology of Clothing and Adornment* (The Hague: Mouton, 1979); Peggy Gilfoy, *Patterns of Life: West African Strip-Weaving Traditions* (Washington, D.C.: National Museum of African Art, 1987); *History, Design, and Craft in West African Strip-Woven Cloth* (Washington, D.C.: National Museum of African Art, 1992); Dale Idiens and I. Ponting, eds., *Textiles in Africa* (Bath: Pasold Research Fund, 1980); Venice Lamb, *West African Weaving* (London: Duckworth, 1975); John Picton and John Mack, *African Textiles: Looms, Weaving, and Design* (London: British Museum, 1979); Renne, *Cloth That Does Not Die*; Roy Sieber, *African Textiles and Decorative Arts* (New York: Museum of Modern Art, 1972).

7. Several important exceptions to this rule are discussed below.

8. The semiological analysis of fashion is exemplified by Roland Barthes, *Système de la Mode* (Paris: Editions du Seuil, 1967). Lee Wright, "Outgrown Clothes for Grown-up

People: Constructing a Theory of Fashion," in Ash and Wilson, *Chic Thrills,* 49–57, typifies the use of qualitative methodology.

9. Dulali Nag, "Fashion, Gender, and the Bengali Middle Class," *Public Culture* 3, no. 2 (Spring 1991): 93.

10. Jennifer Craik, *The Face of Fashion: Cultural Studies in Fashion* (New York: Routledge, 1994), x.

11. Introduction, in *Cloth and Human Experience,* ed. Jane Schneider and Annette B. Weiner (Washington, D.C.: Smithsonian Institution Press, 1989), 4.

12. Many of these have been discussed in previous chapters on tourist art and fine art, including "authenticity," "Westernization," and "modernity."

13. Fred Davis, *Fashion, Culture, and Identity* (Chicago: University of Chicago Press, 1992), 25.

14. Craik, *Face of Fashion,* 16.

15. Ruth Barnes and Joanne B. Eicher, eds., *Dress and Gender: Making and Meaning* (Oxford: Berg, 1992), 1.

16. This reluctance is discussed in Chapters 3 and 5, as it relates to the tourist art and fine art markets for bogolan.

17. Angela Fisher, *Africa Adorned* (New York: Harry N. Abrams, 1984), 9–10. Fisher and her frequent collaborator, Carol Beckwith, have more recently published an extraordinarily lavish, two-volume book of photographs, *African Ceremonies* (New York: Harry N. Abrams, 1999). Their photos from the book were also reproduced at mural scale in an exhibition mounted by the Brooklyn Museum of Art in July 2000.

18. Fisher, *Africa Adorned,* 10.

19. Barbara Brodman, "Paris or Perish: The Plight of the Latin American Indian in a Westernized World," in *On Fashion,* ed. Shari Benstock and Suzanne Ferriss (New Brunswick, N.J.: Rutgers University Press, 1994), 267.

20. Ibid., 269.

21. Phyllis M. Martin, "Contesting Clothes in Colonial Brazzaville," *Journal of African History* 35 (1994): 414–15.

22. Ibid., 408.

23. Ibid., 407.

24. Karen Tranberg Hansen, "Dealing with Used Clothes: *Salaula* and the Construction of Identity in Zambia's Third Republic," *Public Culture* 6, no. 3 (Spring 1994): 503–23; see also eadem, *Salaula: The World of Secondhand Clothing and Zambia* (Chicago: University of Chicago Press, 2000).

25. Hansen, "Dealing with Used Clothes," 504.

26. Ibid., 519.

27. Ibid., 522.

28. Justin Daniel Gandoulou, *Dandies à Bacongo: Le Culte de l'Elégance dans la Société Congolaise Contemporaine* (Paris: L'Harmattan, 1989).

29. Jonathon Friedman, "The Political Economy of Elegance," *Culture and History* 7 (1990): 122.

30. Kobena Mercer, "Black Hair/Style Politics," *New Formations* 3 (Winter 1987): 47.

31. Richard Wilk, "Consumer Goods as Dialogue about Development," *Culture and History* 7 (1990): 79–100.

32. Ibid., 82.

33. Ibid., 84.

34. Ibid., 89.

35. Georg Simmel, "Fashion," *International Quarterly* 10 (October 1904); reprint in *American Journal of Sociology* 57, no. 6 (May 1957): 547.

36. Ibid., 556.

37. Ibid., 557.

38. Ibid., 550.

39. Ali A. Mazrui, "The Robes of Rebellion: Sex, Dress, and Politics in Africa," *Encounter* 34, no. 2 (1970): 27.

40. Ibid.

41. Ibid.

42. Frantz Fanon, "Algeria Unveiled," in *Studies in a Dying Colonialism,* as cited in Mazrui, "Robes of Rebellion," 22.

43. Mazrui, "Robes of Rebellion," 29.

44. Homi Bhabha, "Remembering Fanon: Self, Psyche, and the Colonial Condition," in *Colonial Discourse and Postcolonial Theory,* ed. Patrick Williams and Laura Chrisman (New York: Columbia University Press, 1994), 121.

45. Betty M. Wass, "Yoruba Dress in Five Generations of a Lagos Family," in Cordwell and Schwartz, *The Fabrics of Culture,* 346.

46. John L. and Jean Comaroff, *Of Revelation and Revolution,* vol. 2, *The Dialectics of Modernity on a South African Frontier* (Chicago: University of Chicago Press, 1997).

47. Ibid., 244.

48. Ibid., 235.

49. Ibid.

50. The dominance of imported, mass-produced British cloth came to exemplify the destruction of local industries and, by extension, of local Indian cultures. Through boycotts of British cloth, local textiles were "transformed from an endangered rural craft to a powerful symbol of the moral and spiritual regeneration of India." C. A. Bayly, "The Origins of Swadeshi (Home Industry): Cloth and Indian Society, 1700–1930," in *The Social Life of Things: Commodities in Cultural*

*Perspective,* ed. Arjun Appadurai (New York: Cambridge University Press, 1986), 311.

51. Hillary O'Kelly, "Reconstructing Irishness: Dress in the Celtic Revival, 1880–1920," in Ash and Wilson, *Chic Thrills,* 76.

52. Ibid., 78.

53. Joanne B. Eicher and Tonye Erekosima, "Why Do They Call It Kalabari? Cultural Authentification and the Demarcation of Ethnic Identity," in Eicher, *Dress and Ethnicity.* Interestingly, Eicher and Erekosima note that much of the attire that is marked as specifically Kalabari is based on borrowed forms, originating in Europe or in the Kalabari's many trade contacts within West Africa.

54. Ibid., 159.

55. Misty L. Bastian, "Female 'Alhajis' and Entrepreneurial Fashions: Flexible Identities in Southeastern Nigeria," in Hendrickson, *Clothing and Difference,* 97–132.

56. Wealth and power are associated with the ability to make the *hajj,* the pilgrimmage to Mecca, as all Muslims wish to do. Those who have made the trip are called al-hajjis.

57. Bastian, "Female 'Alhajis,'"104.

58. Ibid., 106.

59. Ibid., 119.

60. To classify such garments as "Western" simplifies a complex, highly nuanced situation. Men's business suits and women's miniskirts have been thoroughly adapted into local fashion systems, made of local fabrics and tailored in local styles.

61. Esther Pasztory, "Identity and Difference: The Uses and Meanings of Ethnic Styles," *Studies in the History of Art* 27 (1989): 35.

62. Mansour Ciss, interview, October 15, 1992.

63. Racine Keita, interview, December 5, 1992.

64. Mamadou Keita, interview, December 6, 1992.

65. I asked young people I encountered at the Centre Culturel Français, on downtown streets, and at social gatherings why they wore bogolan. Some wore bogolan vests, others skirts, shorts, or hats. All replied that they liked the cloth and found it fashionable.

66. Dean MacCannell, *Empty Meeting Grounds: The Tourist Papers* (New York: Routledge, 1989), 68.

67. Ibid., 297.

## 8. MAKING IT MODERN: BOGOLAN CLOTHING'S DUAL DIRECTIONS

1. See Sarah Brett-Smith's forthcoming publication, *Bamana Mudcloths: A Female Language of Power,* in which she discusses past styles of clothing, including specific bogolanfini patterns, being used to identify their wearers' ethnic identity and region of origin. Sarah Brett-Smith, personal communication, September 9, 2000.

2. *Couture* means "sewing" in French.

3. Even second- and third-generation residents of Bamako often maintain family ties in "home" villages, sending their children to visit during holidays and returning for important family events.

4. See the discussion below on Chris Seydou.

5. The wardrobes of many urban Malians include both ready-to-wear clothing and garments that are commissioned from local tailors. Every neighborhood has at least one (and often several) tailoring shops.

6. The obituaries include Maîmouna Traoré, "Chris Seydou: La Mort d'une Etoile," *Nyeleni,* no. 5 (1994): 18–19, 26; K. B. Diakité, "Chris Seydou," *L'Essor,* March 8, 1994, 1, 4; "Hommage à un Grand Créateur," *Les Echos,* March 7, 1994, 1, 3; Rachid N'diaye, "Chris Seydou: La Mort d'un Magicien," *Africa International,* April 1994, 28–29; "Chris Seydou: Le Roman d'une Vie," *Africa International,* July–August 1994. A series of tributes, including a statement by Yves Saint Laurent, were featured in *Revue Noire:* Adam Bâ Konaré et al., "Chris Seydou: Hommage," June–July–August 1994, 55–56; Pauline Awa Bary and Jean Loup Pivin, "Quelques Dates d'une Vie de Chris Seydou," June–July–August 1994, 56; Jean Loup Pivin, "Drapé de Son Manteau Noir/Draped in His Black Cloak," tr. John Taylor, June–July–August 1994, 57.

7. Diakité, "Chris Seydou," 4: "A travers ses créations, le Mali s'est fait mieux connaître dans ses valuers culturelles à travers le monde, jusqu'en Amérique où les Noirs américains font aujourd'hui du bogolan une source d'identification culturelle."

8. N'diaye, "Chris Seydou: La Mort d'un Magicien": "C'était le pionnier de la mode Africaine, l'homme qui a rendu la femme africaine fière de la mode africaine, le premier à . . . honorer les célèbres tissus Bogolan créés par les tisserands d'Afrique."

9. Macy Domingo, "Ciseaux d'Ivoire/Ivory Scissors," *Revue Noire,* September 1991, 6.

10. Pauline Duponchel, "Bogolan: From Symbolic Material to National Emblem," in *The Art of African Textiles: Technology, Tradition, and Lurex,* ed. John Picton (London: Barbican Art Gallery, 1995), 36.

11. Among these are Mansour Ciss, the Senegalese sculptor; Aziz Diop, a Senegalese designer; and Mamadou Keita, owner of the Galerie Indigo.

12. Among these are Abdoulaye Konaté, painter

and museum curator; the members of the Groupe Bogolan Kasobane; and Ismaël Diabaté.

13. Chris Seydou, interview, March 6, 1993.

14. Bary and Pivin, "Quelques Dates d'une Vie de Chris Seydou," 56.

15. "Interview: Chris Seydou," *Grin-Grin: Le Magazine des Jeunes,* April–May–June 1989, 10.

16. Domingo, "Ciseaux d'Ivoire," 6–7.

17. In 1986, Seydou was granted Ivorian citizenship by presidential decree. Bary and Pivin, "Quelques Dates d'une Vie de Chris Seydou," 56.

18. Ibid.

19. "Le Roman d'une Vie," 34.

20. Seydou, interview, March 6, 1993, and "Le Roman d'une Vie," 34.

21. Seydou, interview, March 6, 1993: "J'apporte une sensibilité Africaine."

22. "Le Roman d'une Vie," 35: "Le Mali, c'est presque une punition car Chris souhaite vivre la grande vie citadine sous les sunlights abidjanais, new-yorkais ou parisiens."

23. Seydou, interview, March 6, 1993.

24. Traoré, "La Mort d'une Etoile," 26: "Malgré l'immense richesse de l'art malien, il lui manque des structures capables de lui assurer une compétivité internationale. Je vais m'y mettre dès maintenant pour structurer. Cet art qui ne demande qu'a s'épanouir."

25. Chris Seydou, interview, January 21, 1993.

26. Seydou, interview, March 6, 1993.

27. Seydou referred to the cloth as "souvenirs de mon pays" (souvenirs of my country).

28. Anya Peterson Royce, *Ethnic Identity: Strategies of Diversity* (Bloomington: Indiana University Press, 1982).

29. Valerie Cassel, "Convergence: Image and Dialogue Conversations with Alexander 'Skunder' Boghossian," *Third Text,* no. 23 (Summer 1993): 53–54.

30. Seydou, interview, March 6, 1993: "C'est ma faute."

31. Ibid: "Si un créateur malien comme moi va en France, si je reviens pour dire que moi je suis derrière le bogolan, qu'est-ce qu'on va faire? . . . Je l'ai valorisé."

32. Ibid.

33. Ibid: "Moi je suis un créateur contemporain qui connais techniquement ce que je peux faire et comment je peux le faire. Le bogolan peut être simplement une base culturelle."

34. Seydou, interview, January 21, 1993: "Il y a dix dessins dans un même pagne, on peut enlever dix maquettes dans une seule."

35. Seydou, interview, March 6, 1993: "Même pour tailler ce tissu avec ma technique française et tout, j'avais très peur de le tailler. . . . Le graphisme n'est pas fait pour être couper."

36. Ibid: "Dans la société traditionnelle ça fait ça, mais quand ça sort de là ça n'a aucune signification."

37. Ibid: "C'étais pour moi symbolique. Pour moi, je n'aimais pas tailler le bogolan à l'époque; difficile à mettre les ciseaux dedans."

38. Seydou, interview, March 6, 1993: "Décoder."

39. Seydou, interview, January 21, 1993.

40. Similarly, cloth with repetitive designs in the tourist market communicated nothing to Diarra, for whom they were "nonsense." Tavy Aherne, *Nakunte Diarra: A Bógólanfini Artist of the Beledougou* (Bloomington: Indiana University Art Museum, 1992), 10.

41. Seydou, interview, January 21, 1993.

42. Seydou, interview, March 6, 1993: "C'est beau comme ça, plein d'imperfections; on l'aime comme ça parce que c'est ethnique et c'est ceci et c'est cela, mais on peut aller plus loin."

43. "Le Roman d'une Vie," 36: "le vent de la démocratie entraîne avec lui tous les rêves de réussite minutieusement prépare: adieu centre artisanal, maison de distribution sur le Mali et l'Europe." Despite the setback in his plans that resulted from the change of government, Seydou was certainly a supporter of the new democracy. In fact, Adam Bâ Konaré, the wife of President Alpha Oumar Konaré, was among his close friends.

44. Seydou, interview, March 6, 1993.

45. Seydou, interview, January 21, 1993: Kamali's bogolan blouse and skirt were included in the exhibition *Renewing Tradition: The Revitalization of Bogolan in Mali and Abroad* at the University of Iowa Art Museum in 2000. Thanks to Judith Bettelheim for providing the ensemble.

46. Here again, as in every bogolan market, young men are in the overwhelming majority. Because tailors are almost exclusively male in Mali, as elsewhere in West Africa, the dearth of women involved in "couture" bogolan is not surprising. The few women designers I met only occasionally used bogolan, focusing instead on bazin, a factory-produced cloth distinguished by the tapestry-like designs woven into the cloth, and other industrial fabrics.

47. Youssouf Sidibe, interview, March 1, 1993.

48. Ibid.

49. Ibid. See the discussion on innovation and secrecy in Chapter 6.

50. The two terms refer to the same ethnic group.

51. This is not a fact that I found confirmed elsewhere, though in her forthcoming book on

bogolanfini, Sarah Brett-Smith notes that in
the past the Bamana in the Beledougou and
neighboring Fadugu regions "avoided contact
with the Maures, the Fulani, and the Marka."
See *Bamana Mudcloths*, 107.

52. Sidibe, interview, March 1, 1993.
53. On visiting in 1997, I found that these stalls
had disappeared. They had once provided
space for a variety of artists to sell their work,
including potters, jewelers, and teenaged boys
who made toys out of recycled cans and tires.
54. Mamadou Diarra, interviews, March 6, 1993,
and December 9 and 11, 1993.
55. Diarra, interview, March 6, 1993: "Je n'ai pas
besoin des maquettes. Je peux faire cinq
ensembles par jour."
56. Ibid.
57. Ibid.
58. On the long tradition of using matching attire
as a signal of group solidarity, see Chapter 6,
note 14.
59. "The Pan-African Film Festival of
Ouagadougou" program.
60. Cameron Bailey, *Toronto Film Festival Catalogue* (Toronto: Toronto Film Festival, 1995).
61. Clément Tapsoba, "Les Signes du Bogolan
Comme Base de Créativité," *Ecrans d'Afrique*
24, no. 2 (1998): 100.
62. Ibid., 98
63. David Heathcote, "Aspects of Embroidery in
Nigeria," in Picton, *Art of African Textiles*, 40.
64. Klétigui Dembélé, interview, July 17, 1997.
65. "Un Entretien avec le 'Groupe Bógólan': La
Technique du Bógólan," *Jamana*,
January–February 1987, 17: "Si la teinture à
l'indigo s'est répandue à travers tout l'ouest
africain, il semble indéniable que le 'bógólan'
soit une technique ancestrale spécifique à la
région du Mali."
66. Samuel Sidibe, interview, July 29, 1997. Much
Malian interior decoration is reminiscent of or
directly derived from North African and
Middle Eastern design. In predominantly
Muslim Mali, particularly in Bamako, the
status associated with travel to Mecca (al-hajj)
is certainly, in part, responsible for the
prevalence of pillows, carpets, mirrors, and
other home decor in Middle Eastern styles.
67. Though I visited many homes in Bamako, I
encountered few Malians who made use of
bogolan in their houses; the members of the
Groupe Bogolan Kasobane, Aminata Dramane
Traoré, a leading promoter of Malian art and
culture and founder of the San Toro cultural
center, and Mansour Ciss, the Senegalese
sculptor, were among the few.

68. See Chapter 6.
69. Rokiatou Sow, interview, January 20, 1993.
70. Sekou Traoré, interview, May 24, 1993.
71. Ibid.
72. Alou Traoré's work is discussed in Chapter 4,
with particular attention paid to his stenciled
pagnes, which differ dramatically from the
more monotonous use of stencils that
characterizes much of the cloth sold in the
tourist art market.
73. Alou Traoré, interview, March 3, 1993: "Je ne
suis pas une artiste par formation mais comme
je suis né dans une ville où on fait le bogolan,
quand je suis frappé par le chômage, j'ai
commencé à le faire."
74. Traoré sometimes creates Western-style
garments on commission. He at one point
received a commission to design fabric for
upholstery.
75. Alou Traoré, interview, March 8, 1993.
76. During the 1992 elections, Traoré created shirts
stenciled with the insignia of the winning
political party, ADEMA, the Association
Démocratique du Mali.
77. In 2000, I found that Traoré had built a very
modest but comfortable home on the outskirts
of Bamako; he did not become wealthy
through bogolan but it provided a means of
support for his family. As this book went to
press in 2001, I received news of Traoré's return
to teaching, leaving his bogolan business in the
hands of his employees.
78. Yaya Sylla, interview, March 12, 1993.
79. Ibid.
80. In fact, the Groupe Bogolan Kasobane, Ismaël
Diabaté, and other artists I worked with use
leaves and roots in numerous combinations to
create a wide range of colors.
81. In 1993 Sylla had not yet secured funding for
the project. On my return trips to Bamako in
1997 and 2000, I was unable to find
information on the school Sylla planned to
open, which he may yet succeed in
establishing.
82. Ismaël Diabaté had a studio at San Toro in
1997–98, when he needed a place to work
after leaving a studio at the Centre Culturel
Français. As a close friend of Chris Seydou,
Traoré was a strong proponent of his
bogolan-based fashion, selling his work at
San Toro and providing a venue for fashion
shows.
83. Aminata Dramane Traoré, interview, May 25,
1993.
84. Ibid.: "être nous-mêmes sans rejeter les
autres."

## 9. BOGOLAN ABROAD: REVERBERATIONS IN THE UNITED STATES

1. Thomas McEvilley, *Fusion: West African Artists at the Venice Biennale* (New York: Museum for African Art, 1993), 20.

2. The first two names refer to patterns that adorn towels and bedsheets. Both products were marketed in U.S. outlets, including major department stores such as Dayton's and Marshall Field's. "Zimbabwe" is the name of an upholstery fabric.

3. Anya Peterson Royce, *Ethnic Identity: Strategies for Diversity* (Bloomington: Indiana University Press, 1982), 9.

4. Here, Strother refers to the influential exhibition and catalogue by William Rubin, *"Primitivism" in Twentieth Century Art: Affinity of the Tribal and the Modern* (New York: Museum of Modern Art, 1984). See Z. S. Strother, *Inventing Masks: Agency and History in the Art of the Central Pende* (Chicago: University of Chicago Press, 1998), 147.

5. Norimitsu Onishi, "Gomitogo Journal: Undependable Rains Bring Seasonal Exodus," *New York Times,* January 4, 2000, A4.

6. Ibid.

7. Ibid.

8. The exhibition was organized by Janet Goldner, a sculptor and supporter of Malian arts, and Klétigui Dembélé, a member of the Groupe Bogolan Kasobane. It was presented in the lobby of the Walter Reade Theatre from April 15 to May 15, 1998. The exhibition provided significant exposure and might, one hopes, lead to further attention for contemporary Malian arts.

9. Tavy Aherne, *Nakunte Diarra: A Bógólanfini Artist of the Beledougou* (Bloomington: Indiana University Art Museum, 1992). The exhibition ran from November 7, 1992, to January 8, 1993.

10. *Bogolanfini: The Mudcloth of Mali,* UCLA Fowler Museum of Cultural History, February 10–May 6, 1999.

11. Another U.S. exhibition that featured the work of the Groupe Bogolan Kasobane, along with numerous other contemporary bogolan artists, was *Renewing Tradition: The Revitalization of Bogolan in Mali and Abroad,* at the University of Iowa Museum of Art from March through June 2000. I curated the show.

12. Gaddie McBride, Rentia Hobbs, and Elizabeth Klopper, "African Connexion" catalogue, Ferndale, Calif., 1995.

13. The J. Peterman Company catalogue, "Owner's Manual No. 36b," Summer 1995, 100.

14. Leaflet advertising Turtlewear, Carefree, Ariz., ca. 1998–99. I thank Joan Mannheimer for drawing my attention to this company.

15. "Bloomingdale's By Mail" catalogue, Spring 1999, 10.

16. John Villani, "Tribal Textiles," *Southern Accents,* September–October 1994, 142.

17. "Trade Routes: Alternative Market" catalogue, Winter 1995, 29.

18. "The Daily Planet: Clothing and Gifts from Around the World," Early Summer 1994, 34.

19. "Bloomingdale's By Mail" catalogue, February 1999.

20. I am grateful to Christa Clarke for calling Brooklyn's Bogolan to my attention and to Liz Brown and Melissa Anderson for photographing its street banners.

21. "E-Style," Summer 1994, 24.

22. Kente, strip-woven cloth adorned with elaborate, brightly colored patterns, has long been familiar to students of African textiles. Unlike bogolan, which in its rural, "traditional" form is associated with initiatory contexts and ritual protection, *kente* is associated with royalty and social status in the kingdoms of the Akan, most notably the Ashanti, in Ghana and Côte d'Ivoire. The 1998 Fowler Museum of Cultural History exhibition on kente addressed the cloth's popularity in the United States. See the catalogue, Doran H. Ross, ed., *Wrapped in Pride: Ghanaian Kente and African American Identity* (Los Angeles: UCLA Fowler Museum of Cultural History, 1998).

23. In one illustration of the cloth's symbolic power, former president Bill Clinton and first lady Hillary Rodham Clinton, while on a state visit to Ghana in March 1998, were presented with kente cloths, which they donned to the great approval of Ghanaian crowds. Ghanaian president Jerry Rawlings often wears the cloth, tailored into shirts and other garments.

24. "Fashion Influences from J.C. Penney," Spring 1994.

25. Kerris Wolsky, interview, New York, March 24, 1994.

26. Nii O. Quarcoopome, "Pride and Avarice: Kente and Advertising," in Ross, *Wrapped in Pride,* 194.

27. Amy M. Spindler, "XIII. A Fashion Odyssey," *New York Times Magazine Fashions of the Times,* Fall 2000, 155.

28. Pilar Viladas, "The Artifacts of Life," *New York Times Magazine Fashions of the Times,* Fall 2000, 116–17.

29. Arlene Hirst, "Verdant," *Metropolitan Home,* January–February 2000, 104.

## 10. CONCLUSION: MAKING THE TRADITIONAL MODERN

1. At least half of the audience at the opening were non-Malians, because much of the museum's attendees consists of tourists and foreigners.

2. This was my sole encounter with a hunter's shirt in Bamako outside of art galleries and the Musée National, where such shirts might be displayed for sale or as part of an exhibition on traditional Malian culture.

3. The exhibition was also scheduled for the University Art Museum, University of California, Santa Barbara, July 10–September 2, 2001, and the Neuberger Museum of Art in Purchase, New York, January 27–May 5, 2002.

4. The other two artists, colleagues of Touré, were Boubacar Keita and Soulayeman Soukouna. Also participating in the events surrounding the opening was Baba Wagué Diakité, a Malian artist resident in Portland, Oregon, whose talents include bogolan making, ceramics, and storytelling.

# SELECTED BIBLIOGRAPHY

**BOGOLAN AND BOGOLANFINI**

Aherne, Tavy. *Nakunte Diarra: A Bógólanfini Artist of the Beledougou.* Bloomington: Indiana University Art Museum, 1992.

Becchetti-Laure, Marie-Françoise. "Aperçu de la Jeune Peintre à Bamako, République du Mali, 1960–1990: Formation-Création-Diffusion." Mémoire de Maîtrise, Université de Provence, Aix-Marseille, 1990.

Berthé, Youssouf Kalilou, and Abdoulaye Konaté. *Un Mode de Teinture: "Le Bogolan."* Bamako: Musée National du Mali, 1985.

*Bogolan et Arts Graphiques du Mali.* Paris: ADEIAO and Musée des Arts Africains et Océaniens, 1990.

Brett-Smith, Sarah. "On the Origin of a New *Tapis* Mud-Cloth Design." *African Arts* 27, no. 4 (Autumn 1994).

———. "Speech Made Visible: The Irregular as a System of Meaning." *Empirical Studies of the Arts* 2, no. 2 (1984): 127–47.

———. "Symbolic Blood: Cloth for Excised Women." *RES* 3 (Spring 1982): 15–31.

Desjeux, Catherine and Bernard. "Bogolan Kasobane: Le Pluriel de l'Art." *Balafon,* July 1996, 30–34.

Diabaté, Ismaël. "Monochromies Sacrées: Ouverture sur la Mythologie Bamana." Exhibition pamphlet. Hôtel des Ventes Chave Jean Martin. Marseille, France, June 1992.

Donne, John B. "Bogolanfini: A Mud-Painted Cloth from Mali." *Man* 8, no. 1 (1973): 104–7.

Duponchel, Pauline. "Bogolan: From Symbolic Material to National Emblem." In *The Art of African Textiles: Technology, Tradition, and Lurex,* edited by John Picton, 36–39. London: Barbican Art Gallery, 1995.

———. *Du Bogolan Traditionnel au Bogolan Contemporain.* Bamako: Centre Culturel Français, 1995.

———. "Formes, Fonctions et Significations des Textiles Traditionnels de Coton Tissés et Teints du Mali." Mémoire de DEA, Université de Paris I–Pantheon-Sorbonne, 1990.

———. *Textile de Coton—Bogolan du Mali.* Paris: Ecole Practique des Hautes Etudes, Section des Sciences Religieuse, 1997.

"Un Entretien avec le 'Groupe Bógólan': La Technique du Bógólan." *Jamana,* January–February 1987.

"Groupe Bogolan Kasobane." Review in *La Voix des Artistes,* no. 7 (1989). Bamako, Institut National des Arts.

Imperato, Pascal James. Review of *Nakunte Diarra: A Bógólanfini Artist of the Beledougou,* by Tavy Aherne. *African Arts* 27, no. 2 (April 1994).

Imperato, Pascal James, and Marli Shamir. "Bokolanfini: Mud Cloth of the Bamana of Mali." *African Arts* 3, no. 4 (Summer 1970).

Luntumbue, Toma Muteba. *Bogolan: Un Art Textile du Mali.* Brussels: Editions les Alizés, 1998.

McNaughton, Patrick R. "The Shirts That Mande Hunters Wear." *African Arts* 15, no. 3 (May 1982).

Mouniratou, Arouna. "Rapport de Stage: Bogolan et Batik." Report submitted to the Institut National des Arts, Bamako, May 1993.

Polakoff, Claire. *Into Indigo: African Textiles and Dyeing Techniques.* Garden City, N.Y.: Anchor Books, 1980.

Rovine, Victoria. "Bogolanfini in Bamako: The Biography of a Malian Textile." *African Arts* 30, no. 1 (Winter 1997).

———. *Renewing Tradition: The Revitalization of Bogolan in Mali and Abroad.* Iowa City: University of Iowa Museum of Art, 2000.

Tapsoba, Clément. "Les Signes du Bogolan Comme Base de Créativité." *Ecrans d'Afrique* 24, no. 2 (1998).

## MALI

Amselle, Jean-Loup. "Socialisme, Capitalisme, et Precapitalisme au Mali (1960–1982)." In *Contradictions of Accumulation in Africa: Studies in Economy and State,* edited by Henry Bernstein and Bennie K. Campbell, 249–66. Beverly Hills: Sage Publications, 1985.

Arnoldi, Mary Jo. *Playing with Time: Art and Performance in Central Mali.* Bloomington: Indiana University Press, 1995.

Conrad, David C., and Barbara E. Frank, eds. *Status and Identity in West Africa: Nyamakalaw of Mande.* Bloomington: Indiana University Press, 1995.

*Country Profile: Côte d'Ivoire and Mali.* London: Economist Intelligence Unit, 1994.

Cutter, Charles. *Nation-Building in Mali: Art, Radio, and Leadership in a Pre-Literature Society.* Ann Arbor, Mich.: University Microfilms International, 1980.

"Democracy in Mali." *New York Times,* April 29, 1996, A26.

Diarrah, Cheick Oumar. *Vers la Troisième République du Mali.* Paris: Editions L'Harmattan, 1991.

Dieterlen, Germaine, and Youssouf Cissé. *Les Fondements de la Société d'Initiation du Komo.* Paris: Mouton, 1972.

"Exposition Coloniale Internationale de Paris, 1937–1940." Dossier 1, Doc. IQ-1750, Archives Nationales, Bamako.

Ezra, Kate. "Early Sources for the History of Bamana Art." In *Iowa Studies in African Art.* Vol. 1. Iowa City: School of Art and Art History, University of Iowa, 1981.

Freeman, Julianne. "Muso Korobaya: Practice, Embodiment, Transition, and Agency in the Lives of Senior Bamana Women of Mali." Ph.D. diss., Indiana University, 1996.

Gosselin, Claudie. "Handing Over the Knife: *Numu* Women and the Campaign against Excision in Mali." In *Female "Circumcision" in Africa: Culture, Controversy, and Change,* edited by Bettina Shell-Duncan and Ylva Hernlund, 193–214. Boulder: Lynne Rienner Publishers, 2000.

*Les Gouvernements de la République du Mali, de l'Indépendance à Nos Jours.* Bamako: Editions Imprimerie du Mali, 1993.

Imperato, Pascal James. *Historical Dictionary of Mali.* Metuchen, N.J.: Scarecrow Press, 1977.

———. *Mali: A Handbook of Historical Statistics.* Boston: G. K. Hall, [1982?].

———. *Mali: A Search for Direction.* Boulder: Westview Press, 1989.

Jones, Heidi, Nafissatou Diop, Ian Askew, and Inoussa Kaboré. "Female Genital Cutting Practices in Burkina Faso and Mali and Their Negative Health Outcomes." *Studies in Family Planning* 30, no. 3 (September 1999): 219–30.

McNaughton, Patrick R. *The Mande Blacksmiths: Knowledge, Power, and Art in West Africa.* Bloomington: Indiana University Press, 1988.

———. *Secret Sculptures of Komo: Art and Power in Bamana (Bambara) Initiation Associations.* Working Papers in the Traditional Arts 4. Philadelphia: Institute for the Study of Human Issues, 1979.

Meillassoux, Claude. "The Social Structure of Modern Bamako." *Africa* 35, no. 2 (April 1965): 126–47.

———. *Urbanization of an African Community: Voluntary Associations in Bamako.* Seattle: University of Washington Press, 1968.

N'diaye, Issa. "Jeunesse et Identité Culturelle." *Jamana,* August 1986, 15–17.

Onishi, Norimitsu. "Gomitogo Journal: Undependable Rains Bring Seasonal Exodus." *New York Times,* January 4, 2000, A4.

"Participation du Soudan au Salon de la France d'Outre Mer, 1940." Doc. IQ-1329, Archives Nationales, Bamako.

Perinbam, B. Marie. *Family Identity and the State in the Bamako Kafu, c. 1800–c. 1900.* Boulder: Westview Press, 1997.

Pivin, Jean-Loup. "Le Mémoire en Marche," interview with Alpha Oumar Konaré. *Revue Noire,* September 1991, 2–3.

*Post Report: Mali.* Washington, D.C.: U.S. Department of State, 1992.

*Programmes Officielles.* Bamako: Institut National des Arts, 1988.

*Revue Noire,* June–July–August 1995. Special issue.

Roberts, Richard. *Two Worlds of Cotton: Colonialism and the Regional Economy in the French Soudan, 1800–1946.* Stanford, Calif.: Stanford University Press, 1996.

Touré, Amadou Chab, ed. *Signes et Alphabets au Mali: Synthèse des Semaines de la Calligraphie.* Bamako: Club Ahmed Baba with the support of the Embassy of France to Mali, 1999.

Touré, Baba Moussulu. "Arts et Peuples du Mali: Tradition et Tendances Modernes." Thèse de doctorat d'art, Ecole Supérieur des Arts Industriels du Moscou, 1991.

## TEXTILES

Aronson, Lisa. "Akwete Weaving: Tradition and Change." In *Man Does Not Go Naked: Textilien und Handwerk aus afrikanischen und andern*

*Ländern,* edited by Beate Engelbrecht and Bernhard Gardi. Basel: Ethnologisches Seminar der Universität and Museum für Völkerkunde, 1989.

Bayly, C. A. "The Origins of *Swadeshi* (Home Industry): Cloth and Indian Society, 1700–1930." In *The Social Life of Things: Commodities in Cultural Perspective,* edited by Arjun Appadurai, 285–322. New York: Cambridge University Press, 1986.

Bean, Susan. "Ghandi and *Khadi,* the Fabric of Indian Independence." In *Cloth and Human Experience,* edited by Annette B. Weiner and Jane Schneider, 355–76. Washington, D.C.: Smithsonian Institution Press, 1989.

Bensai, S. "Plantes Tinctoriales et Teintures Indigenes au Soudan." *Notes Africaines* 23, no. 6 (1944): 17–19.

Boser-Sarivaxévanis, Renée. *Recherche sur l'Histoire des Textiles Traditionnels Tissés et Teints de l'Afrique Occidentale.* Basel:Verhandlungen der Naturforschenden Gesellschaft, 1975.

———. *Les Tissus de l'Afrique Occidentale.* Basel: Pharos-Verlag, H. Schwabe, 1972.

Clouzot, Henri. "Le Tissage à la Main dans les Textiles." *La Renaissance de l'Art Français* (1923): 555–57.

———. *Tissus Nègres.* Paris: A. Calavas, [1920–25?].

Cordwell, Justine M., and Ronald A. Schwartz, eds. *The Fabrics of Culture: The Anthropology of Clothing and Adornment.* The Hague: Mouton, 1979.

di Grandi, F. *Assessment and Plan of Action for the Export Development of the Textile, Leather, Apparel, Fruits, and Spices Industries of Mali.* Washington, D.C.: World Bank, 1989.

Drier, Deborah. "African Textiles." *Art News,* November 1983, 202.

Engelbrecht, Beate, and Bernhard Gardi, eds. *Man Does Not Go Naked: Textilien und Handwerk aus afrikanischen und andern Ländern.* Basel: Ethnologisches Seminar der Universität and Museum für Völkerkunde, 1989.

Etienne, Mona. "Women and Men, Cloth and Colonialisation: The Transformation of Production-Distribution Relations among the Baule (Ivory Coast)." *Cahiers d'Etudes Africaines* 65, no. 17 (1977): 41–64.

Fourneau. "Le Pagne sur la Côte Occidentale d'Afrique." *Bulletin d'Etudes Centrafricaines,* nos. 7–8 (1954): 5–22.

Gilfoy, Peggy. *Patterns of Life: West African Strip-Weaving Traditions.* Washington, D.C.: National Museum of African Art, 1987.

Heathcote, David. "Aspects of Embroidery in Nigeria." In *The Art of African Textiles: Technology, Tradition, and Lurex,* edited by John Picton, 138–40. London: Barbican Art Gallery, 1995.

*History, Design, and Craft in West African Strip-Woven Cloth.* Washington, D.C.: National Museum of African Art, 1992.

Hodder, B. W. "Indigenous Cloth Trade and Marketing in Africa." In *Textiles of Africa,* edited by Dale Idiens and K. G. Ponting, 203–10. Bath: Pasold Research Fund, 1980.

Idiens, Dale. "An Introduction to Traditional African Weaving and Textiles." In *Textiles of Africa,* edited by Dale Idiens and K. G. Ponting. Bath: Pasold Research Fund, 1980.

Idiens, Dale, and K. G. Ponting, eds. *Textiles of Africa.* Bath: Pasold Research Fund, 1980.

Johansen, Felicia. *Opportunity Study for the Development of the African Textile Industry.* Doc. no. TF/GLO/89/902. New York: United Nations Industrial Development Organization, 1991.

Johnson, Marion. "Calico Caravans." *Journal of African History* 17 (1976).

Lamb, Venice. *West African Weaving.* London: Duckworth, 1975.

Leidhom, C. "The Economics of African Dress and Textiles." *African Arts* 15, no. 3 (1982).

Mathon, M. Eug. *Le Commerce des Tissus en Afrique Occidentale Française.* Supplement to *Bulletin de l'Office Colonial,* no. 21 (September 1909).

Picton, John, ed. *The Art of African Textiles: Technology, Tradition, and Lurex.* London: Barbican Art Gallery, 1995.

Picton, John, and John Mack. *African Textiles: Looms, Weaving and Design.* London: British Museum, 1979.

Renne, Elisha P. *Cloth That Does Not Die: The Meaning of Cloth in Bùnú Social Life.* Seattle: University of Washington Press, 1995.

Roberts, Richard. "Women's Work and Women's Property: Household Social Relations in the Maraka Textile Industry of the Nineteenth Century." *Comparative Studies in Society and History* 26, no. 2 (April 1984): 229–50.

Ross, Doran H. *Wrapped in Pride: Ghanaian Kente and African American Identity.* Los Angeles: UCLA Fowler Museum of Cultural History, 1998.

Schneider, Jane. "The Anthropology of Cloth." *Annual Review of Anthropology* 16 (1987): 409–48.

Schneider, Jane, and Annette B. Weiner. "Cloth and the Organization of Human Experience." *Current Anthropology* 27, no. 2 (April 1986).

Sieber, Roy. *African Textiles and Decorative Arts.* New York: Museum of Modern Art, 1972.

Smith, Fred, and Joanne Eicher. "The Systematic Study of African Dress and Textiles." *African Arts* 15, no. 3 (1982).

Spooner, Brian. "Weavers and Dealers: The Authenticity of an Oriental Carpet." In *The Social Life* of *Things: Commodities in Cultural Perspective,* edited by Arjun Appadurai. New York: Cambridge University Press, 1986.

Steiner, Christopher B. "Another Image of Africa: Toward an Ethnohistory of European Cloth Marketed in West Africa, 1873–1960." *Ethnohistory* 32, no. 2 (1985): 91–110.

Sundström, Lars. "The Exchange Economy of Pre-Colonial Tropical Africa." In *Textile Trade.* New York: St. Martin's Press, 1974.

Weiner, Annette B., and Jane Schneider, eds. *Cloth and Human Experience.* Washington, D.C.: Smithsonian Institution Press, 1989.

Werbeloff, Arnold. *Textiles in Africa: A Trade and Investment Guide.* London: Alain Charles Publishing, 1987.

Zeltner, Franz de. "Tissus Africains à Dessins Réservés ou Décolorés." *Bulletin et Mémoires: Société d'Anthropologie de Paris,* ser. 16, 1 (1910): 224–27.

## TOURIST ART

Bascom, William. "Changing African Art." In *Ethnic and Tourist Arts: Cultural Expressions from the Fourth World,* edited by Nelson H. H. Graburn, 303–19. Berkeley: University of California Press, 1976.

Ben-Amos, Paula. "Pidgin Languages and Tourist Arts." *Studies in the Anthropology of Visual Communication* 4, no. 2 (Winter 1977): 128–39.

———. "A la Recherche du Temps Perdu: On Being an Ebony Carver in Benin." In *Ethnic and Tourist Arts: Cultural Expressions from the Fourth World,* edited by Nelson H. H. Graburn, 320–33. Berkeley: University of California Press, 1976.

"Fakes, Fakers, and Forgery." *African Arts* 9, no. 3 (April 1976): 21–74.

Graburn, Nelson H. H., ed. *Ethnic and Tourist Arts: Cultural Expressions from the Fourth World.* Berkeley: University of California Press, 1976.

Jules-Rosette, Bennetta. *The Messages of Tourist Art: An African Semiotic System in Comparative Perspective.* New York: Plenum Press, 1984.

MacCannell, Dean. *Empty Meeting Grounds: The Tourist Papers.* New York: Routledge, 1989.

Megaw, Vincent. "Something, but for Whom? Ethnic and Transitional Arts." *Cultural Survival Quarterly* 10, no. 3 (1986): 64–69.

Phillips, Ruth B. *Trading Identities: The Souvenir in Native North American Art from the Northeast, 1700–1900.* Seattle: University of Washington Press; Montreal: McGill-Queen's University Press, 1998.

———. "Why Not Tourist Art? Significant Silences in Native American Museum Representations." In *After Colonialism: Imperial Histories and Post-colonial Displacements,* edited by Gyan Prakash, 98–125. Princeton: Princeton University Press, 1995.

Richter, Dolores. *Art, Economics, and Change: The Kulubele of Northern Ivory Coast.* La Jolla, Calif.: Psych/Graphic Publishers, 1980.

Shiner, Larry. "'Primitive Fakes,' 'Tourist Art,' and the Ideology of Authenticity." *Journal of Aesthetics and Art Criticism* 52, no. 2 (Spring 1994): 225–34.

Silver, Harry R. "Beauty and the 'I' of the Beholder: Identity, Aesthetics, and Social Change among the Ashanti." *Journal of Anthropological Research* 35, no. 2 (1979): 191–207.

———. "Foreign Art and Ashanti Aesthetics." *African Arts* 16, no. 3 (May 1983).

Steiner, Christopher B. "Authenticity, Repetition, and the Aesthetics of Seriality: The World of Tourist Art in the Age of Mechanical Reproduction." In *Unpacking Culture: Art and Commodity in Colonial and Postcolonial Worlds,* edited by Ruth B. Phillips and Christopher B. Steiner, 87–103. Berkeley: University of California Press, 1999.

———. "The Trade in West African Art." *African Arts* 24 (January 1991).

———. "Worlds Together, Worlds Apart: The Mediation of Knowledge by Traders in African Art." *Society for Visual Anthropology* 6, no. 1 (Spring 1990): 45–49.

Waterbury, Ronald. "Embroidery for Tourists: A Contemporary Putting-Out System in Oaxaca, Mexico." In *Cloth and Human Experience,* edited by Annette B. Weiner and Jane Schneider. Washington, D.C.: Smithsonian Institution Press, 1989.

Wollen, Peter. "Tourism, Language, and Art." *New Formations,* no. 12 (Winter 1990): 43–60.

## CONTEMPORARY AFRICAN ART

Antubam, Kofi. "From Ghana Folk Art to Kofi Antubam Art," in *Catalog of an Exhibition Held at Accra Central Library* (December–January 1962). Cited in Marshall Mount, *African Art: The Years since 1920.* Bloomington: Indiana University Press, 1989.

Araeen, Rasheed. "From Primitivism to Ethnic Arts." In *The Myth of Primitivism: Perspectives on Art,* edited by Susan Hiller, 158–82. New York: Routledge, 1991.

Awoonor, Kofi. *Breast of the Earth: A Survey of the History, Culture, and Literature of Africa South of the Sahara.* New York: Nok Publishers International, 1975.

Cassel, Valerie. "Convergence: Image and Dialogue Conversations with Alexander 'Skunder' Boghossian." *Third Text,* no. 23 (Summer 1993): 53–68.

Cotter, Holland. "The Brave New Face of Art from the East." *New York Times,* October 29, 1996, 1, 38.

Delange, Jacqueline, and Roger Fry. *Contemporary African Art.* New York: Studio Museum, 1969.

Deliss, Clémentine. "7 + 7 = 1: Seven Stories, Seven Stages, One Exhibition." In *Seven Stories about Modern Art in Africa,* edited by Clémentine Deliss. New York: Flammerion, 1995.

Ejiogu, Emma. "African Art in Transition." *African Commentary: A Journal of People of African Descent* 2, nos. 4–5 (May 1990): 67.

Enwezor, Okwui. "Redrawing the Boundaries: Towards a New African Art Discourse." *Nka,* no. 1 (1994): 3–7.

Enwonwu, Ben. "Le Point de Vue de l'Afrique sur l'Art et les Problèmes Qui Sont Posents Aujourd'hui aux Artistes Africains." In *Colloque: Fonction et Signification de l'Art Nègre dans la Vie du Peuple et pour le Peuple.* Paris: Editions Présence Africaine, 1966.

Gaudibert, Pierre. *L'Art Africain Contemporain.* Paris: Diagonales, 1991.

Jager, E. J. de. "African Art and Artist: A New Identity?" *African Insight* 18, no. 4 (1988): 202–3.

jegede, dele. "African Art Today: An Historical Overview." In *Contemporary African Artists: Changing Tradition,* 29–43. New York: Studio Museum in Harlem, 1990.

Koloane, David. "The Identity Question: Focus on Black South African Expression." *Third Text,* no. 23 (Summer 1993): 99–102.

*Magiciens de la Terre.* Paris: Editions du Centre Georges Pompidou, 1989.

McEvilley, Thomas. *Fusion: West African Artists at the Venice Biennale.* New York: Museum for African Art, 1993.

McEwen, Frank. "La Peinture et la Sculpture Africaines Modernes." In *Colloque: Fonction et Signification de l'Art Nègre dans la Vie du Peuple et pour le Peuple.* Paris: Editions Présence Africaine, 1966.

———. "Return to Origins: New Directions for African Arts." *African Arts* 1, no. 2 (Winter 1968).

Mount, Marshall W. *African Art: The Years since 1920.* Bloomington: Indiana University Press, 1989.

Mudimbe, V. Y. "'Reprendre': Enunciations and Strategies in Contemporary African Arts." In *Africa Explores: Twentieth Century African Art,* edited by Susan Vogel, 276–87. New York: Center for African Art; Munich: Prestel-Verlag, 1991.

Nettleton, Anitra. "Myth of the Transitional: Black Art and White Markets in South Africa." *South African Journal of Cultural and Art History* 2, no. 4 (1988): 301–10.

Nicodemus, Everlyn. "Inside, Outside." *Seven Stories about Modern Art in Africa,* edited by Clémentine Deliss. New York: Flammerion, 1995.

Njami, Simon. "An African in New York." *Revue Noire,* June–July–August 1992, 47.

Nwoko, Demas. "Contemporary Nigerian Artists and Their Traditions." *Black Art* 4, no. 2 (1980): 48.

Oguibe, Olu, and Okwui Enwezor, eds. *Reading the Contemporary: African Art from Theory to Marketplace.* Cambridge, Mass.: MIT Press, 1999.

Oloidi, Ola. "Abstraction in Modern African Art." *New Culture* (Ibadan) 1, no. 9 (August 1979).

Omibiyi, Miss. Mosunmola. "The Artist in Contemporary Africa." *Pan-African Journal* 8, no. 1 (1975): 103–13.

Pellizzi, Francesco. Review of *Africa Explores: Twentieth Century African Art,* edited by Susan Vogel. *African Arts* 26, no. 1 (January 1993): 24.

Picton, John. "Desperately Seeking Africa, New York, 1991." *Oxford Art Journal* 15, no. 2 (1992): 104–12.

———. "In Vogue or the Flavour of the Month: The New Way to Wear Black," *Third Text,* no. 23 (Summer 1993): 89–98.

Povey, John. "First Word." *African Arts* 23, no. 4 (October 1990).

Rubin, William, ed. *"Primitivism" in Twentieth Century Art: Affinity of the Tribal and the Modern.* New York: Museum of Modern Art, 1984.

Serota, Nicholas, and Gavin Jantjes. *From Two Worlds,* edited by Rachel Kirby and Nicholas Serota. London: Trustees of the Whitechapel Gallery, 1986.

Stanislaus, Grace. *Contemporary African Artists: Changing Tradition.* New York: Studio Museum in Harlem, 1990.

Vogel, Susan, ed. *Africa Explores: Twentieth Century African Art.* New York: Center for African Art; Munich: Prestel-Verlag, 1991.

Willis, Anne-Marie, and Tony Fry. "Art as Ethnocide: The Case of Australia." *Third Text,* no. 5 (1988–89): 3–20.

## FASHION

Ash, Juliet, and Elizabeth Wilson, eds. *Chic Thrills: A Fashion Reader.* Berkeley: University of California Press, 1992.

Barnes, Ruth, and Joanne B. Eicher, eds. *Dress and Gender: Making and Meaning.* Oxford: Berg, 1992.

Barry, Josette. "Chris Seydou Célèbre la Femme Africaine." *Fraternité Matin,* October 26–27, 1986, 21.

Barthes, Roland. *The Fashion System,* translated by Matthew Ward and Richard Howard. New York: Hill and Wang, 1983.

———. *Système de la Mode.* Paris: Editions du Seuil, 1967.

Bary, Pauline Awa, and Jean Loup Pivin. "Quelques Dates d'une Vie de Chris Seydou." *Revue Noire,* June–July–August 1994, 56.

Bastian, Misty L. "Female 'Alhajis' and Entrepreneurial Fashions: Flexible Identities in Southeastern Nigeria." In *Clothing and Difference: Embodied Identities in Colonial and Post-Colonial Africa,* edited by Hildi Hendrickson, 97–132. Durham, N.C.: Duke University Press, 1996.

Brodman, Barbara. "Paris or Perish: The Plight of the Latin American Indian in a Westernized World." In *On Fashion,* edited by Shari Benstock and Suzanne Ferriss, 267–83. New Brunswick, N.J.: Rutgers University Press, 1994.

"Chris Seydou: Le Roman d'une Vie." *Africa International,* July–August 1994, 31–37.

Comaroff, John L., and Jean. *Of Revelation and Revolution.* Vol. 2, *The Dialectics of Modernity on a South African Frontier.* Chicago: University of Chicago Press, 1997.

Craik, Jennifer. *The Face of Fashion: Cultural Studies in Fashion.* New York: Routledge, 1994.

Davis, Fred. *Fashion, Culture, and Identity.* Chicago: University of Chicago Press, 1992.

Diakité, K. B. "Chris Seydou" (obituary). *L'Essor,* March 8, 1994, 4.

Domingo, Macy. "Ciseaux d'Ivoire/Ivory Scissors." *Revue Noire,* September 1991, 6–7.

Eicher, Joanne B., ed. *African Dress: A Select and Annotated Bibliography of Subsaharan Countries.* East Lansing: Michigan State University, 1970.

———, ed. *Dress and Ethnicity: Change across Space and Time.* Washington, D.C.: Berg, 1995.

Eicher Joanne B., and Tonye Erekosima. "Why Do They Call It Kalabari? Cultural Authentification and the Demarcation of Ethnic Identity." In *Dress and Ethnicity: Change across Space and Time,* edited by Joanne B. Eicher. Washington, D.C.: Berg, 1995.

Finkelstein, Joanne. *The Fashioned Self.* Philadelphia: Temple University Press, 1991.

Friedman, Jonathon. "The Political Economy of Elegance." *Culture and History* 7 (1990): 101–25.

Gandoulou, Justin Daniel. *Dandies à Bacongo: Le Culte de l'Elégance dans la Société Congolaise Contemporaine.* Paris: L'Harmattan, 1989.

Hansen, Karen Tranberg. *Salaula: The World of Secondhand Clothing in Zambia.* Chicago: University of Chicago Press, 2000.

Hay, M. J. *Western Clothing and African Identity: Changing Consumption Patterns among the Luo.* Discussion Papers in the African Humanities 2. Boston: African Studies Center, Boston University, 1989.

H.D.Y. "Chris Seydou et CFCI Textiles." *Fraternité Matin,* October 16, 1985, 16.

Hendrickson, Hildi, ed. *Clothing and Difference: Embodied Identities in Colonial and Post-Colonial Africa.* Durham, N.C.: Duke University Press, 1996.

"Hommage à un Grand Créateur" (obituary for Chris Seydou). *Les Echos,* March 7, 1994, 3.

Hyland, John. "Clothes Meet World." *New York Times Magazine Fashions of the Times,* Fall 2000, 168–83.

"Interview: Chris Seydou." *Grin-Grin: Le Magazine des Jeunes* (Bamako), April–May–June 1989, 10.

Konaré, Adam Bâ, et al. "Chris Seydou: Hommage." *Revue Noire,* June–July–August 1994, 55–59.

Labbe, Claude. "Chris Seydou: Le Tourbillon des Etoffes Africaines." *Demain l'Afrique,* June 18, 1979, 12–13.

Lurie, Alison. *The Language of Clothes.* New York: Random House, 1981.

Martin, Phyllis M. "Contesting Clothes in Colonial Brazzaville." *Journal of African History* 35 (1994): 401–26.

———. "Power, Cloth and Currency on the Loango Coast." *African Economic History* 15 (1986): 1–12.

Mazrui, Ali A. "The Robes of Rebellion: Sex, Dress, and Politics in Africa." *Encounter* 34, no. 2 (1970).

McCracken, Grant. *Culture and Consumption: New Approaches to the Symbolic Character of Consumer Goods and Activities.* Bloomington: Indiana University Press, 1988.

McLaughlin, Patricia. "Style with Substance: Black Style Is a Fashion Statement and a Political Statement." *Philadelphia Inquirer Magazine,* March 8, 1998, 18.

Menkes, Suzy. "A Touch of Modern Exotica: At the Fashion Shows, Ethnic Clothing Meets the Twenty-first Century." *New York Times,* April 24, 1994, C1.

Mercer, Kobena. "Black Hair/Style Politics." *New Formations* 3 (Winter 1987): 33–54.

Messing, S. "The Nonverbal Language of the Ethiopian Toga." *Anthropos* 55 (1960): 558–61.

Nag, Dulali. "Fashion, Gender, and the Bengali Middle Class." *Public Culture* 3, no. 2 (Spring 1991): 93–115.

N'diaye, Rachid. "Chris Seydou: La Mort d'un Magicien." *Africa International,* April 1994, 28–29.

O'Kelly, Hillary. "Reconstructing Irishness: Dress in the Celtic Revival, 1880–1920." In *Chic Thrills: A Fashion Reader,* edited by Juliet Ash and Elizabeth Wilson. Berkeley: University of California Press, 1992.

Perani, Judith, and Norman H. Wolff. *Cloth, Dress and Art Patronage in Africa.* New York: Berg, 1999.

Pivin, Jean Loup. "Drapé de Son Manteau Noir/Draped in His Black Cloak," translated by John Taylor. *Revue Noire,* June–July–August 1994, 57.

———. "Rebirth of an African Style," translated by Gail de Courcy-Ireland. *Revue Noire,* December 1997–January 1998.

Polhemus, Ted. *Fashion and Anti-Fashion: Anthropology of Clothing and Adornment.* London: Thames and Hudson, [1978?].

Roach, Ellen, and Joanne Eicher. *The Visible Self: Perspectives on Dress.* New York: Prentice Hall, 1973.

Seydou, Chris. Promotional feature. *Nyeleni,* no. 5 (1994): 18–19.

Simmel, Georg. "Fashion." *International Quarterly* 10 (October 1904). Reprinted in *American Journal of Sociology* 57, no. 6 (May 1957).

Tarlo, Emma. "Traders as Trend-Setters: The Marketing of Village Embroidery in Gujarat." Paper presented at the conference "Cloth, the World Economy, and the Artisan," Dartmouth College, April 1993.

Traoré, Aminata Dramane. "African Fashion: A Message." In *The Art of African Fashion,* edited by Els van der Plas and Marlous Willemsen, 8–9. Trenton, N.J.: Africa World Press; The Hague: Prince Claus Fund, 1998.

Traoré, Maîmouna. "Chris Seydou: La Mort d'une Etoile." *Nyeleni,* no. 5 (1994): 26.

van der Plas, Els, and Marlous Willemsen, eds. *The Art of African Fashion.* Trenton, N.J.: Africa World Press; The Hague: Prince Claus Fund, 1998.

Wass, Betty M. "Yoruba Dress in Five Generations of a Lagos Family." In *The Fabrics of Culture: The Anthropology of Clothing and Adornment,* edited by Justine M. Cordwell and Ronald Schwartz, 331–48. The Hague: Mouton, 1979.

Wipper, Audrey. "African Women: Fashion and Scapegoating." *Canadian Journal of African Studies* 6, no. 2 (1972): 329–49.

Wright, Lee. "Outgrown Clothes for Grown-up People: Constructing a Theory of Fashion." In *Chic Thrills: A Fashion Reader,* edited by Juliet Ash and Elizabeth Wilson. Berkeley: University of California Press, 1992.

## AUTHENTICITY AND IDENTITY

Anderson, Benedict. *Imagined Communities: Reflections on the Origin and Spread of Nationalism.* London: Verso, 1983.

Appadurai, Arjun. "Disjuncture and Difference in the Global Cultural Economy." *Public Culture* 2, no. 2 (Spring 1990): 1–25.

———. "Introduction: Commodities and the Politics of Value." In *The Social Life of Things: Commodities in Cultural Perspective,* edited by Arjun Appadurai, 3–64. New York: Cambridge University Press, 1986.

———. *Modernity at Large: Cultural Dimensions of Globalization.* Minneapolis: University of Minnesota Press, 1996.

Appiah, Kwame Anthony. "Is the Post- in Postmodernism the Post- in Postcolonial?" *Critical Inquiry* 17 (Winter 1991): 336–57.

———. "The Postcolonial and the Postmodern." In *In My Father's House: Africa in the Philosophy of Culture.* New York: Oxford University Press, 1992.

Bhabha, Homi. "Remembering Fanon: Self, Psyche, and the Colonial Condition." In *Colonial Discourse and Postcolonial Theory,* edited by Patrick Williams and Laura Chrisman. New York: Columbia University Press, 1994.

Clifford, James. "The Others: Beyond the Salvage Paradigm." *Third Text,* no. 6 (Spring 1989): 73–79.

———. *The Predicament of Culture: Twentieth Century Ethnography, Literature, and Art.* Cambridge, Mass.: Harvard University Press, 1988.

Cohodas, Marvin. "Elizabeth Hickox and Karuk Basketry: A Case Study in Debates on Innovation and Paradigms of Authenticity." In *Unpacking Culture: Art and Commodity in Colonial and Postcolonial Worlds,* edited by Ruth B. Phillips and Christopher B. Steiner, 143–61. Berkeley: University of California Press, 1999.

Cornet, Joseph. "African Art and Authenticity." *African Arts* 9, no. 1 (October 1975): 52–55.

Drewal, Henry. "Contested Realities: Inventions of Art and Authenticity." *African Arts* 25, no. 4 (October 1992).

Frank, Barbara. "Open Borders: Style and Ethnic Identity." *African Arts* 20, no. 4 (August 1987).

Hobsbawm, Eric. "Introduction: Inventing Traditions." In *The Invention of Tradition,* edited by Eric Hobsbawm and Terence Ranger, 1–14. New York: Cambridge University Press, 1983.

Hobsbawm, Eric, and Terence Ranger, eds. *The Invention of Tradition.* New York: Cambridge University Press, 1983.

Houlberg, Marilyn Hammersley. "Collecting the Anthropology of African Art." *African Arts* 19, no. 3 (April 1976).

Kasfir, Sidney. "African Art and Authenticity: A Text with a Shadow." *African Arts* 25, no. 2 (April 1992).

———. "One Tribe, One Style: Paradigms in the Historiography of African Art." *History in Africa* 11 (1984): 163–93.

———. "Taste and Distaste: The Canon of New African Art." *Transition,* no. 57 (1992): 52–70.

Kopytoff, Igor. "The Cultural Biography of Things: Commodification as Process." In *The Social Life of Things: Commodities in Cultural Perspective,* edited by Arjun Appadurai, 64–91. New York: Cambridge University Press, 1986.

Manning, Patrick. "Primitive Art and Modern Times." *Radical History Review* 33 (1985): 165–81.

Marcus, George E., and Fred R. Myers, eds. *The Traffic in Culture: Refiguring Art and Anthropology.* Berkeley: University of California Press, 1992.

Miller, Sebastian. "Real or Fake? The Ellusive Chi Wara." *World of Tribal Arts* (Spring 1995): 80–81.

Pasztory, Esther. "Identity and Difference: The Uses and Meanings of Ethnic Styles." *Studies in the History of Art* 27 (1989): 35–36.

Phillips, Ruth B., and Christopher B. Steiner. "Art, Authenticity and the Baggage of Cultural Encounter." In *Unpacking Culture: Art and Commodity in Colonial and Postcolonial Worlds,* edited by Ruth B. Phillips and Christopher B. Steiner. Berkeley: University of California Press, 1999.

Phillips, Ruth B., and Christopher B. Steiner, eds. *Unpacking Culture: Art and Commodity in Colonial and Postcolonial Worlds.* Berkeley: University of California Press, 1999.

Price, Sally. *Primitive Art in Civilized Places.* Chicago: University of Chicago Press, 1989.

Royce, Anya Peterson. *Ethnic Identity: Strategies of Diversity.* Bloomington: Indiana University Press, 1982.

Steiner, Christopher B. *African Art in Transit.* New York: Cambridge University Press, 1994.

——. "Can the Canon Burst?" *Art Bulletin* 128, no. 2 (June 1996): 213–17.

Stewart, Susan. *On Longing: Narratives of the Miniature, the Gigantic, the Souvenir, the Collection.* Baltimore: Johns Hopkins University Press, 1984.

Willett, Frank. "True or False? The False Dichotomy." *African Arts* 9, no. 3 (April 1976): 8–14.

Wolff, Janet. *The Social Production of Art.* New York: New York University Press, 1984.

**OTHER WORKS CITED**

Algotsson, Sharne, and Denys Davis. *The Spirit of African Design.* New York: Clarkson Potter Publishers, 1996.

Bailey, Cameron. *Toronto Film Festival Catalogue.* Toronto: Toronto Film Festival, 1995.

Ben-Amos, Paula. "African Visual Arts from a So-cial Perspective." *African Studies Review* 32, no. 2 (1989): 1–53.

Benedict, B. *The Anthropology of World's Fairs.* London: Scolar Press, 1983.

Celenko, Theodore. *Art and Technology: Africa and Beyond.* Indianapolis: Indianapolis Museum of Art, 1996.

Crowley, Daniel J. "The Contemporary-Traditional Art Market in Africa." *African Arts* 4, no. 1 (1970).

Fisher, Angela. *Africa Adorned.* New York: Harry N. Abrams, 1984.

Gallotti, Jean. "Les Arts Indigènes à l'Exposition Coloniale." *Art et Decoration,* July 1931, 69–100.

Guillaume, Paul, and Thomas Munro. *Primitive Negro Sculpture.* 1926. Reprint, New York: Hacker Art Books, 1968.

Hartt, Frederick. *Art: A History of Painting, Sculpture, Architecture.* 2d ed. Englewood Cliffs, N.J.: Prentice-Hall; New York: Harry N. Abrams, 1985.

*Jamana,* October–December 1984, editorial, 1.

Janneau, Guillaume. "Le Mouvement Moderne: Nos Colonies Inspiratrice d'Art." *La Renaissance de l'Art Français* (June 1923): 379–85.

Johnson, Marion. "Technology, Competition, and African Crafts." In *The Imperial Impact: Studies in the Economic History of Africa and India,* edited by Clive Dewey and A. G. Hopkins, 259–69. London: University of London, 1970.

Nooter, Mary H. "The Aesthetics and Politics of Things Unseen." In *Secrecy: African Art That Conceals and Reveals,* 23–40. New York: Museum for African Art, 1993.

Phillips, Tom. *Africa: The Art of a Continent.* Munich: Prestel, 1996.

Picton, John. "In Vogue or the Flavour of the Month: The New Way to Wear Black." *Third Text,* no. 23 (Summer 1993): 89–98.

Ravenhill, Philip. *Dreams and Reverie: Images of Otherworld Mates among the Baule, West Africa.* Washington, D.C.: Smithsonian Institution Press, 1996.

Rubin, Arnold. "Artists and Workshops in Northeastern Zaire." In *Iowa Studies in African Art.* Vol. 2. Iowa City: School of Art and Art History, University of Iowa, 1987).

Tomlinson, John. *Cultural Imperialism.* Baltimore: Johns Hopkins University Press, 1991.

Vogel, Susan. *The Art of Collecting African Art.* New York: Center for African Art, 1988.

Wilk, Richard. "Consumer Goods as Dialogue about Development." *Culture and History* 7 (1990): 79–100.

# INDEX

Page numbers in **boldface** refer to illustrations